ENDORSEMENTS FOR *THE BURNOUT BIBLE*

As I sat and read Rachel's book, I couldn't help but stop and reflect on the personal moments of burnout that I have experienced in my own life. Yet, in feeling the expectation to be 'always on' and in experiencing the challenges of burnout, there is also an opportunity to learn that taking downtime and looking after your health is, indeed, productive too. Rachel's book will open your mind to thinking about your approach to burnout in a whole new way. We all want to know how to feel more energised so that we can be at the top of our game, but how can we if we don't address the root cause of why we're burnt out? This book puts the power back in your hands and will become your bible on the road to recovery, giving you the opportunity to address your symptoms and find a solution!
—**Tracey Raye, Health editor,** *BBC Good Food* **and** *Olive*

Rachel and I have followed each other on Instagram for a number of years, and I have always been impressed by her hands-on approach and her genuine focus on the individual, both of which are very evident in *The Burnout Bible*. The book is a deep dive into the overwhelm that so many of us experience at times in our lives, and clearly explains what burnout is, how to recognise the signs and what lifestyle changes we can make to redress the balance in favour of our health and sanity. *The Burnout Bible will* be invaluable for anyone looking to regain control and lead a calmer, more authentic life.
—**Sam Rice, Food and Health columnist,** *The Telegraph,* **and author of** *The Midlife Method, Supercharge Your Diet* **and** *The Midlife Kitchen*

T0283769

As someone who's personally struggled with burnout, I know how debilitating it can be. That's why this book is an absolute lifeline for any woman who feels exhausted, stressed out and emotionally overwhelmed. Rachel unpacks the root causes of burnout and gives you practical and natural solutions to help you either prevent it happening or recover from it if you're already there. This is such an important book for the modern-day woman who needs to be at her best.

—Nicki Williams, nutritionist and author of *It's Not You, It's Your Hormones*

As a business owner, burnout is the biggest problem I must deal with. Struggling to turn the mind off and neglecting physical and emotional health when life gets 'busy' is a massive hinderance to daily performance. *The Burnout Bible* has become a truly valuable tool I turn to when my health starts to breakdown. The recipes are all amazing and the team have all benefitted from the guidance around managing chronic stress.

—Sam Higgins, CEO and co-founder, Nu Mind Wellness

Before reading *The Burnout Bible* I thought that feeling tired or drained most of the time was an inevitable part of being successful. After reading the wealth of knowledge within this book, I identified some immediate changes that I could make to strike a better balance. Taking care of yourself doesn't have to be an extra chore. *The Burnout Bible* will give you simple and achievable ideas that flow into your existing environment. Truly grateful that Rachel took the time to share so much wisdom; this book is going to be life changing for so many people.

—Clare Bowers, psychotherapist and co-founder, Leading Ladies in Business

As someone who previously knew very little about burnout, I found this book to be invaluable. Not only is there thorough description and case studies that describe the common signs, symptoms and stages, more importantly there are practical steps, ideas, recipes and support, making self-help through burnout or pre-burnout accessible for everyone. As a busy mum of three and owner of two businesses, I found this book enlightening, honest and easily digestible! This book makes the science behind burnout accessible for all and most importantly gives the tools and techniques to effectively prevent or work through it. Your body will thank you for reading it!

—Carolyn Whitehead, co-founder, Leading Ladies in Business, and founder of Beautiful New Beginnings CIC

This book is a must-read for those experiencing or at risk of burnout, as well as those who generally feel that they have too much stress in their lives. All in all, a lot of us would benefit from reading this book and it could not come at a better time given the mental health crisis of today. This book is a well-written, well-referenced, accessible navigation of how stress impacts the body and how this can tip into burnout, and the promise of functional medicine for helping to protect ourselves from and better manage burnout. Rachel's accessible explanation of the microbiome-gut-brain axis is especially worth a read. I truly hope this book helps to break the stigma surrounding burnout and I have no doubt that it will contribute to the gathering momentum about the importance of nutrition and lifestyle for improving mental health and wellbeing alongside conventional strategies. Well done, Rachel, for bringing your clinical expertise, deep knowledge and personal insight about this important subject to the masses.

—Emily Blake, registered nutritional therapy practitioner and clinical educator, Invivo Healthcare

Am I right? Rachel asks on page 17 of this book. *Yes!* is the resounding answer. *The Burnout Bible* helps women understand burnout and what to do about it. After all, it takes one to know another that has been there, one who has reached the other side to embrace life with energy and vitality again. Rachel has summarised the complexities of burnout to provide insight into how our bodies work and guidelines to help us with practical nutrition and lifestyle suggestions. *The Burnout Bible* is a must-read for anybody with a foggy brain or feels like they are scraping the bottom of the energy barrel.

—Satu Jackson, business leader, CEO and nutrition and lifestyle medicine advocate

The Burnout Bible

How to tackle fatigue and emotional overwhelm naturally

RACHEL PHILPOTTS

First published in Great Britain by Practical Inspiration Publishing, 2023

ISBN   9781788603768   (print)
        9781788603782   (epub)
        9781788603775   (mobi)

Cover image: Wild Kind Photography
Mood Boosting Method infographic: Louise Mora Creative

Want to bulk-buy copies of this book for your team and colleagues? We can customize the content and co-brand The Burnout Bible to suit your business's needs.

Please email info@practicalinspiration.com for more details.

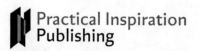

TABLE OF CONTENTS

INTRODUCTION

Picture a fierce female. To all intents and purposes, she is at the top of her game, killing it at work and spinning all the plates at home. Now really look at her. Her eyes are vacant, her smile is forced and her clothes are tight. She is constantly run down and tired all the damn time. She has lost her glow. Behind closed doors she is tearful and withdrawing from social activities. She is frustrated and cannot seem to tap into the same motivation and energy reserves she had previously. She knows something is wrong but she keeps going, just doing what she can to survive. She can't see it, but she is on the brink of burnout.

How many of us, if we are honest, recognize ourselves in this picture, whether now or in the past? If not us then we all know someone else who has felt this way. Taking it one step further, how many of us are brave enough to admit it out loud?

If it helps, I'll go first. I was that girl: fierce on the outside, broken on the inside. I burnt out.

My story

I'd always been a high achiever and academically bright. That kid who seemed to be good at everything; a generalist without much sense of direction other than onwards and upwards. Achieve, achieve, achieve. I went off to uni to study law, popped out the other end and threw myself into a corporate career without much real thought as to whether these choices were the right ones. It was just what you did when you were considered 'brainy'. Maybe you were the same?

Something else you should know about me – a little more personal but important for context – is that I experienced generalized anxiety from an early age. I hated conflict and I worried way too much about what other people thought of me. At times it was like my brain would not switch off. It turns out that this was how my brain had learned to keep me safe – by keeping me in a high state of alert. It was constantly scanning for threats so that I could be ready to protect myself at any given moment. Unbeknown to me at the time, this 'hyper-vigilance' would predispose me to burnout when exposed to the right environment and the right set of triggering events.

Anyway, back to my story. For ten years I was a typical career girl, a workaholic who thrived on stress and success. At the same time, I played hard, cramming in as many social commitments as I could into my limited spare time; over-compensating for being 'Little Miss Sensible' in my teenage years. At one point the best sleep I had during a whole week was on the Monday morning red-eye flight to Amsterdam. I survived on processed food grabbed between meetings and ate out most nights. I spun the plates and rushed through life.

Fast forward to my 30s and this lifestyle began to take its toll. The workload and pressure became relentless at a time when I was already feeling the isolation of senior management and the frustration of the ever-present glass ceiling. My mood plummeted and I was plagued by negative self-talk – telling myself that I wasn't good enough and, even worse (deep breath for this one), that I was a failure. I found myself missing personal appointments and disengaging from my family and friends. I instinctively knew something was wrong but didn't want to admit it to myself out of fear.

I just tried to keep going, keep working, keep achieving – until one day I couldn't anymore. I broke.

It wasn't dramatic. There was thankfully no public meltdown or physical collapse requiring hospitalization (I've heard many stories like these). It all happened behind closed doors. I just woke up one day unable to function. I didn't go to work, instead hiding myself away for several months. Even then I didn't know what had happened. The doctors said I was depressed, and I believed them. I felt depressed. Well, actually, I felt nothing. I was too damn exhausted. I had burnt out.

These were some of the symptoms I experienced before and at the point of burnout:

- Exhaustion
- Overwhelm
- Nervous tension
- Mood swings
- Insomnia
- Anxiety
- Depression
- Difficulty concentrating
- Brain fog
- Loss of motivation and drive
- Weight gain
- Bloating/IBS (irritable bowel syndrome)
- Sugar cravings
- PCOS (polycystic ovary syndrome)
- Irregular menstrual cycles and heavy bleeding
- Anaemia
- Frequent infections (coughs/colds)
- Low blood pressure
- Blurred vision and dizziness
- Random black outs and fainting fits

I dutifully took my prescribed antidepressant and began psychotherapy, neither of which I particularly enjoyed but found helpful in the short term. I was mainly grateful that someone had given me permission to rest. I was medically signed-off for six months so I was officially 'allowed' to rest – the doctor said! (Have you ever felt like you needed permission to admit you were not feeling OK?)

It was during my time of convalescence that I discovered the concept of functional medicine. I learned what a total bitch stress can be to all biological function, especially our brain function. I learned how essential nutrition is for health. Perhaps most importantly, I learned about myself. Specifically, how the combination of my individual biochemistry, genetic predisposition and life thus far could determine my personal diet and lifestyle needs, and also explain how I had arrived at burnout. I was fascinated.

I began eating a whole-food diet and practising self-care through exercise, yoga and relaxation. After a few months, the dark clouds lifted and my weight also began to normalize. I was no longer bloated and I had more energy than I'd had in years. I was starting to feel like me again.

With this renewed mental clarity, I took the decision to leave the corporate world and go back to university for retraining. I had a special interest in how to treat – and, more importantly, prevent – stress-related mood disorders such as burnout, so I immersed myself in health and nutrition science, biochemistry and neurobiology. Three years of clinical training and a master's degree later I was ready to fulfil my life's purpose: to help other 'tired and wired' career women to combat the fatigue and emotional overwhelm of burnout, naturally.

I now run my own functional medicine clinic doing just that. In my clinic, we look at each client's unique health history alongside state-of-the-art functional and genetic test results to uncover what's really going on. Based on all this data, we create ultra-personalized health programmes incorporating therapeutic supplements, diet and lifestyle change and stress-management techniques.

The results we see never cease to amaze me and I am humbled every time we receive feedback like this:

I've got so much more energy. My depressive feelings and brain fog have significantly reduced. I'm sleeping better and doing more exercise, which I really enjoy. My mood is overall more positive and I feel excited for the future. Thank you, Rachel. (Becky)

My mood has lifted, and I am able to focus again at work. I feel less bloated and my IBS symptoms have significantly improved. But by far the biggest win for me is the improvement in my overall energy levels. I am able to get up in the morning and feel energised. Working with Rachel was the best thing I ever did. (Abbie)

I love what I do. I'm finally channelling all that energy and brain power into something I care deeply about. However, it wasn't long before I realized that I wanted to do more. I wanted to help more women like Becky and Abbie to step off the emotional rollercoaster of burnout; to wake up feeling energized and thinking clearly; to give them back their mood mojo and enable them to fulfil their career (and life) potential.

That was when I decided to write this book. Although a book can never replicate the clinic experience, it is my hope that in sharing my knowledge of burnout, its root causes and how it can be managed naturally, I can help women globally to combat the fatigue and emotional overwhelm of burnout. So here it is: your very own Burnout Bible.

About this book

Burnout is a hot topic, yet it receives little medical recognition or support. This book delves into the research in order to convey what is possible when approaching burnout naturally, and how to get to the root cause of your symptoms. I hope that this book will arm you with the knowledge to either prevent burnout or stop it in its tracks by making manageable changes to your diet and lifestyle.

The book is divided into four parts that together explain what burnout is, what's going on at a biochemical level when you burn out, what you can do to relieve the symptoms and what to do next if you need some additional support. After the four main parts, you will discover a collection of recipes and a list of resources. The book is designed to be read in order but if you have a desire to jump in at a certain section, be my guest.

Science is fascinating and health and nutrition science is no exception. However, understanding it often involves deciphering techie terms and complex scientific concepts. Fear not: I'm here to translate the science for you. But occasionally, I will need to use some biochemical terminology. I hope you will bear with me. If you get stuck, feel free to make use of the glossary at the back of the book.

Throughout the book I have used client stories like Abbie's and Becky's to help bring the science to life. These stories are based on real people who have attended my clinic (well, virtually attended – we see clients online) but I have changed their names and some details of their story so as to preserve confidentiality.

This book cannot replicate the individualized experience you would receive by working with a practitioner. Most of the suggestions put forward in this book will help someone, but not all of the suggestions will help everyone. Scientific research is limited in that it can only tell us about an effect on or an association with the particular group studied. The study subjects might be very like you or they may not be like you at all. Either way, they are not you. Each individual's experience of burnout will be unique. This is the whole premise of functional medicine.

This book is about the burnout experience of women. That being said, many of the biochemical imbalances discussed can and do occur in men. Burnout is not a uniquely female experience.

There are three main reasons I decided to write a book about burnout for women:

1. Burnout is more likely to affect women than men.
2. The majority of my clients are women.
3. I am a woman and have personal experience of burnout.

Societal norms about the way we define womanhood have changed over the years, and unfortunately the scientific research has not caught up with this shift. My expertise and the current clinical evidence lie with cisgender women (that is, women who were assigned a female gender identity at birth, as opposed to transgender women, who were not). Consequently, within this book, references to 'women' and scientific studies on female burnout may not always be applicable for transgender women. That being said, it is my hope that whatever your gender, you will find something that is relevant to your unique experience of burnout in this book.

You will also see that I talk about anxiety and depression alongside burnout in this book. There are a number of reasons for this. First and foremost, feeling anxious and experiencing a depressed mood are both common symptoms of burnout. Secondly, anxiety and depression are often stress-induced conditions; and finally, anxiety and depression often co-occur with burnout, as was my own experience. In the current body of research there is some disagreement about whether burnout is the same as, overlapping with, or an entirely separate condition to either generalized anxiety disorder or major depressive disorder. While the scientists continue to argue about this, I felt it best to cover all bases. Consequently, the information presented here may be relevant to burnout and/or stress-induced mood disorders more broadly.

Disclaimer

Before we begin, I need to let you know that the information and guidance provided in this book is for information purposes only. This book is not a substitute for the consultation of and diagnosis and/or medical treatment by your doctor or other healthcare provider.

You must not rely on any information or guidance provided in this book as an alternative to medical advice from your doctor or healthcare provider. The author and publishers expressly disclaim all responsibility, and shall have no liability, for any damages, loss, injury or liability whatsoever suffered by you or any third party as a result of your reliance on any information or guidance we provide in this book.

If you think you may be suffering from any medical condition, you should seek immediate medical attention from your healthcare provider. Do not delay seeking medical advice, disregard medical advice or discontinue medical treatment because of information or guidance provided in this book.

Nothing in this disclaimer will limit or exclude any liability that may not be limited or excluded by applicable law.

Now that all the formalities are done: let's begin.

PART 1

WHAT IS BURNOUT?

When coming to write this first part of the book, I started to consider how to define burnout. 'Burnout' is a term that has become synonymous with occupational exhaustion, the end-state following a long period of chronic stress. I have seen burnout described as a 'pervasive mental health problem in the workforce', a description that personally resonated with me.

In clinical literature, burnout has been investigated for over 50 years, with modern definitions largely based on the work of two independent researchers: clinical psychologist Herbert Freudenberger and social psychologist Christina Maslach. However, references to the concept of burnout can be found in the historical record as far back as the Old Testament (Exodus 18: 17–18; the irony of this book's title is not lost on me) and even Shakespeare used the concept of burnout as a metaphor for exhaustion in his poem *The Passionate Pilgrim*. So, burnout isn't a new or trendy construct.

Today, most researchers define burnout based on the three-dimensional model proposed by Maslach, namely:

1. emotional exhaustion,
2. occupational cynicism or 'depersonalisation', and

3.   reduced personal achievement.[1]

However, I am most intrigued by Freudenberger's work in the 1970s, where he highlighted the physicality of burnout that goes beyond what we experience psychologically:

'There is a feeling of exhaustion, being unable to shake a lingering cold, suffering from frequent headaches and gastrointestinal disturbances, sleeplessness and shortness of breath.'[2]

I asked a group of high-achieving career women to tell me what they thought of when they heard the word 'burnout'. They described exhaustion, anxiety and overwhelm. When we dug a little deeper, feelings of fear, frustration and failure emerged. Some, who felt they had experienced burnout or had been on the cusp of it, described feeling depressed, lacking in motivation and losing interest in their career. I heard stories of horrible bosses, being overlooked for promotion and confrontational colleagues, accompanied by consequent strained relationships at home and social withdrawal. When I asked what other symptoms they had noticed at the time, many reported problems sleeping, IBS, menstrual disturbances, infertility and frequent infections. But they had not connected these symptoms to stress and were surprised to learn that these are all symptoms of burnout.

In the UK, burnout is not medically recognized. If you type 'burnout' into the NHS website search function, it returns no results. Despite the absence of distinct medical classification, however, there is widespread recognition of burnout as an occupational syndrome. The World Health Organization classifies burnout as an 'occupational phenomenon' in the 11th revision of its International Classification of Diseases (ICD-11), but do not go so far as to recognize it as a distinct

---

[1]   Maslach, Schaufeli, and Leiter, 'Job Burnout.'
[2]   Freudenberger, 'Staff Burn-Out.'

medical condition: 'Burnout is a syndrome conceptualized as resulting from chronic workplace stress that has not been successfully managed.'[3]

The biochemical causes and effects of burnout are complex and unique to each individual. However, there is one common driver: chronic stress. This is the kind of stress that is persistent, the kind that spills over into your personal life and leaves you increasingly cynical and unable to perform at your best, at work or at home!

So, before we can fully understand burnout, we must fully understand stress. Let's delve a little deeper.

[3] World Health Organization, 'ICD-11 for Mortality and Morbidity Statistics.'

CHAPTER 1

STRESS

Stress is a frequently (perhaps over-) used term that we have come to associate with the pressures of life. We use the term interchangeably to refer to both things that have got us worked up: an incessant workload, an irate stakeholder or a presentation to the board; and the (usually negative) feelings we associate with that pressure: anxiety, tension, fatigue, overwhelm and so on. The former we might refer to as *stressors* and the latter a *stressed-out* psychological state.

We also use the term stress for both good stress and bad, good stress being the excitement and challenge that comes with a new project or the motivational effect of a deadline; bad stress usually associated with overload (feeling *stressed-out*) or a negative situation (*distress*).

Stressors come in many forms. Most of us know that work can, and will, be stressful at times. High achievers generally face a more demanding workload and increasing pressure as they climb the corporate ladder. It is this occupational stress that arguably makes burnout unique compared to depression or anxiety. However, most of us recognize that stress can extend beyond the workplace. We may have a stressful home life or have experienced stressful, traumatic events over the course of our lives. Watching the news, scrolling on social media, poor health, illness or injury, nutrient deficiencies, stimulants, loneliness, exercise and junk food are all environmental stressors that many of us are exposed to daily. The main thing to grasp here is that your brain doesn't care what the stressor is. It puts them all in the 'threat' category and responds accordingly.

In the body, stress is a physiological state that occurs in response to an external or internal challenge or threat. It is our body's way of making adjustments to ensure survival. It is an adaptive process and, through this adaptation, we develop resilience so that we are better able to anticipate and cope with the same challenge next time around. In this way, we can view 'stress' – or rather, 'adaption' – as a both positive and protective mechanism.

Scientists have coined a stress-specific term to describe this adaptive process: 'allostasis'. Allostasis essentially means 'the ability to achieve stability through change'.[4]

Problems occur when the body's systems are chronically challenged or stressed. This can lead to inappropriate adjustments and a maladaptive state, which can contribute to chronic disease.

1.1 Stress and the brain

The brain is the key organ that orchestrates our stress response. The brain:

a. Determines what is stressful.
b. Regulates our physiological and behavioural responses to cope with the stressor.
c. Rewires itself to function differently next time – learning from the experience.

The brain's ability to rewire itself – or change – as a result of experience is known as *neuroplasticity*. This rewiring can either be:

---

[4] Sterling and Eyer, 'Allostasis: A New Paradigm to Explain Arousal Pathology.'

- helpful (adaptive): for example, the next time we present to the board our brain will remind us we have done this before and reduce the amount of worry we feel beforehand; or
- unhelpful (maladaptive): for example, after a huge failure at work our brain tells us to worry excessively or disproportionately when asked to undertake a similar project.

In executing the stress response the brain is supported by various biological systems, chief among them being:

- The hypothalamic–pituitary–adrenal (HPA)-axis (part of our endocrine or hormone system, which we will explore properly below).
- The autonomic nervous system.
- The metabolic system.
- The immune system.
- The gut.

Each of these systems produces biochemical mediators of the stress response (hormones, neurotransmitters, cytokines and so on), which collectively regulate one another.

How we respond to stress is a very individual experience. It is influenced by our:

- Genes – our inherited stress resilience/ability to cope.
- Life history – events that have happened to us that may have altered our resilience/ability to cope.
- Current behavioural and physiological state – our diet, lifestyle and other environmental factors that can influence our current resilience levels/ability to cope.

The result is that some of us are hyper- (over-active) responders to stress, whereas others are hypo- (under-active) responders.

1.2 The stress response

Exploring our physiological response to stress a bit further: let's assume that your brain recognizes a threat. It will initiate a response that we have historically referred to as 'fight or flight'.

During this response, two key things immediately happen. First, lightning-fast signals are sent via the autonomic nervous system to the adrenal medulla instructing it to release noradrenaline and adrenaline. These neurotransmitters act to raise the internal threat level to high.

Secondly, the adaptive coping mechanism is launched by the neuroendocrine system, known as the 'HPA-axis'. Specifically, the adrenal cortex releases our stress hormone cortisol in response to signals from the hypothalamus and pituitary glands in the brain.

The result of HPA-axis activation is a cascade of physiological effects that prepare the body to deal with perceived threat or danger. For example:

- Mobilization of energy.
- Relaxation of the airways.
- Dilation of pupils.
- Increase in heartrate.

At the same time, the fight or flight response inhibits non-essential biological processes such as digestion, reproduction and repair. I am just going to repeat that so that it sticks: our natural stress response down-regulates digestion, reproduction and repair. We will see why that is important later.

Historically, this response enabled humans to flee from predators or fight off a bear. Once the perceived danger has passed, cortisol levels return to normal and digestive, reproductive and immune function resume.

Today, our genes and physiology are almost identical to our hunter-gatherer ancestors, yet they are exposed to a very different environment. The persistent stressors of modern life such as

- psychological and emotional stress,
- information overload/overwhelm,
- poor nutrition,
- excess stimulant use, and
- a stressful job/home life

can provoke the repeated over-activation of the fight or flight response, placing the body in continuous survival mode. This may explain why, when we are chronically stressed, we experience symptoms of IBS (a digestive disorder) or feel tired, run down, anxious and unable to concentrate. It can also inhibit fertility, which is why some women struggle to get pregnant when they are chronically stressed.

1.3 The process of adaption/maladaptation: An evolutionary view

Bruce McEwen, one of the current thought leaders in science on the stress response, states that adaption has a price, namely 'wear and tear' on the body and brain.[5]

For the most part, our stress response and this process of adaption is designed to happen over a short period of time. A bear attack was never prolonged. It happened, we ran away to safety or we fought it and (hopefully) won.

---

[5] McEwen, 'Structural Plasticity of the Adult Brain: How Animal Models Help Us Understand Brain Changes in Depression and Systemic Disorders Related to Depression.'

Either way it was over quickly. The brain recognized that the threat had passed and hit the stop button on the stress response. We went back to normal until the next threat, and thankfully these were relatively infrequent.

Fast forward to the 21st century. Now stress is a daily, perhaps hourly, occurrence. To be sure, it is rarely as life-threatening as a bear attack, but now we might experience:

- Frequent stressors throughout the day, necessitating the brain to frequently activate/deactivate the stress response. Like flicking a light switch on/off, on/off, on/off.
- Prolonged stressors with no apparent ending, so the brain doesn't know when or if it is over and never presses stop.
- Overwhelm and a total inability to cope with the load. Consequently, the brain is unable to muster an adequate response from its partner systems.

All of these scenarios can lead to unhelpful rewiring of the brain and leave us lacking the protective effects of a normal adaptive stress response.

In summary, our stress response is most useful when it is rapidly mobilized and rapidly terminated. Problems arise when the stress is chronic, either due to the frequency or duration of the stressor, relative to our level of resilience.

We must also remember that what our brains consider to be stressful is all a matter of perception and is regulated by different areas of our brain, upstream, if you like, from the hypothalamus and the HPA-axis. The prefrontal cortex is responsible for receiving information from the environment and internally interpreting and categorizing this data. It will decide whether a disgruntled customer is worth stressing about. If yes, it will alert the hypothalamus to initiate the stress response. We will explore the brain areas involved in resilience more in Chapter 5.

Spotlight on: The adrenal glands

Your adrenal glands are located above each kidney and form a key part of your 'neuroendocrine' (chemical messaging) system. Your adrenals comprise two main sections: the adrenal medulla and the adrenal cortex.

The adrenal glands are perhaps most widely known for regulating our response to stress; however, they also secrete hormones that are responsible for:

- Regulating our circadian rhythm (sleep–wake cycle).
- Regulating blood pressure and electrolyte balance.
- Regulating blood sugar balance and metabolism.
- Suppressing the immune system and controlling inflammation.

Chronic stress places considerable strain on the adrenal glands and ultimately affects the body's ability to adapt and cope. This can lead to HPA-axis dysregulation, adrenal insufficiency* and what is commonly termed 'burnout'.

*In the recent past it has become quite trendy to talk about 'adrenal fatigue', with some researchers suggesting that the adrenals can become worn-out from overuse. Debate still rages about whether chronic stress can cause the adrenals to become fatigued. The current consensus is that the dysregulation observed in the adrenal glands from burnout is more likely to be due to dysregulated signalling from the brain.

1.4 The three stages of burnout

Burnout doesn't just happen overnight. HPA-axis dysregulation and adrenal insufficiency build up over time with a collection of physiological effects that can be grouped together in three stages. Think of these like a Venn diagram, where the distinct states of feeling anxious or 'wired' and exhausted or 'tired' meet to form a third category:

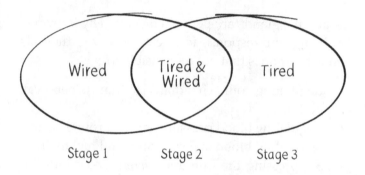

Stage 1   Stage 2   Stage 3

I've called them stages 1–3 but this doesn't mean they occur in this precise order in a path to burnout.

Stage 1: Wired

This is the coping stage.

Most of us recognize the 'typical' feelings of being stressed. That sensation of being on high alert, perhaps a little anxious. This is your body doing its job: screening for threats and responding accordingly to keep you safe. The first stage of burnout is noticing that you are feeling this way constantly. You are experiencing mild/moderate stress on a frequent basis. You might even identify as a 'stress bunny', operating under the limiting belief that you thrive on stress and need it to perform at your best. (We will talk more about limiting beliefs that may not be serving you in Part 3, Chapter 16.) Full disclosure: this was me. I spent most of my early career 'wired'.

I'd like to introduce you to Dee, a 'wired' 26-year-old project manager. Her friends call her 'Duracell Dee' as she is always on the go, with boundless energy. She thinks resting is for wimps. Dee's job is demanding and there are frequent deadlines to be met, but she has the best team and a supportive boss. She gets up at 5am so she can go for a run every day before work. Dee has always been a bit of a worrier; she thinks this makes her better at her job, but when she isn't working she finds it difficult to switch off and relax. Lately, she has noticed that her busy mind is preventing her from falling asleep easily – but she still musters enough energy to get through the day.

At a physiological level, Dee's adrenals are in constant demand from repetitive stress signals received in her brain. There are prolonged periods of raised cortisol levels, which are making her feel restless and anxious and occasionally disrupting her sleep. But other than this, Dee feels healthy.

Your body can respond in this way for a surprisingly long time, especially when the stressors are mild. This is adaption: the wear, before the tear. Consequently, the first stage of burnout can be a long one and can largely go undetected as burnout. The health consequences of this stage may appear mild compared to the later stages, but I would argue that Stage 1 is actually the most critical phase of burnout. If you can recognize yourself in this stage, you have the best chance of both preventing burnout and offsetting the effects of chronic stress.

Stage 2: Tired AND wired

At some stage, the body loses resilience and is less able to cope, disturbing the delicate balance of the HPA-axis. The brain doesn't know when or if to press the stop button on the stress response.

Meet Hannah, a 'tired and wired' 33-year-old employment lawyer at an international law firm. Pre-pandemic, she was travelling a lot with work – up and down to London and often abroad. She describes her life as 'go-go-go', with high stress levels par for the course. Recently, Hannah has noticed that she is struggling to get going in the mornings and finds it difficult to concentrate in client meetings. It's a running joke in the office to avoid Hannah before lunchtime! Her peers are mostly men and they are all jostling for the same promotion. Privately, Hannah is worried that her health is affecting her performance and with it her ability to make partner in the firm.

Hannah's adrenal glands are still receiving signals from her brain and continue to pump out cortisol; however, her cortisol receptors are becoming 'resistant' or less sensitive. This means she needs to produce even more cortisol to achieve the same energy levels and focus she had pre-pandemic. As a result, she is starting to feel agitated, on edge and tired. Physiologically, she is in a high-cortisol or *hypercortisolaemic* state.

The point at which this loss of resilience occurs is different for everyone and can be influenced by a number of genetic, diet and lifestyle factors.

[Note this stage is not to be confused with the cortisol excess observed in Cushing's syndrome.]

Stage 3: Tired

Well, 'tired' is putting it mildly – it is more like total exhaustion and emotional overwhelm. This is the stage that most of us associate with outright burnout.

Meet Abbie, a 'tired' 35-year-old corporate accountant. Abbie is exhausted and finds herself frequently tearful. Most days she struggles to get into the office and when she does get there, she feels unable to function. At weekends she sleeps until midday and still doesn't feel rested. Abbie has always described herself as a happy person but now finds it difficult to even smile. Alongside this she has put on weight, which no amount of dieting has been able to shift. She feels overwhelmed and trapped in a miserable cycle of poor health. She has lost all confidence in herself.

For Abbie, the demand on her stress response has outstripped supply and sub-optimal adrenal function has occurred. Signalling from her brain is dysregulated and cortisol production has declined. She feels mentally and physically exhausted. Physiologically, she's in a low cortisol or *hypocortisolaemic* state.

[Note this stage is not to be confused with the primary adrenal insufficiency observed in Addison's disease.]

It is at this stage that an individual might notice a change in their mental health. Once anxious, now disinterested, exhausted and feeling low – the classic symptoms of depression. This may explain why many who burn out also experience depression and why there is such a significant link between chronic stress and mood disorders.

1.5 Detecting which stage of burnout you are at

As well as regulating our response to stress, the hormone cortisol regulates our circadian rhythm. When functioning optimally, the adrenal glands will ensure that cortisol levels are at their peak just before we wake up – giving us our 'get-up and go' – and decline steadily throughout the day in preparation for sleep. This pattern of cortisol levels can be detected in both saliva and urine. In Stages 1 and 2, the pattern may appear dysregulated, whereas in Stage 3 it will appear flat. This type of testing helps functional medicine practitioners tailor therapeutic support to their patients' needs.

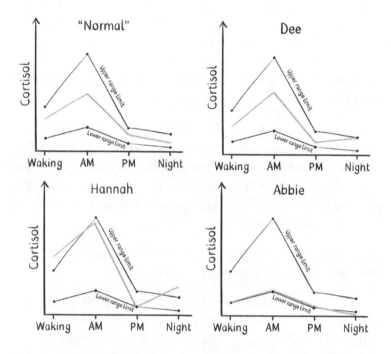

Even without testing, your symptoms provide an indication as to what stage of burnout you might be at. You can determine which stage of burnout you might be at by visiting our website www.re-nutrition.co.uk and taking our burnout quiz (see resources at the back of this book for more information).

CHAPTER 2

WHY WOMEN EXPERIENCE BURNOUT

Burnout is not a uniquely female experience; however, women are more likely than men to experience emotional exhaustion in business and are at increased risk of burnout.[6] We ladies are also struggling more with our mental health post pandemic.[7] Who hasn't felt overwhelmed, am I right?

But why are women more vulnerable than men? Well, that's something we don't fully understand yet. It may be linked to the way we have evolved to handle stress. Frustratingly, most of the historical research on stress has been conducted by men on male subjects (or on male rodents). This has given science a very thorough understanding of the male stress response, and it is from this body of evidence that the concept of 'fight or flight' derives.

The phrase 'fight or flight' is used interchangeably to describe both the *physiological* response to stress, i.e. the activation of the sympathetic nervous system and the ensuing cascade of physiological effects described in Chapter 1, and as a metaphor for the human *behavioural* response, i.e. the decision to either stay and fight the aggressor or flee the scene.

Modern science tells us that while 'fight or flight' *physiology* does not differ across the genders, the female *behavioural*

---

[6] Beauregard et al., 'Gendered Pathways to Burnout: Results from the SALVEO Study.'

[7] Pierce et al., 'Mental Health before and during the COVID-19 Pandemic: A Longitudinal Probability Sample Survey of the UK Population.'

response to stress is less likely to have evolved as physical fighting (acts of aggression) or fleeing.

Psychologist Shelley Taylor has proposed the concept of the 'tend and befriend' response, whereby, under stress, women have evolved to tap into biological care-giving and attachment systems that push us to focus not only on the survival of ourselves but also of our offspring.[8] In this model:

- **Tend** means to nurture ourselves and/or our children in a way that calms the nervous system, makes us feel safe and reduces the negative effects of stress.
- **Befriend** means to create, maintain and lean on your 'girl gang' (or any social group) in times of need. This functions both as a protective mechanism (strength and safety in numbers) and as a way of managing stress.

In certain occupational contexts, women may find their natural need to 'tend and befriend' impeded, which will increase their vulnerability to burnout. For example, climbing the career ladder can be an isolating experience that reduces women's capacity for socializing outside of work. It may also result in either delaying starting a family or having less time to spend with them. On the flip side, this model also offers methods to reduce the risk of burnout.

Research suggests that women are more likely than men to become anxious in stressful situations, remembering that the brain ultimately decides what is stressful and that our perception becomes our reality.[9] In one study, women

---

[8] Taylor et al., 'Biobehavioral Responses to Stress in Females: Tend-and-Befriend, Not Fight-or-Flight.'
[9] McLean et al., 'Gender Differences in Anxiety Disorders: Prevalence, Course of Illness, Comorbidity and Burden of Illness.'

reported lower self-esteem than men, which in turn was associated with higher levels of burnout.[10] There are also some animal studies that suggest women may not be able to adapt as well to acutely stressful situations. In one such animal study, it was noted that, in response to an acute stressor, male rodents showed improved behavioural performance after adapting to the situation, whereas the females behaved differently and did not adapt as well.[11]

But burnout risk doesn't just come down to gender or individual vulnerability. Environmental factors both at work and at home can influence susceptibility to burnout. At work, burnout-related factors can be classified as either increasing the risk of burnout (work demands) or mitigating the risk of burnout (work resources). Typical demands that we all recognize as stressful include long hours or irregular shift patterns, job uncertainty, abusive supervision and interpersonal conflict. Remember Hannah from Chapter 1? Her fellow lawyers were not her friends. Her peers were competitive and her team was afraid of her. This is an added stressor that, unbeknown to Hannah, may have made her more vulnerable to burnout.

These stressors – or work demands – can be eased or offset to a degree by appropriate remuneration, rewards and recognition; alongside appropriate skill utilization, decision-making authority and support. Beyond the working environment, the demands and support of family can also influence susceptibility to burnout. When conflict arises between work and family life, this creates an additional stressor that can increase the risk of burnout.

---

[10] Beauregard et al., 'Gendered Pathways to Burnout: Results from the SALVEO Study.'

[11] Wood and Shors, 'Stress Facilitates Classical Conditioning in Males, but Impairs Classical Conditioning in Females through Activational Effects of Ovarian Hormones.'

Research indicates that differential gender exposure to these environmental factors may adversely influence female burnout. A 2018 study of 2,162 workers from 63 workplaces in Canada (the SALVEO study) assessed levels of burnout alongside work, non-work and individual factors.[12] In this study, the female participants who experienced burnout reported lower levels of decision-making authority and skill utilization, alongside higher levels of child-related strain and higher instances of single parenthood.

Even in an age of so-called gender equality, it is easy to see how the balance might be tipped unfavourably against women. Despite ongoing efforts to equalize pay, the gender pay gap still exists and, interestingly, becomes wider as we enter our 30s and 40s. And just as that gap begins to widen, we face major life decisions about careers and babies. Having chosen a path, we risk dissatisfaction in the life area we leave behind – or we try to do it all, each path increasing the risk of burnout in susceptible women. As Joy Burnford points out her book, *Don't Fix Women: The Practical Path to Gender Equality at Work*, there are just too many obstacles on the path![13]

If we decide to start a family, and assuming we are successful in this venture (stress being a major factor in both fertility and fertility treatment – more about that later), we as women are more likely to be the primary caregiver and therefore more likely to experience work–home conflict. Women are also more likely to take on work they are overqualified for in an attempt to strike a better work–life balance and are more likely to be overlooked for promotion, which reduces decision-making latitude and skill utilization at work.

---

[12] Beauregard et al., 'Gendered Pathways to Burnout: Results from the SALVEO Study.'
[13] Burnford, *Don't Fix Women: The Practical Path to Gender Equality at Work*.

Part-time and flexible working is the modern way of attempting to address the issue of work–life balance and, indeed, these arrangements can offer protective effects in the short term. (Beauregard et al. found that female burnout levels were reduced when participants had more time outside of work to invest in domestic tasks.[14]) However, part-time work also presents with career limitations that may not be helpful to female occupational mental health and a sense of fulfilment in the long term.

And then we arrive at mid-life: battle worn and scarred, staring down the menopause. All while getting paid less than our male counterparts. Taken together, it is easy to imagine why women are more stressed and more likely to experience occupational exhaustion, cynicism and reduced efficacy – the core characteristics of burnout.

---

[14] Beauregard et al., 'Gendered Pathways to Burnout: Results from the SALVEO Study.'

CHAPTER 3

THE BURNOUT EFFECT

Cortisol is toxic to the brain and can cause atrophy (or wasting away) of brain tissue. Stress can literally kill neurons (brain cells). This is particularly true in areas of the brain that are responsible for our emotional response to stress as well as cognition, learning, memory and mood, such as the prefrontal cortex, hippocampus and hypothalamus. Conversely, cortisol can increase the volume of the fear centre of our brain – the amygdala – in a condition known as hypertrophy. My telling you this is not intended to cause you stress or to activate your HPA-axis! But I think it is important to know that stress really can alter the size of your brain!

Now that I have your attention, I am pleased to report that these effects are reversible with the right action and interventions. As you will later learn, certain nutrients and activities – such as exercise and mindfulness – have been scientifically proven to increase brain volume in the prefrontal cortex, hypothalamus and hippocampus, while also reducing the size of the amygdala.[15] Yay! But what happens if we don't take action?

Well, let's not forget that your brain is running the show when it comes to your physiological response to stress. How you think and feel – your psychology – can literally determine

---

[15] Jacka et al., 'Western Diet Is Associated with a Smaller Hippocampus: A Longitudinal Investigation'; Wilckens et al., 'Exercise Interventions Preserve Hippocampal Volume: A Meta-Analysis'; Hölzel et al., 'Mindfulness Practice Leads to Increases in Regional Brain Gray Matter Density.'

your physiology and therefore your overall health. Consider that the physiologic response to stress involves the whole body. In turn, chronic stress can influence disease in various body systems. Stress is serious stuff and while it can be a lifesaver in some situations, it is also a killer.

Let's look at some health conditions associated with chronic stress, HPA-axis dysfunction and burnout.

3.1 Health conditions associated with burnout

Unsurprisingly, chronic stress and the resultant changes in brain structure have been linked with mood disorders and cognitive decline.

Mood disorders

Both high- and low-cortisol states have been linked with major depressive disorder. Specifically, over-production of the stress hormone cortisol (as seen in Stage 1 and 2 burnout) have been linked with 'melancholic depression', which is characterized by feeling anxious throughout the day, insomnia, feelings of dread and lack of appetite. Under-production of cortisol, meanwhile, is associated with 'atypical depression', characterized by overwhelming fatigue, lethargy, excessive sleep and increased appetite/overeating.[16] Remember Abbie from Chapter 1? This was her experience of Stage 3 burnout.

As well as atypical depression, suppressed cortisol patterns have been linked with other mood disorders such as seasonal affective disorder, panic disorder, bipolar II,

---

[16] Lamers et al., 'Evidence for a Differential Role of HPA-Axis Function, Inflammation and Metabolic Syndrome in Melancholic versus Atypical Depression.'

postpartum depression and generalized anxiety disorder.[17] Post-traumatic stress disorder (PTSD) has been observed in both high- and low-cortisol states.[18]

Cognitive decline and dementia

The stress response is designed to make us more alert in the short term, and when adrenaline and cortisol are at the right levels the brain will respond positively. However, if it becomes overwhelmed by cortisol, or if cortisol is produced in insufficient amounts, the brain will struggle to function. At work this is flipping frustrating and impacts our performance as we struggle to recall information or take new information on board. And, over time, it can have serious consequences.

A persistent stressed state not only shrinks the areas of the brain that support learning and memory but also perpetuates low levels of inflammation. This chronic, low-level inflammation is associated with the build-up of plaques in the brain, which are believed to be the primary cause of dementia and Alzheimer's disease. Cognitive decline does not happen overnight, and although it is primarily associated with older age (ages 65+), cases of early-onset dementia (arising between the ages of 30 and 64) are on the rise.[19] In fact, signs of Alzheimer's have been detected as

[17] Mantella et al., 'Salivary Cortisol Is Associated with Diagnosis and Severity of Late-Life Generalized Anxiety Disorder'; Cervantes et al., 'Circadian Secretion of Cortisol in Bipolar Disorder.'
[18] Wahbeh and Oken, 'Salivary Cortisol Lower in Posttraumatic Stress Disorder'; Kasckow, Baker, and Geracioti, 'Corticotropin-Releasing Hormone in Depression and Post-Traumatic Stress Disorder.'
[19] Vieira et al., 'Epidemiology of Early-Onset Dementia: A Review of the Literature.'

early as 18 years before a formal diagnosis is given.[20] This is a slow-burn disease.

Stressful life events are associated with increased risk of cognitive decline. One study has highlighted that mid-life job strain is associated with reduced cognitive performance in later life and an increased risk of cognitive impairment.[21]

Muscular-skeletal health

Brain tissue is not the only tissue to be affected by stress. In an effort to fuel the stress response, cortisol recruits energy and nutrients stored in bone and muscular tissue. Consequently, chronic stress has been associated with reduced bone mineral density, and burnout increases the risk of developing muscular skeletal pain in otherwise healthy individuals.[22]

Chronic fatigue syndrome

The occupational exhaustion of Stage 3 burnout shares many characteristics with chronic fatigue syndrome, or myalgic encephalomyelitis (ME), a long-term, debilitating condition that leaves sufferers unable to engage effectively in day-to-day tasks. Common symptoms include extreme fatigue, sleep issues, cognitive issues, muscle aches, palpitations and headaches. The exact causes are unknown, but psychological stress, hormone imbalance and immune dysregulation are thought to play a role. Sound familiar?

---

[20] Rajan et al., 'Cognitive Impairment 18 Years before Clinical Diagnosis of Alzheimer Disease Dementia.'

[21] Andel et al., 'Indicators of Job Strain at Midlife and Cognitive Functioning in Advanced Old Age.'

[22] Armon et al., 'Elevated Burnout Predicts the Onset of Musculoskeletal Pain among Apparently Healthy Employees.'

Autoimmune conditions

Perhaps one of the biggest impacts of chronic stress is on our immune system. Physiologic stress is pro-inflammatory and decreases our ability to launch an anti-inflammatory counter response. Low levels of chronic stress that persist for years leave us susceptible to frequent infections and colds and vulnerable to developing chronic disease.[23] We've just looked at the effects of stress on the brain, including mood disorders, cognitive decline and dementia. Out in the rest of the body, or the periphery, chronic stress may play a role in the development of autoimmune conditions such as Hashimoto's thyroiditis.[24] Remember Hannah from Chapter 1? We will meet her again in Chapter 8 when we explore burnout and its effect on thyroid function.

You can read more about stress and inflammation in Chapter 10.

IBS, 'leaky gut' and beyond

The brain and the gut can communicate bidirectionally in what is known as the gut–brain axis (more about this in Chapter 9). Consequently, stress can influence gut functioning and has been linked with irritable bowel syndrome (IBS) and irritable bowel diseases (IBD) such as Crohn's and ulcerative colitis.[25] Stress may also be a factor in changing the composition of the gut microbiome, which

---

[23] Glaser and Kiecolt-Glaser, 'Stress-Induced Immune Dysfunction: Implications for Health.'
[24] Mizokami et al., 'Stress and Thyroid Autoimmunity.'
[25] Brzozowski et al., 'Mechanisms by Which Stress Affects the Experimental and Clinical Inflammatory Bowel Disease (IBD): Role of Brain-Gut Axis'; Chang, 'The Role of Stress on Physiologic Responses and Clinical Symptoms in Irritable Bowel Syndrome.'

may lead to the gut becoming 'leaky' or more permeable.[26] 'Leaky gut' has been linked with systemic conditions such as arthritis, migraine and acne.[27]

Cardiovascular disease

The stress response also raises our blood pressure and dilates blood vessels so that oxygen from the lungs can rapidly reach our muscles to enable fight or flight. Chronic activation of the stress response has been linked with hypertension (high blood pressure) and diminished endothelial function, where the arteries narrow instead of remaining open. Both hypertension and cardiovascular disease increase the risk of heart attack and stroke. In these cases, stress can be fatal.[28]

Obesity and the metabolic syndrome

Chronic stress increases the risk of obesity and a collection of conditions known as metabolic syndrome – the precursors of type 2 diabetes and cardiovascular disease.

Cortisol stimulates our appetite and increases our preference for sugary, high-fat foods. Consumed in excess, these types of foods may contribute to blood sugar dysregulation and increased fat storage, particularly around the abdomen (see Chapter 7 for more about blood sugar dysregulation).[29]

---

[26] Kelly et al., 'Breaking down the Barriers: The Gut Microbiome, Intestinal Permeability and Stress-Related Psychiatric Disorders.'

[27] Fasano, 'All Disease Begins in the (Leaky) Gut: Role of Zonulin-Mediated Gut Permeability in the Pathogenesis of Some Chronic Inflammatory Diseases.'

[28] Tawakol et al., 'Relation between Resting Amygdalar Activity and Cardiovascular Events: A Longitudinal and Cohort Study.'

[29] Hackett et al., 'Diurnal Cortisol Patterns, Future Diabetes, and Impaired Glucose Metabolism in the Whitehall II Cohort Study'; Kumari et al., 'A Nonlinear Relationship of Generalized and Central Obesity with Diurnal Cortisol Secretion in the Whitehall II Study.'

Excess cortisol is converted into cortisone, which is stored in fat cells – particularly in the abdominal area. In a vicious circle, excess abdominal fat equals more space to store cortisol, and increased cortisol increases fat. This is why we often develop a 'burnout belly'. It can take years to get rid of this. Believe me, I'm still working on mine!

Infertility and pregnancy

In survival mode, reproduction is considered non-essential and hormone production is downregulated. Our libido is decreased, and our menstrual cycle might go on the fritz or disappear altogether. With this in mind it is easy to predict that chronic stress may impair fertility outcomes.

If pregnancy is achieved, stress and elevated cortisol has also been associated with early pregnancy loss, miscarriage, foetal distress and pre-term birth.[30] Maternal stress can impact the temperament and cognitive function of the baby once born, and may even reduce their resilience to stress and increase their susceptibility to disease in adulthood.[31]

Wow. This highlights why it is super important to tackle burnout and get stress under control before thinking about pregnancy.

---

[30] Nepomnaschy et al., 'Cortisol Levels and Very Early Pregnancy Loss in Humans'; Wainstock et al., 'Prenatal Stress and Risk of Spontaneous Abortion'; Sandman et al., 'Corticotrophin-Releasing Hormone and Fetal Responses in Human Pregnancy.'

[31] Lambertini, Chen, and Nomura, 'Mitochondrial Gene Expression Profiles Are Associated with Maternal Psychosocial Stress in Pregnancy and Infant Temperament'; Wu et al., 'Association of Elevated Maternal Psychological Distress, Altered Fetal Brain, and Offspring Cognitive and Social-Emotional Outcomes at 18 Months'; Drake, Tang, and Nyirenda, 'Mechanisms Underlying the Role of Glucocorticoids in the Early Life Programming of Adult Disease.'

Cancer

Finally, the dreaded big one. Emerging research suggests that chronic daily stress, severe life events and social isolation, which are all stressors on the human body, may play a role in the growth and spread of cancer. The human stress response suppresses immune function, creating the right environment for cancer cell growth, while simultaneously preventing the natural process of cell die-off. In one study, female rodents, exposed to the psychosocial stress of isolation, experienced increased growth and malignancy of breast cancer, compared to rodents who lived in a group.[32] As well as being more tumour-prone, the stressed rodents exhibited hyper-vigilant behaviours like anxiety and fearfulness. In humans, dysregulated or flattened cortisol patterns (like those observed in Stage 3 burnout) have been associated with increased mortality rates from metastatic breast cancer.[33]

3.2 The cost of burnout

You will probably have noticed that all these conditions are what are known as *lifestyle diseases*. By this, I mean diseases that have a strong environmental influence on their onset and progression (unlike like cystic fibrosis or Huntington's disease, which sufferers are born with, or infectious diseases like the plague or coronaviruses). These lifestyle diseases are chronic conditions that are typically prolonged in duration, require long-term treatment and are rarely completely curable. They are diseases that have become more prevalent in the 21st century and have an enormous cost burden,

---

[32] Hermes et al., 'Social Isolation Dysregulates Endocrine and Behavioral Stress While Increasing Malignant Burden of Spontaneous Mammary Tumors.'

[33] Sephton et al., 'Diurnal Cortisol Rhythm as a Predictor of Breast Cancer Survival.'

both in terms of an individual's quality of life and on the economy. In the UK, chronic disease costs the tax payer £54 billion a year according to the latest data from the Office of National Statistics.[34]

Burnout itself is also an expensive business. A survey published by Deloitte in 2022 estimated the total cost of burnout to UK employers at £56 billion, compared to £45 billion in the 2019 survey. As well as absenteeism and reduced performance, burnout is contributing to increased levels of staff turnover, with 61% of leavers citing poor mental health as their reason for leaving.[35]

3.3 Symptoms to look out for

Having read this far, you are probably sitting up now and wondering what signs and symptoms you should be looking out for if you suspect you may be burning out.

The most obvious signs that stress is affecting your health are changes in your energy levels, brain function and sleep, alongside changes in your mood, thoughts and feelings. Symptoms such as:

- Fatigue/exhaustion
- Energy slumps during the day
- Brain fog
- Difficulty concentrating
- Poor short-term memory/recall
- Insomnia
- Night waking
- Emotional overwhelm

---

[34] Office for National Statistics, 'Healthcare Expenditure, UK Health Accounts: 2020.'
[35] Deloitte, 'Poor Mental Health Costs UK Employers up to £56 Billion a Year | Deloitte UK.'

- Anxiety
- Negative thinking
- Low mood
- Mood swings
- Irritability
- Agitation
- Anger
- Low motivation
- Disinterest
- Frustration
- Despair
- Cynicism

However, because the stress response involves the whole body, we may also notice symptoms of immune, circulatory, metabolic, gut and reproductive dysregulation. These are perhaps the less obvious signs and symptoms of burnout, but all could have stress at the root cause. Symptoms might include:

- Frequent infections
- Joint/muscle pain
- Slow-healing wounds
- Rashes
- Acne
- Migraines/headaches
- Palpitations
- Dizzy spells
- Weight loss or weight gain
- Sugar cravings
- Constipation
- Diarrhoea
- Bloating
- Nausea
- Irregular or missing periods
- Heavy periods
- Fertility issues

This list is not exhaustive, but I think you get the idea that burnout is not fun and stress is a force to be reckoned with.

Of course, not all these symptoms will present themselves with every case of burnout, and symptoms may vary depending on which stage of burnout you are at. Equally, these symptoms could have multiple other root causes.

We all want to improve our lifespan – but equally important is improving our 'health span'. No one wants to live until they are 100 if they spend 40 years of that life debilitated by mental, cognitive or physical disease. In this book, I am sharing my tried-and-tested Mood Boosting Method, designed to improve the way you feel *and* the way you think in order to increase your resilience to stress. By increasing your resilience, you will also be improving the function of your brain, your immune system, your communication systems, your digestive system and your cardiovascular system, and supporting the structural integrity of your body's musculo-skeletal system. And with all of that you are reducing your risk of chronic disease.

CHAPTER 4

MANAGING FATIGUE AND EMOTIONAL OVERWHELM

Let's say you were to go to the doctor with your symptoms: what would happen? Well, despite recognition by the World Health Organization as an occupational syndrome, burnout is not classified as a medical condition.[36] This makes diagnosis and appropriate treatment of burnout tricky.

Unsurprisingly, many are misdiagnosed with general anxiety or major depressive disorder. To be fair, it is easy to see why as there is significant overlap in symptomology: low mood, fatigue, anhedonia (loss of interest), sleep disturbances and so on.

4.1 The traditional approach

The traditional medical approach to managing mental health disorders is the provision of psychotherapy and/or antidepressant drugs. For some with burnout, when anxiety and/or depression are part of the picture, this approach can literally be lifesaving.

However, waiting times for psychotherapy in England can stretch up to 229 days and recovery rates are reported at less than 50%.[37] Similarly, the literature indicates that pharmacological drugs have sub-optimal efficacy (50%) and

---

[36] World Health Organization, 'ICD-11 for Mortality and Morbidity Statistics.'

[37] Baker and Kirk-Wade, 'Mental Health Statistics: Prevalence, Services, and Funding in England.'

low remission rates (*c.* 30–40%), and can be accompanied by undesirable side effects such as nausea, constipation, hypotension, weight gain and sexual dysfunction.[38]

Why might this be? Well, the former is based on a historical lack of recognition that mental health warrants an equal focus to physical health. This has led to woeful underfunding and, consequently, an overstretched service. There is also a tendency to a one-size-fits-all approach to talking therapy, which has failed to recognize that not everyone is suited to cognitive behavioural therapy or counselling (or even talking at all!).

In terms of drug treatment, most pharmacological drugs work on the assumption that the cause of mood disorders is an imbalance in brain chemistry; the drugs have been designed to redress this balance. However, the causes of depression and anxiety are not fully understood, and there are multiple other functional imbalances cited by scientists as being associated with mood disorders (we'll get into this in Part 2). If the root cause(s) have not been correctly identified, this will inherently reduce the efficacy of the treatment.[39]

What this tells us is that the traditional approach will only help half of us (the 50% reported to recover following psychotherapy and/or antidepressants), *assuming* we have been correctly diagnosed and can access the services we need. Hmm. How frustrating. It is hardly any wonder that

---

[38] Gaynes et al., 'The STAR*D Study: Treating Depression in the Real World'; Wang et al., 'Addressing the Side Effects of Contemporary Antidepressant Drugs: A Comprehensive Review.'

[39] This isn't me having a go at the NHS, by the way. I think they are amazing at what they do, especially in emergency and acute healthcare. I only wish that functional (or lifestyle) medicine could be accessed under the same banner to help with chronic illness and preventative healthcare.

nutrition and lifestyle interventions are increasingly being sought to modulate mental health.[40]

If a mood disorder is ruled out, we are typically sent on our way and told to 'just relax'. Now, there is nothing wrong with a holiday or a spa-day; I'm sure you love them as much as I do. But how many times have you taken a short break, then gone back into work and ended up right back where you were before you left? This quick-fix approach to 'self-care' leaves us none the wiser as to how we got here in the first place, nor does it equip us with the tools we need to thrive through stress in the long term. We can't just 'Eat, Pray, Love' our way back to health. Most of us need to work!

4.2 An alternative

What if there was an approach that recognized that no two of us are the same? And what if the solution could be as individual as we are? Well, I would like to introduce you to the concept of **functional medicine.**

Functional medicine is centred around two key principles:

Principle 1: The human body is one big, interconnected system. If all the body's systems are functioning optimally and in balance with one another, then we shouldn't see any signs and symptoms of disease.

Principle 2: Every human body is different. What brings one person to burnout could (and probably will) be entirely different to the next.

You may already be familiar with the functional approach and may have heard it described as 'lifestyle medicine', 'complementary medicine', 'preventative medicine' or

---

[40] Parletta, Milte, and Meyer, 'Nutritional Modulation of Cognitive Function and Mental Health.'

'integrative medicine'. This may have influenced your thoughts and feelings about what functional medicine is (or isn't).

Here are some things that you need to know about functional medicine:

- It is evidence based and rooted in science. The solutions offered by functional medicine practitioners have been meticulously researched and are backed by a broad range of scientific evidence. This is not 'hocus-pocus' magic or 'woo-woo' theoretical health.
- It is person-centred and recognizes individuality. Functional medicine treats the person rather than the disease.
- It is a root-cause approach. It seeks to understand the drivers behind symptoms, and to address those rather than just treating the symptoms.
- It isn't a replacement for traditional medicine; rather a partner. There will be times when an individual needs both medical and functional interventions to support them with burnout.

The root-cause therapy practised in functional medicine is always personalized to the individual. It considers a wide array of contributing factors, which are grouped under the headings 'Antecedents', 'Triggers' and 'Mediators'.

Antecedents refer to your genetic predisposition and early life exposures. For example, how and where you were born, whether you experienced any birth trauma or had to be treated with antibiotics, whether you have a genetic variation that increases your vulnerability to stressful events, and even the diet and lifestyle of your mum when she was pregnant with you, as this may have altered your own gene expression.

Triggers are identified by considering your personal life journey to date and whether any significant events may have triggered your current state of health. Triggers can be as varied as involvement in a car accident, the sudden death of a loved one, being bullied at school, contracting an illness or disease, or a change in diet and lifestyle.

Mediators are the environmental, biochemical and even spiritual factors that perpetuate the way you are feeling. Environmentally, this includes things like diet, stress, sleep, exercise and relationships; biochemical mediators could include nutrient deficiency, hormone and brain chemistry imbalance, inflammation, pathogens, gut dysbiosis (either suspected or identified through testing); and spiritual mediators derive from your belief systems and the way you think and feel. All of these can contribute to your current state of health.

Collectively, these factors – referred to as your ATMs – make up you as a person and are the first step towards finding a tailored solution to help you beat burnout.

PART 2

WHAT IS ACTUALLY GOING ON?

Fluctuating moods and declining energy levels do not happen by themselves. One of the founding principles of functional medicine is that if all our biological systems were functioning optimally, we would not experience ill health.

However, we become out of balance all the time! That's life. And the beauty of the system that is our complex and amazing human body is that we do not become immediately ill when something isn't quite right. We adapt and the brain instigates corrective action.

But when an imbalance is perpetual, it creates the optimal environment for ill health and disease. The symptoms we experience are actually our body's warning signs, prompting us to change our behaviour in order to restore balance. When these symptoms are just ignored, burnout is able to flourish.

In this section we are going to explore what is actually going on at a functional level in our bodies when we feel tired, wired and overwhelmed.

CHAPTER 5

OUR MOOD-REGULATING BRAIN CHEMISTRY

The most obvious place to start is the nervous system, given the central role the brain plays in orchestrating our stress response. Remember that it is your brain that determines what you consider stressful, regulates your stress response and learns from the stressful experience. Your brain is there to keep you safe, but it isn't infallible. The nervous system requires TLC to protect you from burnout: imbalanced brain chemistry can both contribute to and result from burnout. Let's take a take a closer look at how the brain functions so that we can understand how to nurture it.

5.1 Overview of the brain

The nervous system is your body's information superhighway: a vast network of nerves delivering essential messages across the whole body. This intricate web utilizes billions of specialist cells called 'neurons' to transmit electrical signals around the body, regulating our biological functions and enabling us to experience our environment. The nervous system affects every aspect of your health, including:

- Your thoughts, memories and feelings.
- Your sleep pattern.
- Breathing and heartbeat.
- Digestive, reproductive and immune function.
- Your senses and how you interpret the world around you.
- Your response to stress and threat.

You could spend years studying this mysterious and complex system, but you probably didn't pick up this book to become a neuroscientist. So let's keep this on a 'need to know' basis and stay focussed on burnout.

First, the basics: a map, if you like, to the nervous system.

Central nervous system (CNS): the brain and your spinal cord.

Peripheral nervous system: everything else – the nerves that branch out from your CNS to your organs, reaching right down to your fingers and toes. This system further divides as follows:

- *Somatic nervous system*: controlling voluntary movement, in other words when you *decide* to get up and go for a walk.
- *Autonomic nervous system*: all the clever stuff that happens without you even thinking about it. This system is heavily involved in the stress response and divides even further into two systems that we really do need to sit up and pay attention to:
  - The *sympathetic* nervous system: active when we are in a state of alertness and responding to a stressful situation.
  - The *parasympathetic* nervous system: active when we are at rest and feeling calm.

At the centre of all of this, commanding the whole show, is what I consider the most beautiful organ of all – your brain.

The brain is a complex and tissue-dense organ, home to:

- Eighty billion **neurons** or nerve cells (wow!) that transmit instructions to the rest of the nervous system.
- Approximately three times as many **glial cells** – specialist cells that form a protective and insulating

fatty layer around our neurons to improve their function.

- Blood cells – delivering oxygen-rich blood to the brain so it can function.
- Chemical messengers (hormones and neurotransmitters).

Each of these elements relies on optimal nutrition to function. Key vitamins, minerals, amino acids from protein and fatty acids from dietary fat provide the building blocks and the co-factor enzymes (helper molecules that support chemical reactions) the brain needs to maintain its structure and carry out its job. In fact, the brain consumes 20% of everything you eat: your brain is food. A poorly fed brain cannot function properly and becomes more susceptible to stress. Nourish the brain and it will protect you from burnout.

In this book I refer to various parts of the brain in turn and explain how each particular region is linked to your health and biological function. But before I begin, there are a couple of specific brain areas worth mentioning, insofar as they relate to burnout and our understanding of what is happening to the brain when we are under stress. I am, to a degree, over-simplifying: the brain is complex and no one part is responsible for one thing, but I think a basic understanding is helpful.

Historically, science told us that we were born with a finite number of neurons and that once we reached adulthood we wouldn't be making any more. We believed that, unlike other cells in our body that are constantly reproducing, our neurons did not regrow or form new connections. Fortunately, modern research has revealed we were wrong: the brain *can* continue to grow and adapt as we age – a concept known as 'neuroplasticity'. Importantly, this 'plasticity' can be influenced by environmental factors such as your diet, lifestyle and life experiences.

One especially plastic area of the brain where new neurons are formed is the hippocampus, which is unsurprising considering its key role in learning and memory formation.

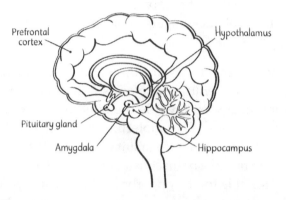

The hippocampus (or hippocampi – you actually have two, one on either side of the brain, deep inside the temporal lobe) is a small, seahorse-shaped region of the brain. It forms part of the limbic system, which regulates survival behaviours (feeding, reproduction, fight or flight) and emotional responses. The hippocampus specifically helps us to process short-term memories into long-term memories and connect these memories to sensations and emotions. It also helps us to recall emotional and sensory memories: that feel-good song that always perks you up, or the smell of baking that reminds you of your gran – that is your hippocampus at work. The hippocampus also plays a role in spatial memory and navigation: MRI scans of London cabbies revealed increased hippocampal volume compared with the brains of individuals without any extensive navigational experience.[41]

The hippocampus is highly susceptible to damage from chronic stress. Chronic stress induces cell death and damages tissue in the hippocampus, reducing its overall

[41] Maguire et al., 'Navigation-Related Structural Change in the Hippocampi of Taxi Drivers.'

volume. At the same time, chronic stress depletes a brain chemical called brain-derived neurotrophic factor, or BDNF, which supports the growth and survival of brain cells. BDNF also helps neurons to form new synaptic connections, enabling our brains to flex and adapt. BDNF is basically our plasticity chemical. Both the hippocampus and BDNF play a crucial role in mental health: studies show that individuals with major depressive disorder have reduced hippocampal volume and reduced levels of BDNF. Early symptoms of dementia (poor short-term recall and disorientation) are also associated with hippocampal deterioration.

Fortunately, studies have found that nourishing the brain with powerful 'mood foods' and engaging in exercise and mindfulness can all increase the volume of the hippocampus.[42] Happy days!

The prefrontal cortex (PFC) is the area of the brain that controls the highest levels of cognitive function and our thoughts, behaviours and emotions. When you are bossing it at work, the PFC is firing. It helps you to think strategically, critically evaluate information and make shit-hot decisions. It provides you with emotional intelligence about your team, deep insight into your own performance and keeps you motivated to pursue your most challenging 'stretch' goals. At the same time, the PFC is quietly keeping you resilient to *controllable* stress and helping to regulate your mood. All functions, I think you would agree, that enable high achievers to perform at their best.

As you can imagine, this level of cognitive function is pretty energy intensive and the PFC relies on being alert

---

[42] Jacka et al., 'Western Diet Is Associated with a Smaller Hippocampus: A Longitudinal Investigation'; Wilckens et al., 'Exercise Interventions Preserve Hippocampal Volume: A Meta-Analysis'; Hölzel et al., 'Mindfulness Practice Leads to Increases in Regional Brain Gray Matter Density.'

for optimal function. Tired or wired? Forget it! The PFC is affected by both fatigue and anxiety.

Neuroscientists have discovered that both sleep deprivation and *uncontrollable* stress can detrimentally affect PFC function, as a result of inadequate or excessive production of the chemicals that modulate our alert state – known as neurotransmitters (more about them later). PFC dysfunction results in:

- Difficulty concentrating.
- Poor decision making.
- Poor recall / forgetfulness.
- Reduced insight and judgement.
- Reduced empathy and compassion.
- Reduced optimism and persistence.
- Reduced self-regulation and inhibitory control.

All of these impair professional performance and increase occupational cynicism, both of which define burnout. Perhaps more concerningly, chronic stress can actually destroy grey matter, reducing prefrontal cortex volume while simultaneous activating more primitive brain circuitry.[43] Which brings me nicely on to....

The amygdala. The amygdala and the PFC couldn't be less alike. If the PFC is the sophisticated, evolved area of your brain, the amygdala is your cave woman – your basic instincts, if you like. Like the hippocampus, the small almond-shaped amygdala forms part of your brain's limbic system. If you have read Professor Steve Peters' *Chimp Paradox* you may be familiar with this brain system being described as your 'chimp', or your 'monkey mind'.[44] It is

---

[43] Arnsten and Shanafelt, 'Physician Distress and Burnout, the Neurobiological Perspective.'
[44] Peters, *The Chimp Paradox: The Mind Management Programme to Help You Achieve Success, Confidence and Happiness.*

your subconscious and is the area of your brain where you develop habits and limiting beliefs that may not be serving you well. We will look at ways to tackle these in Chapter 16.

The amygdala is also your fear centre and controls emotional responses such as anxiety, anger and pleasure. Any scary or traumatic experiences – your amygdala not only remembers but makes them your strongest memories. Under chronic, uncontrollable stress, the fear circuit in your brain is strengthened and subconscious thoughts, feelings and behaviours are re-enforced. The volume of the amygdala grows and a biological state of chronic stress is perpetuated; you persistently respond to your environment as if you are under threat.[45] When this happens, your *perception* of stress, in addition to the stress itself, can make you more vulnerable to burnout. This is the link between burnout and generalized anxiety.

You will have seen that I emphasize controllable as opposed to uncontrollable stress. A sense of control helps us to classify stress and manage it more effectively. Feeling out of control and anxious all the time leads to emotional overwhelm and a sense that we cannot cope.

Fortunately, a sense of control can be restored by following my four-step Mood Boosting Method:

1. Restoring the body, getting enough sleep and practising active relaxation.
2. Nourishing the brain – providing access to vital nutrients to meet the PFC's energy needs; removing 'anti-nutrients' – those short-term fixes that we believe serve us but have damaging effects in the long run.

---

[45] Savic, Perski, and Osika, 'MRI Shows That Exhaustion Syndrome Due to Chronic Occupational Stress Is Associated with Partially Reversible Cerebral Changes.'

3. Engaging in activities that help you to gain perspective, feel more in control and restore grey matter (exercise, walking in nature, mindful contemplation).
4. Reframing thoughts and developing emotional intelligence that helps your brain to regulate its response to threat and changes your *perception* from the uncontrollable to the controllable.

5.2 The role of neurotransmitters in mood regulation

The way we feel is regulated by chemicals in the brain called 'neurotransmitters'. Neurotransmitters form a key part of the communication process between the brain and the rest of the body. They enable the body to act upon the brain's instructions and also communicate feedback from the body to the brain to establish how we are feeling.

Neurotransmitters perform their role by hanging out in synapses – the space between nerve cells – and transferring information across this space from one cell to another. They must bind to a receptor site at the destination cell to deliver their message. Once they have performed this task, the neurotransmitters are recycled out of the synapse space until they are needed next time – a process known as 'reuptake'. Imbalances occur when:

- there are not enough neurotransmitters available at the synapse, or
- there are insufficient receptors at the receiving cell for the neurotransmitters to bind to, or
- the reuptake process is defective in some way – either too fast or too slow – preventing effective communication.

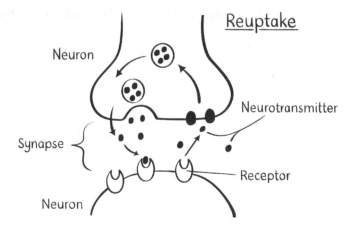

The building blocks of almost all neurotransmitters are amino acids, which are derived from protein.

Obtaining the right amount of protein in the diet is crucial for mood balance. Too little or too much at the expense of other nutrients is not helpful.

Often, the women I see in clinic aren't eating enough protein. They perceive protein as something body builders use to build muscle and are fearful that if they increase their intake they will gain weight. Less commonly, some women are eating too much protein – often at the expense of carbohydrates – which is also not helpful: the amino acids from our food need carbohydrates to cross what is known as the 'blood–brain barrier' – in other words, to get into the brain and perform their crucial mood-regulating functions.

So here we are, having barely scratched the surface, and already we are talking about how crucial a basic aspect of our diet is for regulating our mood.

Neurotransmitters perform a beautiful and fascinating role, and of course I have over-simplified their function, but already we can see how sub-optimal nutrition and lifestyle factors may affect our mood. We will explore this further when we consider some specific neurotransmitters in the next section.

5.3 The key neurotransmitters involved in regulating mood

There are some specific neurotransmitters that are involved in regulating our mood and cognitive function, some of which you may have heard of and some that may be less familiar. Let's begin with one that most of you will have heard of.

Serotonin

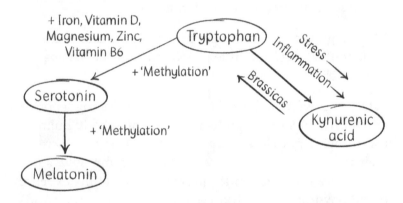

Serotonin is our happy neurotransmitter. When functioning optimally, serotonin will foster feelings of happiness, contentment and overall wellbeing.

As you can see from the diagram, serotonin is derived from the amino acid tryptophan. Tryptophan is known as an essential amino acid, which simply means it cannot be produced in the body and therefore must be obtained from the food we eat. Unfortunately, tryptophan is one of the least abundant amino acids in our food supply and it competes with other amino acids for absorption and transfer across the blood–brain barrier, making us vulnerable to deficiency.

This is why it is super important to eat protein – and particularly protein sources that are higher in tryptophan. Some good sources of tryptophan include eggs, salmon, turkey and other poultry, chickpeas, nuts and organic soy.

Assuming there is sufficient tryptophan available to make serotonin, certain 'helper' vitamins and minerals are also needed as 'co-factors' to undertake the conversion process from tryptophan to serotonin. We will see that this is the case with most neurotransmitters. For serotonin, adequate iron, magnesium, zinc and vitamin B6 are required for conversion. Already we are painting a picture that optimum nutrition is needed for optimal mood.

In the absence of these nutrients from our diet, tryptophan can be diverted down a different pathway resulting in less tryptophan available to make serotonin. Our stress hormone cortisol plays a key role in this diversion, which goes someway to explaining why chronic stress and burnout can leave you feeling utterly depressed and highlights how important it is to manage stress to foster happy moods. More about this in Part 3. Equally problematic is inflammation, as this can also divert tryptophan away from converting to serotonin. We will discuss the role of inflammation in more detail in Chapter 10. Fortunately, you can help your tryptophan to stay at optimum levels and right where you need it by eating plenty of veggies from the brassica family like broccoli and kale. Just one of the reasons I dub broccoli 'a girl's best friend'.

The serotonin hypothesis

For years, researchers postulated that a deficit of serotonin in the brain was the cause of depression. Based on this hypothesis, serotonin became the target of a modern type of antidepressant known as 'selective serotonin reuptake inhibitors', or SSRIs. You may have heard of some: Prozac, citalopram, sertraline and so on. These drugs exert their effect by delaying the recycling process and keeping serotonin in play at the synapse for longer. However, in 2022, a systematic umbrella review published in *Molecular Psychiatry* cast doubt on the popular theory, calling into question decades of SSRI use when it concluded that there was 'no convincing evidence' that low serotonin causes depression.[46]

Serotonin is not just used to make us feel happy; it also has other key functions, for example supporting gut motility. You need to keep your gut healthy – it's your second brain (more about that in Chapter 9).

Melatonin

As you may have noticed from the diagram, serotonin is not the only neurotransmitter reliant on tryptophan for conversion. Melatonin, our sleep hormone, is downstream from serotonin in the neuro-hormone production line. Melatonin is produced in the pineal gland in the brain.

There is a reciprocal relationship among sleep, energy levels and mood. Have you ever felt so wired or emotionally overwhelmed that you just couldn't fall asleep, only to then feel tired, grumpy and tearful the next morning because

---

[46] Moncrieff et al., 'The Serotonin Theory of Depression: A Systematic Umbrella Review of the Evidence.'

you haven't slept? You just manage to get going by mid-afternoon only to find yourself in the same spiral later on. It's an exhausting cycle that can take its toll on our mental health and can ultimately contribute to burnout.

Melatonin works in tandem with our old friend cortisol and has an opposing circadian (or 24-hour) rhythm. Whereas cortisol is designed to peak in the morning to give us our 'get-up and go' and then steadily decline throughout the day, melatonin is designed to be at lower levels in the morning and higher in the evening to prepare us for sleep. An imbalance in one or both of these signalling hormones can contribute to insomnia or disrupted sleep patterns.

One of the best ways to support your melatonin levels is to take steps to regulate your sleep cycle. Jump to Chapter 13 to find out more. There are actually very few food sources of melatonin, however it does occur naturally in cherries – tart Montmorency cherries to be specific – and is present in moderate amounts in almonds and pistachios. Unfortunately, you would need to eat 90–100 cherries to obtain therapeutic levels that may support sleep, which isn't exactly practical (or advisable). Clinical trials have shown that drinking 30ml of concentrated Montmorency cherry juice diluted with 240ml of water twice daily (once in the morning and once in the evening) improves sleep quality and efficiency as well as increasing tryptophan availability.[47] Drinking cherry juice may therefore be helpful if you struggle to sleep; however, proceed with caution if you have imbalanced blood sugar levels (see Chapter 7). You can buy active cherry juice in your local health store – head over to my website to see my recommended brands. In the USA and some other countries, melatonin is available to buy as a supplement – but it is classified as a prescription-only drug here in the UK.

---

[47] Losso et al., 'Pilot Study of Tart Cherry Juice for the Treatment of Insomnia and Investigation of Mechanisms.'

Dopamine

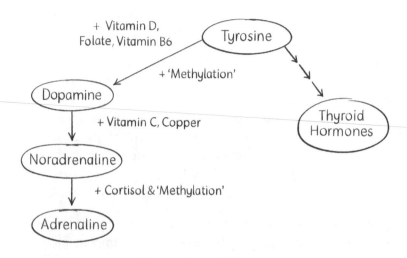

Dopamine is our anticipation and reward neurotransmitter; it is closely linked to how much pleasure we feel and our motivation levels. Imbalances in dopamine may present as some of the symptoms we have now become familiar with: difficulty concentrating, disinterest, low motivation levels, agitation and reward-seeking/addictive behaviours (are you reaching for the chocolate or the wine when you are feeling stressed?). Both low and high dopamine levels – influenced by genetics, diet and/or lifestyle – have been linked with anxiety, lethargy, mood swings and depression in the scientific literature.[48]

Like other neurotransmitters, dopamine is derived from an amino acid – in this case tyrosine – and requires key nutrients as co-factors in its synthesis: folate and vitamins D and B6. Low dopamine levels may result from nutrient deficiency.

---

[48] Zarrindast and Khakpai, 'The Modulatory Role of Dopamine in Anxiety-like Behavior'; Belujon and Grace, 'Dopamine System Dysregulation in Major Depressive Disorders.'

You may have spotted from the diagram that dopamine sits ahead of noradrenaline and adrenaline in the synthesis pathway. These neurotransmitters play a key role in our fight or flight response, readying the body and mind for action. Persistent stress activates this response in a disproportionate fashion, lowering dopamine levels in favour of adrenaline. In this way, chronic stress can also lower dopamine levels.

When dopamine levels are low, we can lack energy and motivation. We may experience anxiety and low mood and derive less pleasure from life. In this state, we may seek to increase our dopamine by engaging in reward-seeking behaviours; this may explain why some women on the path to burnout increase their alcohol intake and eat more sugary foods.

Dopamine and serotonin are closely linked and imbalances in one of these neurotransmitters may affect the levels of the other. Both utilize monoamine oxidase (MAO) enzymes in their metabolism. A shortage of this enzyme can result in a build-up of one or both neurotransmitters. High dopamine levels can result in agitation, hyperactivity and an inability to concentrate. It can also, confusingly, result in anxiety. This is why it is so important to understand what is driving your symptoms – the root cause.

Like cortisol, dopamine also inhibits gastric motility and could be a contributing factor in constipation and IBS.

Abbie's story

Remember Abbie from Chapter 1? Abbie is our overwhelmed 35-year-old corporate accountant, who was feeling exhausted and depressed. Most days she struggled to get into the office and, when she got there, she could barely muster the motivation to function.

Abbie also complained of bloating, frequent diarrhoea and brain fog. She had put on weight, which no amount of dieting and intense workouts seemed able to shift. She said she experienced intense sugar cravings and drank alcohol to relax and feel good.

Abbie undertook testing to assess her stress response and neurotransmitter function. The standout result was her cortisol profile, which was flat to the bottom end of the range. Years of occupational stress and the physical stress of yo-yo dieting, nutrient depletion and over-exercising had left her struggling to mount a sufficient stress response. Her low levels of cortisol had resulted in no 'get-up and go'. She was essentially revving her engine but there was no fuel in the tank. Typical of Stage 3 burnout.

Abbie's noradrenaline and adrenaline metabolites were within range, but her dopamine metabolites were low, suggesting she was converting any dopamine she was making into her stress neurotransmitters. Her lack of motivation and her reward-seeking behaviour with sugar and alcohol consumption could both have been linked to this low dopamine.

To support Abbie, we created an ultra-personalized plan that included a robust set of therapeutic supplements to support her adrenal and neurotransmitter function and energy levels. As she started to feel better, we flooded her system with adrenal- and brain-nourishing foods and changed her mindset around food restriction. We gave her stress-management tools and worked with her personal trainer to adapt her exercise routine – to help her take the foot off the gas while she recovered.

Abbie was amazed at the transformation. Within a few months, she was jumping out of bed in the mornings and bossing it at work. Her mood lifted and she achieved increased mental clarity. She actually said to me that she didn't realise just how exhausted she had been until her energy levels had started to normalize. After six months or so, Abbie also noticed she was beginning to lose her 'stress belly'. She was eating more than ever but, because she had calmed her nervous system and removed dietary stressors, her brain was getting the message that the 'threat' was subsiding and it was safe to let that excess fat go.

GABA and glutamate

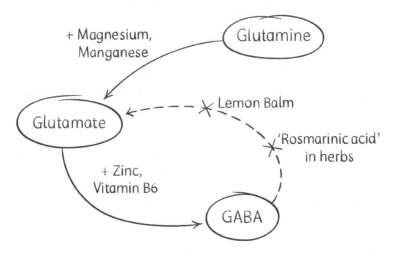

We are now entering territory that you might be less familiar with. GABA (or gamma aminobutyric acid) and glutamate are two neurotransmitters that work with opposing effects. Whereas glutamate is an excitatory, or stimulating, neurotransmitter, GABA is inhibitory, or calming.

As with the other neurotransmitters we have discussed, balance is key. Low GABA leaves glutamate unopposed, which means neurons can be over-stimulated. In this scenario, individuals are at higher risk of anxiety disorders, phobias, obsessive-compulsive disorder and hyperactivity. Conversely, too much GABA, or lower levels of glutamate, can result in reduced transmission of vital chemical messages in the brain and is associated with lethargy, chronic fatigue and low motivation.

Both GABA and glutamate originate from yet another amino acid: glutamine. (Have I mentioned that protein is important for mood balance?) The initial step requires magnesium and manganese to support synthesis of glutamate and then zinc and activated vitamin B6 are required to convert glutamate to GABA. I hope that by now you are starting to see some key nutrients appearing time and time again in the synthesis of our mood-regulating chemicals.

Keeping GABA at the synapses for longer may be beneficial for those with anxiety disorders as it has a sedative and calming effect. Interestingly, this is how alcohol and other sedative drugs like benzodiazepines (such as diazepam) exert their effects: they act on our GABA receptors. However, we know that alcohol is detrimental to health; both alcohol and sedative drugs have undesirable side effects, such as drowsiness, confusion, poor co-ordination and tremors and both have been linked to addiction. Alcohol also depletes the brain of those vital co-factors needed for neurotransmitter synthesis (B vitamins, zinc, magnesium and so on).

Fortunately, there are natural alternatives. Rosmarinic acid (a compound found in herbs such as peppermint, rosemary, thyme, basil and sage) and lemon balm can exert the same relaxing effect – namely by keeping GABA in play at the synapse for longer. This may explain why peppermint tea is so calming or why, when you cook a roast dinner with herbs, the smell is so comforting and relaxing. I always encourage my anxious clients to drink herbal teas for this reason and to grow their own herb garden and sit outside and inhale the smells for an instant anti-anxiety effect.

Yoga and meditation can also support GABA, while at the same time decreasing cortisol (see Chapter 13 for more on this).

Acetylcholine

Acetylcholine is our cognition neurotransmitter and plays a key role in learning, memory and focus. Unsurprisingly, it is heavily expressed in the hippocampus, where it supports conversion of short-term memories into long-term storage.

Sub-optimal acetylcholine activity can result in:

- Impaired visual memory leading to a reduced capacity to take on new information and learn.
- Impaired verbal memory and difficulty recalling information.
- Slow mental speed, poor comprehension and difficulty processing numbers.
- Reduced creativity.

As you can see, impaired acetylcholine can certainly diminish our professional performance, hence the potential link with the third dimension of burnout (reduced personal achievement; see the Introduction to Part 1 for a reminder of the other dimensions). More seriously, low levels are associated with cognitive decline and Alzheimer's disease.

The name 'acetylcholine' gives us clues as to what is required for its synthesis:

- Choline – an essential nutrient found in (primarily animal-derived) fatty foods, like liver and organ meats, egg yolk, beef and full fat dairy.

- An 'acetyl' group – derived from glucose metabolism in the brain.

Vitamin B5 (pantothenic acid) is also required as a co-factor for acetylcholine synthesis.

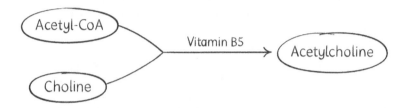

Insufficient choline availability will prompt the brain to breakdown its own fatty neuron tissue to synthesize acetylcholine, which is neither ideal nor efficient. Following a low-fat or plant-based diet may contribute to choline deficiency, although some choline can be found in nuts and tofu. Likewise, poor energy production in the brain will also impair the availability of acetylcholine. Fasting, calorie restriction and/or blood sugar dysregulation may also be factors in impaired acetylcholine activity (more about dietary patterns and their influence on mental health in Chapter 17).

5.4 Other brain chemicals

As I have already mentioned, there is no single cause of mood disorders such as depression. Some researchers believe that other chemicals in the brain may be involved, and these are worth looking at as they can be both affected by chronic stress and influenced by diet and lifestyle factors.

Neurotrophins

Neurotrophins are a family of proteins involved in brain function at a cellular level. Brain derived neurotrophic factor (or BDNF) is one such signalling protein involved in the formation of new neurons, cell growth, cell survival and synapse formation.

BDNF and its receptors are found ubiquitously in areas of the brain linked with mood disorders, such as the hippocampus, prefrontal cortex and amygdala.

Chronic stress can lower levels of BDNF in the brain, which can result in the loss of brain cells and the reduction of new brain cell formation – both of which have been associated with lowered mood and loss of interest.[49] Lowered BDNF has also been observed post-mortem in the brains of suicide victims, leading researchers to infer that reduced or imbalanced BDNF may be involved in mood disorders.[50]

As well as taking steps to reduce stress, which we shall discuss in Chapter 13, you may be able to support your BDNF levels through certain foods, according to some interesting and emerging research.[51]

Saffron is one food type being studied. Clinical trials using concentrated forms of saffron (in supplement form) have found it to improve symptoms of depression and anxiety to a degree that is equal or superior to traditional antidepressants.[52] Early research into this has shown that saffron is able to increase levels of BDNF.

---

[49] Leal, Bramham, and Duarte, 'BDNF and Hippocampal Synaptic Plasticity.'

[50] Erickson, Miller, and Roecklein, 'The Aging Hippocampus'; Zhang, Yao, and Hashimoto, 'Brain-Derived Neurotrophic Factor (BDNF)-TrkB Signaling in Inflammation-Related Depression and Potential Therapeutic Targets.'

[51] Akbari-Fakhrabadi et al., 'Saffron (Crocus Sativus L.), Combined with Endurance Exercise, Synergistically Enhances BDNF, Serotonin, and NT-3 in Wistar Rats.'

[52] Tóth et al., 'The Efficacy of Saffron in the Treatment of Mild to Moderate Depression: A Meta-Analysis.'

Endorphins

Endorphins are 'feel-good' hormones that are released in your brain in response to pain or stress. They act as neurotransmitters and send signals to the rest of the body, helping us to cope with pain and continue functioning in stressful situations. Much like the 'fight or flight' response, endorphin release can be viewed as a survival mechanism.

In the brain's reward centre, endorphins attach to opioid receptors and block pain signals. The word 'endorphin' is derived from the words 'endogenous', which means 'inside the body', and 'morphine', an opiate pain reliever. There are more than 20 different types of endorphins produced in the body, grouped in three categories: alpha-endorphins, beta-endorphins and gamma-endorphins. Beta-endorphins have a stronger effect than morphine in the body, and also act to suppress our stress hormone, cortisol.[53]

Endorphins work in tandem with dopamine, helping us to seek out pleasurable activities. When endorphins attach to their receptors, dopamine is released. Exercise, massage, food and having sex can all boost endorphins. Perhaps the most famous endorphin effect is the 'runners' high' – but running isn't the only way to release endorphins. Other forms of exercise are equally as effective.

Oxytocin

Oxytocin is a neuropeptide commonly referred to as the 'love' hormone or (and I prefer this one) the 'cuddle' hormone. It plays a role in social bonding and helps us to feel connected with others.

---

[53] Taylor, Dluhy, and Williams, 'Beta-Endorphin Suppresses Adrenocorticotropin and Cortisol Levels in Normal Human Subjects.'

Oxytocin is released by the brain as part of the stress response and serves to increase stress resilience, particularly in women. (Notably oxytocin is released during childbirth and helps mothers to bond with their newborns.) Oxytocin reduces activity in the amygdala – the fear centre of the brain – and moderates HPA-axis reactivity.[54]

Oxytocin can be increased through touch, hugging, massage, kissing and sex being prime examples. But it can also be increased by taking part in communal activities like yoga, playing in a band or just spending time with friends. Remember: isolation is stressful, particularly for women. The release of oxytocin may be one explanation for why spending time with others can have an anti-stress effect (see Chapter 15 for more on this).

Endocannabinoids

The endocannabinoid system is a complex cell-signalling system that is thought to play a role in regulating stress, mood, cognitive function and sleep.[55] It works when endocannabinoids (chemicals produced naturally inside the body, not to be confused with the plant-derived cannabinoids found in marijuana) bind to cannabinoid receptors. 'Anandamide' is one of two endocannabinoids identified so far and is sometimes referred to as the 'bliss' molecule as it enhances motivation and mood. The second identified endocannabinoid is '2-Arachidonoylglycerol', which experts believe is a key regulator of neurotransmitter release.

The endocannabinoid system is not yet fully understood and is the subject of much research at the time of writing,

---

[54] Love, 'The Impact of Oxytocin on Stress: The Role of Sex.'
[55] Zou and Kumar, 'Cannabinoid Receptors and the Endocannabinoid System: Signaling and Function in the Central Nervous System.'

particularly as to the therapeutic potential of exogenous cannabinoids (cannabidiol and Tetrahydrocannabinol, the components of cannabis) in stress-related mood disorders and other conditions.

For now, we need to be aware that endocannabinoids are derived from omega-6 fatty acids and therefore diet may be a factor influencing this system. There are also genetic variations that may influence our ability to synthesize and metabolize (breakdown) endocannabinoids. These genes can be up-/down-regulated by diet and lifestyle factors like stress!

My top tips for supporting healthy brain chemistry

- Ensure your diet is protein rich. Protein provides access to the amino-acid building blocks required to synthesize many neurotransmitters. Protein can be obtained from high-quality animal-derived sources, such as free-range poultry, grass-fed beef, wild fish and organic dairy, as well as plant-based sources such as beans, legumes, pulses, nuts and seeds.
- Ensure your diet contains adequate fat. Fats protect brain cells and support cognitive function through the synthesis of neurotransmitters like acetylcholine. Healthy fats can be found in olives, olive oil, coconut oil, avocado, nuts, seeds and oily fish.
- Fill half your plate with green and brightly coloured plants. Fruits and vegetables provide access to the co-factor vitamins, minerals and micro-nutrients that support neurotransmitter synthesis. You will

discover in Chapter 14 that almost all my Top 10 Mood Foods are plants!

- Follow a Mediterranean dietary pattern – more about this and why it is so good for your mood in Chapter 17.
- Avoid foods that disrupt brain chemistry – discover my list of mood disrupters in Chapter 14, chief among them sugar and alcohol.
- Manage stress! See Chapter 13.
- Exercise – one of *the* best things you can do for the short- and long-term health of your brain. See Chapter 15 for more on this.
- Spend time with others to promote the feel-good oxytocin hormone.

Let's recap some essential takeaways from this section:

1. The brain controls the show; it will determine what you perceive as stressful, your response to stress and your ability to learn from the experience.
2. Chronic stress can shrink the parts of the brain that help us to focus and perform at our best, while increasing the volume of parts of the brain that makes us feel fearful and anxious.
3. Your mood is regulated by chemicals in the brain called neurotransmitters. Neurotransmitters are susceptible to up/down regulation by stress; conversely, sub-optimal levels may contribute to the symptoms of burnout.
4. Neurotransmitters require optimal nutrition for their synthesis and breakdown.

By now I think you have got the picture that the brain runs the show and can help or hinder you when it comes to burnout. Operating alongside the nervous system is the endocrine system, which, when in balance, creates hormone harmony. When it's out of balance, however, the effects can wreak havoc on our hormones – as we shall see in the next chapter.

CHAPTER 6

HORMONE HAVOC

Your hormones can play havoc with your mood. And working and playing hard can take its toll on how well your hormones function. Basically, balanced hormones are the key to successful communication in the body. Mixed-up chemical messaging leads to mental (and physical) chaos and confusion.

Hormones also have a starring role in burnout prevention and the stress response. If the brain is the director, then cortisol is the leading lady. We met cortisol in Chapter 1. Cortisol is your survival hormone. Like any other diva, cortisol calls the shots.

When cortisol is active, the production of many other hormones is affected. This is a natural part of adaption to keep you safe. But when cortisol levels are chronically high, like we see in Stage 2 burnout, or woefully low like in Stage 3 burnout, wider hormone dysregulation is possible. This is why the symptoms of burnout can extend way beyond feeling 'tired and wired'.

As I am sure you can appreciate, hormones and endocrinology are such vast topics that they could be (and have been) the subject of many standalone books. If you want to delve deeper into this topic, I have included some great titles for you to consider in the Resources section at the back of this book. For the purpose of this book, however, I am going to focus on the hormones that I see having the biggest impact on mood balance in my clinic and those that are affected the most by burnout. These are:

- Cortisol, discussed extensively in Chapter 1 and throughout this book – because of its role in our stress responses.
- Insulin (Chapter 7) – because of its interplay with cortisol in regulating our blood sugar levels.
- Thyroid hormones (Chapter 8) – because of their influence on the chemicals in our autonomic nervous system (dopamine, noradrenaline, adrenaline).
- Reproductive hormones (this chapter) – because of their influence on our mood and energy levels (these are the hormones you first think of when I say 'hormone havoc', right?).

As women, we are perhaps predisposed to think negatively about our hormones, mainly because we are told we got a raw deal in having to face menstruation each month. I believe that the more informed we can become about hormone health, the more we can reframe our thinking about hormones and begin to embrace them as the life-giving, burnout-protective chemicals that they are.

But firstly, let's look at the basics.

6.1 What are hormones?

Much like neurotransmitters, hormones are communication chemicals. However, they are distinct from neurotransmitters in the way they deliver their message.

Hormones travel around the body, not in the central nervous system but in the 'periphery', specifically in the bloodstream or in the fluid around our cells. They are on the look-out for target cells. Once they find their target, they bind to a receptor inside or on the surface of that cell and deliver their instructions, thereby changing the activity of that cell. There is a high degree of specificity involved; hormones can't just land anywhere. It is very much like a lock and key scenario, where the cell receptor site is the lock and the hormone is the key.

Remarkably, some communication chemicals can function as both a neurotransmitter (remember, these work by travelling across the synapses in the brain) *and* a hormone. Serotonin is a prime example.

Hormone receptor cells are located all over the body and can influence our mood and the way we feel at any given time. Hormones are also produced all over the body in endocrine glands, some of which will be very familiar to you:

- The ovaries produce our sex hormones.
- The thyroid gland produces our thyroid hormones.
- The pancreas produces insulin, our blood-sugar-regulating hormone.
- The adrenal glands, as we have already heard, produce our stress hormones. They also takeover sex hormone production when we hit menopause – another super important reason to nurture your adrenals!

We can even produce hormones in peripheral tissue: half of female testosterone is produced in the periphery from precursor hormones produced in the ovaries and the adrenal glands. The largest hormone-producing organ of all is the gut, both in size and in the amount of hormone-producing cells located in the gut tissue (see Chapter 9 for more about the gut).

Given what we have learned so far, it won't surprise you to hear that many hormones are produced in the brain. In fact, the brain is where ovarian, adrenal and thyroid hormone production begins, in the pea-sized pituitary gland. The pituitary produces hormones that signal other endocrine glands to stimulate or inhibit their own hormone production. For this reason, the pituitary is often referred to as the 'master' endocrine gland.

For example, it is the pituitary gland that produces adrenocorticotropic hormone (ACTH), which in turn stimulates cortisol production in the adrenal glands when you're stressed. It also produces thyroid-stimulating hormone (TSH), which instructs the thyroid to produce thyroid hormones; and follicle-stimulating hormone (FSH) and luteinising hormone (LH), which help regulate ovarian function. The pituitary gland also produces other hormones, such as prolactin and growth hormone.

However, the pituitary gland does not run the hormone show on its own. It is connected to, and often acts upon instructions from, the hypothalamus. The hypothalamus is the part of the brain that controls homeostasis (a state of balance between all body systems) and is the interface between the nervous system and the endocrine system. The pituitary can also release hormones produced by the hypothalamus, such as our bonding and childbirth hormone, oxytocin. Complicated, right? But brilliantly beautiful.

We saw in Chapter 1 that this partnership between the hypothalamus and pituitary gland is super important for mounting an effective stress response; and also how dysregulation in the hypothalamic–pituitary–adrenal (HPA) axis can contribute to burnout. As this duo are responsible for initiating broader hormone production, a clear link between burnout and hormone havoc emerges.

Let's first explore how this plays out in the reproductive system hypothalamic–pituitary–ovarian (or HPO) axis.

6.2 Female reproductive hormones and burnout

> **Carly's burnout story**
>
> Carly was a 44-year-old chief engineer with a young family, trying to do it all without any notable support network. She was exhausted, unable to focus at work and she hadn't had a period in three months. In terms of her mood, she reported anxiety, despair, low motivation, lack of drive and tearfulness. She was visibly distressed and repeatedly told me she felt overwhelmed and burnt out.
>
> Unfortunately for Carly, her GP was quite dismissive of her burnout symptoms and was not prepared to undertake any investigations. Instead, he wanted to prescribe an antidepressant and refer her for psychotherapy for depression. But Carly instinctively knew that this didn't feel right – there must be some other explanation for the way she was feeling – so she sought me out.

Carly is not alone. Many frazzled career women come into my clinic and tell me that whereas previously they experienced that one 'shitty' day a month, they can now count on one hand the number of good days they have, if any. To understand Carly's burnout story, we first need to understand a bit more about our reproductive hormones and how they are influenced by stress.

In Chapter 1, I made you aware that our stress response down-regulates non-essential biological functions to enable the body to focus on survival. One of these non-essentials is reproduction. This is Team HP (hypothalamus–pituitary) at work. While they are telling the adrenals to 'make cortisol,

I can see a bear', they are simultaneously telling the ovaries to 'stop what you're doing, I can see a bear'. In simple terms, the more active your HPA-axis, the less active your HPO axis will be.

This kind of makes sense from an evolutionary perspective: we don't want to be making babies when there is a bear hanging around outside our cave. But it is less helpful nowadays, when the stressor is occupational and not quite so life-threatening.

The thing is, we need our reproductive hormones to protect us from the symptoms of burnout. Although famed for regulating our monthly cycles and preparing the body for pregnancy, our sex hormones also influence the mood-regulating chemicals in our brain and our energy levels.

Reproductive hormone	Primary reproductive function	Other burnout-protective functions	Symptoms of imbalance
Oestrogen	Stimulates ovulation; vaginal lubrication	Supports nervous system function; helps the brain to maintain homeostasis; supports memory recall	PMS; insomnia; night-waking; irritability; anxiety; menstrual migraine; painful/heavy/absent periods; breast tenderness; low mood; low libido; hot flushes; fertility issues
Progesterone	Prepares uterus for pregnancy	Supports brain function; supports sleep, balanced mood and relaxation in second half of menstrual cycle	
Testosterone	Increases libido around ovulation	Supports balanced moods; helps us to handle stress	Lack of motivation; irritability; mood swings

In balance, these hormones help us to feel 'in the zone' and achieve total focus. Out of balance, they can lead us to feel out of control, fearful or just downright flat: symptoms synonymous with burnout. If sex hormone imbalance is at the root cause of these symptoms, then no antidepressant and / or psychotherapy will fix that!

To start to make sense of how burnout can send our sex hormones awry, we need to get back to basics. What follows is what I call the 'why were we never taught this at school' information about our sex hormones.

Our 'monthlies'

During our reproductive years, women cycle through a hormonal rinse-and-repeat-like pattern each month, with one goal in mind: pregnancy. This is all tightly regulated by Team HP via the HPO axis. The menstrual cycle lasts on average 28 days but some women have naturally slightly shorter or longer cycles. Assuming they are regular and functioning optimally, a typical cycle is as follows.

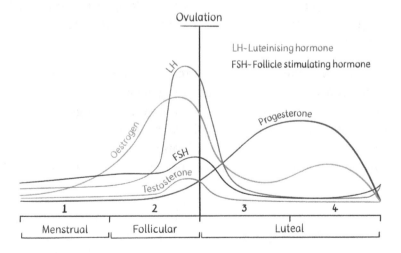

Week 1 is the *menstrual phase*. During this phase we get our periods and our female sex hormones – oestrogen and progesterone – are at their lowest. But, unbeknown to us, the baby-making process is starting again behind the scenes. Team HP release the hormone FSH to trigger the ovaries to recruit egg-containing follicles in preparation for ovulation.

Week 2 is the *follicular phase*. As these follicles mature, oestrogen levels rise in preparation for ovulation. FSH hormone levels decrease while rising oestrogen levels signal to the brain that it is time to release a surge of LH to initiate ovulation. In parallel, LH triggers an increase in testosterone production, peaking just before ovulation and bringing with it an increase in our sex drive – handy! Remember, FSH and LH are pituitary hormones: this is a busy week for the HPO axis.

At the mid-cycle point, *ovulation* occurs: the dominant follicle releases an egg from the ovary that will survive for 24–48 hours if it is not fertilized. But the follicle is not done yet. It goes on to form a temporary endocrine gland, called the 'corpus luteum', from which the majority of our progesterone is produced. So, to be clear, ovulation and progesterone production are the direct result of HPO axis activity.

Weeks 3–4 is the *luteal phase*. After ovulation, FSH, LH and oestrogen levels decline while progesterone levels rise to help prepare the uterus for pregnancy. Oestrogen levels rise again at the end of this phase; however, if there is no pregnancy, both progesterone and oestrogen drop off dramatically, triggering menstruation. And around we go again.

If you are stressed *at any point* during this cycle, there is potential for disruption. If you are stressed all of the time, then there is huge scope for HPO axis dysregulation and sex hormone imbalance. This leaves you vulnerable to burnout as well as some of the broader health issues associated with it, such as:

Menopause mimicry: persistent chronic stress has been associated with menopause-mimicking symptoms, theoretically due to persistently high circulating cortisol levels outweighing the amount of oestrogen, causing the body to respond as if there were not much oestrogen going around. One study in South Korea found that woman who experience high levels of stress in daily life had a lower natural menopause age compared to those who had lower stress levels.[56] Whether burnout can actually cause early-onset menopause is yet to be established, but it is a hot topic of research at the time of writing.

Fertility issues: the HPO is the reason that stress and burnout are closely linked with female fertility issues in the literature. Optimizing your health for fertility is a whole other book, but Part 3 of this book describes the first step to helping prevent burnout and develop stress resilience, which in turn may help optimize hormone balance and fertility outcomes.

Balancing cortisol can be the key to balancing all other hormones. This is where stress management techniques can be super helpful in deactivating the HPA-axis, bringing a sense of calm to the body and allowing the HPO axis function to resume. We will discuss how in Chapter 13.

---

[56] Choi et al., 'The Association between Stress Level in Daily Life and Age at Natural Menopause in Korean Women: Outcomes of the Korean National Health and Nutrition Examination Survey in 2010-2012.'

6.3 Other causes of sex-hormone imbalance

Aside from chronic stress, our sex hormones can become imbalanced for a variety of other reasons, including:

- Inadequate hormone production – creating a hormone shortage.
- Inadequate hormone elimination – creating a hormone surplus.
- Exposure to endocrine-disrupting chemicals (EDCs) in our environment.
- Genetic variations.

None of these variables are ideal for preventing or recovering from burnout, but happily all can be supported with a functional medicine approach.

Inadequate hormone production

In order for your burnout-protective sex hormones to help you out each month, you need to be making enough of them. But there are a couple of reasons why you might not be. Let's look at these in turn.

You're lacking the building blocks

Just as with neurotransmitters, hormones require key nutritional components for synthesis. All hormones are derived from fat. So guess what? If you aren't eating enough fat-containing foods, you may well be lacking the raw materials required to produce hormones. Here, I am talking about the lovely monounsaturated fats you can obtain from nuts, seeds, olive oil and avocados, and omega-rich foods like oily fish.

Maybe you're fearful of fats? Well, you wouldn't be alone. It is quite common for women who attend my clinic to be either avoiding fats or following a 'low-fat diet', mainly due to an inaccurate belief that fat makes you fat, or a fear about the number of calories fat-rich foods contain. Let me assure you of two things:

1. The 'fat makes you fat' messaging, which started in the 1960s, was based on some now discredited research, funded by the sugar industry! They profited handsomely from the low-fat diet culture that ensued.
2. Food is SO MUCH MORE than its calorie content. Sorry (not sorry) for shouting. Like many other functional medicine practitioners, I consider food as information. The information wrapped up in an avocado is phenomenal and is why it features as one of my Top 10 Mood Foods (see Chapter 14). Compare this to, say, an ultra-processed sugary snack of equal calorific value and, well, there is no comparison. You'll see that sugar is my number 1 mood disrupter (also in Chapter 14).

Myth busting: Calorie counting

The 'calories in vs the calories out' theory is massively oversimplified and does not reflect the complexities of human biology.

Firstly, calorie labels are a crude *estimate* of the calories contained in a food, based on the proportions of protein, carbohydrates and fat a food is believed to contain *on average.*

Secondly, it does not take into account how the nutrients are chemically bound within the food, nor how the food will behave when it enters the body – for example, whether those nutrients are likely to be absorbed or not.

Finally, it does not take into account your unique biology and how that food will interact *with you*.

In one study that looked at almond consumption, the number of calories absorbed varied from 56 calories for one person to 168 calories for another and on average the actual number of calories extracted was 32% less than the number on the label.[57]

There are many other books that debunk both the 'energy in/energy out' and the 'fat makes us fat' myths, so I won't elaborate further here (see list of books in the Resources) section.

I'm not saying energy balance is not important. It is. But it is nowhere near as important as nutrient density or food quality. Especially when it comes to supporting burnout: calorie restriction is perceived by the brain as yet another stressor on the body (see Chapter 17). The take-home message is that healthy, monounsaturated fats are great for hormone balance and great for your mood.

Your age

Your age certainly affects hormone production, with prime output occurring during your reproductive years. For us ladies it is a fact of life: the menopause is coming. Menopause occurs naturally between ages 45 and 55 and is usually confirmed by absent menstruation for 12 months or more and an elevated FSH blood test reading.

---

[57] Novotny, Gebauer, and Baer, 'Discrepancy between the Atwater Factor Predicted and Empirically Measured Energy Values of Almonds in Human Diets.'

Symptoms of menopause can commence and last up to ten years before menopause proper – collectively known as perimenopause syndrome. During this phase, female hormones can fluctuate. Generally, the first to decline is progesterone. As follicle maturation and ovulation becomes more sporadic, there are fewer of those special little endocrine glands (corpus lutea) being produced to release progesterone in the second half of our cycle. Oestrogen surges can also occur in perimenopause, left unchecked by progesterone. Later, oestrogen levels decline as egg reserves and ovulation peter off.

Fluctuating hormones are not helpful for burnout prevention, as we lose access to their protective, brain- and mood-supportive effects (see table on page 74). Emerging research suggests that menopause transition may even be a risk factor for burnout: oestrogen plays a role in regulating internal cortisol levels, and with less of it to go around as we enter menopause transition one effect can be cortisol levels running riot.[58]

Reassuringly, there is plenty we can do to support hormone balance in the body from a diet and lifestyle perspective. Hormone replacement therapy (HRT) has also advanced remarkably in recent years, offering vital support to women who are struggling with (peri)menopause. Gone are the days when synthetic HRT was always derived from horse urine (yuck!). Now it is available as body- or bio-identical HRT, which is both naturally derived (from the yam plant) and chemically identical (i.e., has the same molecular structure) as the hormones you produce naturally from your ovaries.

In the UK, some forms of body-identical HRT are available on the NHS. If you are working with us in clinic, we can

---

[58] Converso et al., 'The Relationship between Menopausal Symptoms and Burnout. A Cross-Sectional Study among Nurses.'

advise you on which forms are body identical and which are not, or you can speak to your GP. Dr Louise Newson's website offers some great HRT guidance – see the link in the Resources section.

Carly's burnout story continued

Testing in my clinic revealed that Carly's sex hormones were on the floor! It also revealed dysregulated cortisol akin to Stage 2 burnout. Carly's HPA-axis was chronically over-activated at the expense of her HPO axis.

Carly told me she didn't feel able to make much dietary change to begin with, so we focussed on managing stress using breathing and mindset techniques. I also put her on a therapeutic supplement plan to support her hormones. Most importantly, I wrote to Carly's GP with her test results and armed Carly with the information she needed to have an informed conversation with a menopause nurse about body-identical HRT.

After eight weeks, Carly was markedly improved. She had started a new job and felt able to cope with the learning curve. Most significantly, she felt like she had the energy and motivation to start to make healthy changes to her diet and lifestyle for herself and her family, which she hadn't been able to contemplate before. Uncovering the root cause of her symptoms had given her control back over her life.

Inadequate hormone elimination

Once it has done its job, oestrogen needs to be efficiently removed from the body. This is a three-phase process:

- Phases 1 and 2 occur in the liver (detoxification).
- Phase 3 happens in the gut (elimination via the stool).

If any one phase is not operating effectively, or if all three phases are not in balance with one another, oestrogen and/or its reactive metabolites (by-products of oestrogen metabolism) can recirculate and contribute to the overall oestrogen load. High oestrogen relative to progesterone (sometimes referred to as 'oestrogen dominance') can be problematic for exacerbating symptoms of Stage 2 burnout, in particular anxiety, sleep issues and migraines.

You may have had your hormones tested and been told your oestrogen levels were normal or maybe even at the lower end of the range. So why all the symptoms? Well, one possible explanation is that some of those used-up oestrogens have come back into play because they have not been effectively detoxified or eliminated from the body.

So, we need to support detoxification and elimination, to minimize impact on our burnout recovery. We do this in two ways, which we look at in turn below. I have started with the gut, as this is what we would address first in clinic – even though biochemically the gut phase comes second to the liver function.

Supporting gut function
Put bluntly, you need to be pooping every day to eliminate used-up hormones. This is true not only of oestrogen but cortisol too! If you're blocked up, this is problematic. Neatly packaged hormones, ready for disposal, can become 'unwrapped' in the colon with the help of certain bacteria and re-enter circulation, disrupting hormone balance. Consider whether you are drinking enough water and consuming enough fibre to support bowel motility. (More

about the role of our microbial friends and how to support a healthy gut, and why, in Chapter 9.)

Supporting liver function

The liver requires adequate nutrients for optimal function. Phase 1 of hormone detoxification/elimination relies on compounds found in cruciferous vegetables. You've heard me say it before (and I'll say it again): broccoli is a girl's best friend – and this is a prime example of why. But *fresh* broccoli only, ladies! The process of freezing broccoli often involves blanching, which destroys the detoxification-supporting compound indole-3-carbinol (sometimes referred to as I3C) that we need. Phase 2 requires amino acids (from protein) and B vitamins to function optimally.

Phase 2 of hormone detoxification/elimination also requires you to be an effective 'methylator'. A what?! I talk more about methylation in Chapter 11 but, in short, methylation is a biochemical reaction in the body that adds 'methyl groups' to molecules to support hundreds of different biological processes. In this case, methylation is supporting oestrogen clearance by synthesizing an enzyme called catecholamine-*methyl*-transferase, or COMT. Your ability to make COMT will determine whether you are a fast, slow or optimal processor of oestrogen and, in turn, whether Phase 2 is fast, slow or optimal, assuming the right nutrients are present!

I want to quickly mention alcohol here. I cover it again as a mood disrupter in Chapter 14, but it is important to note that alcohol is also processed in the liver and while your liver is distracted detoxifying alcohol (a lot more toxic than oestrogen), there is reduced capacity for hormone clearance. Alcohol also depletes us of the nutrients vital for Phase 1 and Phase 2 of hormone detoxification and impedes methylation (see Chapter 11). So, in other words, alcohol and hormone imbalance is not a good combination.

Research also highlights a persistent link between alcohol consumption and the risk of hormone-related cancers.[59] If you suspect a hormone imbalance and/or you are aware you have one then take a serious look at how much you drink and consider quitting, at least in the short term.

Exposure to hormone-disrupting chemicals

Sex-hormone balance can also be derailed by endocrine-disrupting chemicals (EDCs) in our environment, some of which can act as 'xenoestrogens'. What are xenoestrogens? Simply put, they are a group of synthetic chemicals that can mimic oestrogen in the body. Much like our natural oestrogens, xenoestrogens circulate looking for target cells to attach to. Their similar size and shape mean they are recognized by oestrogen receptors as oestrogen: they fit the lock and turn the key. Concerningly, though, the instructions xenoestrogens carry are very different from those conveyed by a natural oestrogen molecule. In this way, EDCs can mess-up hormone signalling and wreak havoc on our nervous system – not at all helpful for mood balance, stress resilience or burnout prevention.

Where are these pesky chemicals found? Everywhere! In plastics, medications, pesticides, cosmetics, household cleaning products. They are in the air we breathe, they are wrapped around or sprayed onto the foods we eat and used in the production of the products we put on our skin. Oh dear!

We can't avoid EDCs entirely, but we can reduce our exposure with the choices we make. Some suggestions include:

---

[59] Chen et al., 'Moderate Alcohol Consumption During Adult Life, Drinking Patterns, and Breast Cancer Risk.'

Eat organic

Prioritize:

- Meat and dairy in order to reduce exposure to synthetic hormones and antibiotics. Chat to your local butcher. They may not be certified organic, but you can tell by asking a few questions about how the animals are raised and whether they are grass or naturally fed.
- Fish. Sadly, fish is one of our most polluted food sources. Choose organic or wild-caught fish and minimize consumption of larger fish like tuna and swordfish, which can be high in toxic mercury.
- Fruit and veg without a skin, which are most vulnerable to pesticides. Useful resources for prioritizing which organic fruit and veg to buy are The Dirty Dozen and The Clean Fifteen, updated annually by The Environmental Working Group, www.ewg.org.

Avoid Plastics
Store food in glass containers and don't wrap food or microwave in plastics. Drink water out of stainless-steel bottles or glass. Use a glass jug water filter.

Download the 'Think Dirty' app
Get to know how toxic your household cleaning and personal care products are by scanning their bar codes in this app. Start to make gradual swaps for natural products. I recommend some natural brands on my website, www.re-nutrition.co.uk.

Genetics

Scientists have identified certain genes that can predispose us to how much hormone we produce and how much we can clear.[60] Fortunately, in many cases, these genes can be up-/down-regulated by nutrition and lifestyle factors. Contrary to popular belief, our genes do not equal unavoidable fate. See Chapter 12 for more information on genetics.

My top tips for supporting female hormone health

1. Support hormone synthesis by consuming healthy fats:

- Consume monounsaturated fats every day, for example avocado, olives, extra-virgin olive oil, seeds, nuts and their unsweetened butters, coconut and coconut oil.
- Consume three to four portions of oily fish a week, for example salmon, mackerel, sardines, herring, anchovies or pilchards. Oily fish is an excellent source of the omega-3 fatty acids Eicosapentaenoic acid (EPA) and Docosahexaenoic acid (DHA)..
- Vegetarians/vegans should consume daily chia, flax, pecans and walnuts and/or consider a high-quality vegan EPA/DHA supplement.

2. Consume phytoestrogens.

Phytoestrogens are compounds derived from plants that can exert a mild oestrogenic effect in the body by binding to oestrogen receptors. Examples are flaxseed, chickpeas, lentils and organic soy products (edamame beans, soya yoghurt, miso paste/soup, tempeh, tofu). They may have an oestrogen-balancing effect.

---

[60] Ghisari et al., 'Polymorphisms in Phase I and Phase II Genes and Breast Cancer Risk and Relations to Persistent Organic Pollutant Exposure: A Case-Control Study in Inuit Women.'

3. Get your hormones tested and consider hormone replacement therapy if hormones are low.

4. Support detoxification and elimination of excess hormones.

- Phase 1 – liver: consume 1–2 portions of cruciferous vegetables daily (broccoli, cauliflower, cabbage, kale, Brussel sprouts, watercress, rocket, radishes). Cruciferous vegetables contain a compound called indole-3-carbinol, which is required by the liver to breakdown oestrogen. These foods are also rich in sulphur, which supports broader liver health.
- Phase 2 – liver: consume good-quality protein and dark-green leafy veg to provide the amino acids and B vitamins needed for the detoxification process in the liver.
- Phase 3 – gut: drink plenty of filtered water and consume fibre-rich foods (veggies, fruit, pulses, wholegrains, legumes, nuts, seeds. See also Chapter 9.

5. Reduce alcohol: alcohol increases the toxic burden on the liver.

6. Support broader hormone health.

- Manage stress (cortisol levels): see Chapter 13 for tips.
- Balance blood sugar levels (insulin): see Chapter 7 for tips.

7. Exercise.

Exercise is not only great for your mood; it can also support hormone balance. Resistance training is particularly good for hormone balance; it supports the retention of muscle mass as we age, which, in turn, supports testosterone levels and the health of our bones. See Chapter 15 for more about this.

8. Reduce exposure to EDCs and xenoestrogens.

Aside from cortisol, there is another big-hitter hormone that can influence sex-hormone balance – particularly our male hormones, androgens. I'm talking about our blood sugar hormone, insulin. Blood sugar imbalance and insulin resistance are often at the root cause of androgen excess (think symptoms like irritability and aggression) and have been linked to conditions like PCOS. Unfortunately, when we are burnt out, it is likely we are riding what I call the 'sugar rollercoaster'.

CHAPTER 7

THE BURNOUT SUGAR ROLLERCOASTER

Are you familiar with that temporary high you get when you eat a bar of chocolate or drink a cup of coffee? You feel a rush of energy, you become more alert and your mood lifts? Yet, in what seems like no time at all, it all comes crashing down. You feel tired, unable to concentrate, anxious, irritable, sleepy and you just want to eat, *now*!

Maybe the pounds are piling on and, no matter what you try, that stubborn weight around the middle just won't budge? This really isn't helping your mood or self-esteem. These are signs that you are riding the sugar rollercoaster – and you need to step off.

But that's easier said than done when you are burnt out. Why? Let me explain.

7.1 Your blood sugar control hormone(s): Insulin and cortisol (again!)

The hormones insulin and our now familiar friend cortisol work together to control blood sugar balance in the human body. They are teammates: if you piss off cortisol, insulin won't be happy and vice versa. Remember that if you're on the road to burnout, it's likely that your stress signalling has got mixed up and you may already be producing too much or not enough cortisol. Consequently, cortisol's buddy insulin may be getting a bit agitated and, well, spikey. Imbalanced blood sugar and insulin dysregulation can be both a contributing factor to and effect of burnout. Making insulin your friend and blood sugar balance a priority may therefore prove very helpful in your road to burnout prevention or recovery.

Blood sugar balance is life and death stuff. Both extreme highs and extreme lows in blood sugar levels can be life-threatening and fatal. Insulin is a big-hitter hormone and we rely on it for survival almost as much as we do cortisol.

Mild fluctuations in blood sugar levels are normal and occur within a narrow range that the brain considers safe. When we consume food, it is broken down into smaller components as part of digestion. The digestion of carbohydrates produces glucose (or blood sugar), which is easily absorbed into the bloodstream and acts as the main energy currency for the brain and the rest of the human body. In response to rising glucose levels, the pancreas releases the hormone insulin, which signals to the body that any excess glucose not immediately required for energy should be removed from the blood and stored for later use. Depending on the amount, some will be placed into short-term storage as *glycogen* and some into long-term storage as *fat*. In terms of accessibility, think of glycogen like cash under the mattress – ready to be grabbed in case of emergency – and fat as your savings, only to be dipped into when you're a bit skint. Thus, insulin enables our blood sugar to return to normal levels and keeps us safe. Happy days.

Assuming the correct amount of insulin is produced in response to a rise in blood sugar, levels will return to normal until the next meal. Problems occur when too much insulin is produced. Rapid spikes in blood sugar from a carbohydrate-dense meal, for example, can lead to too much insulin being released. This can have the effect of quickly shunting too much glucose into storage and pushing blood sugar levels too low. When blood sugar levels drop, this triggers the release of cortisol from the adrenal glands.

Cortisol's job is to recruit energy in the face of threat – and a drop in blood sugar is just as threatening to survival as a bear! It will trigger the conversion of glycogen back into glucose and stimulate our appetite, signalling us to eat to help restore normal blood sugar levels.

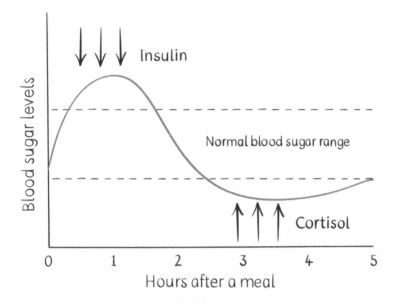

It's more than likely that cortisol is going to get you to eat the quickest and most energy-dense food you can find, as it needs your energy to rise rapidly. Nothing is going to send you to the junk cupboard quicker than cortisol.[61] However, if the next thing we eat also triggers a rapid spike in blood sugar, then yet more insulin is produced and a cycle of imbalanced blood sugar can be triggered. Before you know it, you're riding the sugar rollercoaster, crippled by cravings and consuming all the foods that we know make us feel like crap. The pounds pile on and we feel trapped by this sugar monster. It's a miserable feeling; I know, I've been there.

---

[61] I know you have one of these. Ain't none of us perfect. In our house, it's called the 'shit shelf'.

Some signs and symptoms that you are riding the blood sugar rollercoaster are:

- Fatigue, energy slumps and feeling sleepy during the day.
- Poor concentration and brain fog – the brain needs glucose to function.
- Irritability, anxiety and changes in mood, brought on by increased consumption of 'mood disrupters' and inadequate brain energy.
- Poor sleep and night waking – is cortisol waking you up? (read on for more info…)
- Uncontrollable food cravings and increased preference for energy-dense, processed foods.
- Weight gain and weight-loss resistance – insulin causes excess blood sugar to be stored as fat, particularly in the abdominal area.
- Wider hormone imbalance – just like cortisol, insulin can mess with your thyroid, sex hormones and adrenals (just what you need!).

When these symptoms occur, not only do we feel lousy but beneath the surface a state of dysfunction is developing. You may have heard of it – it's called 'insulin resistance'. Put simply, insulin resistance means that our body's cells are not being sensitive to the message that our hormone insulin is trying to convey, namely: 'remove this sugar from the bloodstream and place it into safe storage, please'. Consequently, we become less efficient at removing glucose from the blood and we need to produce even more insulin to have the same effect. Insulin resistance has been linked with prediabetes and type 2 diabetes. It is also thought to play a role in mood disorders, cognitive decline and broader hormone dysregulation.

I think it is important to recognize that dysregulated blood sugar is not just problematic for those with diabetes. Elevated blood sugar levels, below the diabetes threshold, have been linked with impaired cognitive function.[62] There is also a reason why Alzheimer's is nicknamed type III diabetes – the result of dysregulated blood sugar and insulin resistance in the brain. So it is not something to just worry about later. We can begin a preventative approach now, the first step being to understand your blood sugar levels and whether they are optimal – not just 'normal', or in other words 'not diabetic'. The best indicator of this is an HbA1c blood test, which gives us a good idea of levels over the past two to three months.

Becky's burnout story

Meet Becky. Becky is a 38-year-old regional recruitment manager. Prior to the global pandemic, Becky travelled regularly to the branches she managed. When COVID-19 sent us into lockdown, Becky was forced to work from home and has pretty much been working from home ever since. Becky lives alone.

I first started working with Becky during the second lockdown. Becky told me she had been struggling with her mood. She presented with insomnia, night-waking, brain fog and sugar cravings. She struggled to concentrate during online meetings and her boss had raised it in her performance review.

There were a few things about Becky's current diet and lifestyle worth noting:

- Becky never ate breakfast.
- Despite being a vegetarian, her diet was low in green vegetables.

---

[62] Convit et al., 'Reduced Glucose Tolerance Is Associated with Poor Memory Performance and Hippocampal Atrophy among Normal Elderly.'

- After a light lunch, Becky grazed on food until she went to bed.
- Becky was eating quite a lot of chocolate in the afternoon and evening.
- She drank eight cups of coffee throughout the day.
- Becky told me that she regularly worked or watched Netflix on her laptop in bed before trying to sleep.

During our first consultation, Becky broke down into floods of tears and told me that she was worried she had left it too late to settle down and start a family. She said she saw her former school friends posting pictures of their children on social media and this left her feeling disconnected and low. Her thoughts were overwhelming her, but she said she didn't want to speak to her GP. She said they were too busy and she didn't want to be a burden. She also said she felt nervous about her ability to make dietary and lifestyle change because of the way she was feeling.

7.2 Cortisol and our circadian rhythm

As well as controlling our stress response and blood sugar balance, cortisol has a key role to play in regulating our sleep–wake cycle, aka our 'circadian rhythm'. Cortisol is naturally produced in high quantities just before we wake up. Levels hit their peak the minute we open our eyes and let the light in. This is called our 'awakening response' and is what gives us our 'get-up and go' and motivates us to get our asses out of bed!

Stressors and/or huge plummets in blood sugar aside, levels of cortisol should naturally fall throughout the day and reach their lowest point just before bed. They should then remain low overnight to support sleep.

Now, let's imagine you are riding the sugar rollercoaster. You have eaten a late meal, or maybe you get sugar cravings before bed and snack on chocolate. You go to bed and try to go to sleep.

Here you face your first potential problem – the sugar rush has gone to your brain and has made you temporarily more alert and you cannot fall asleep! Second problem: you eventually fall asleep, only to find yourself awake again at the witching hour (3am) and cannot for the life of you get back off again. Behind the scenes, your digestive system, liver and hormones are processing this late snack. The spike in glucose levels induced an insulin surge, followed by a speedy dumping of glucose into storage. While you slept, your blood sugars dropped too low, so cortisol began the process of converting it back from storage. The surge in cortisol tricked your body into thinking it must be morning and – bing! – you're wide awake. If you do manage to fall back asleep you are then left wondering why the hell you feel pretty dreadful when the alarm goes off. Not only are you dog tired from lack of sleep, but you've also got minimal hormonal support to get you up, as your cortisol peak already happened at the wrong time! Poor sleep, poor mood, more cravings and round and round the rollercoaster you go.

7.3 Burnout and blood sugar imbalance

Imbalanced blood sugar and/or insulin resistance is yet another stress on the human body that you just don't need when you are feeling stressed. Dealing with imbalanced blood sugar increases demand on adrenals that are already over-activated as a result of chronic stress, accelerating

HPA-axis and adrenal malfunction. Burnt out adrenals are less equipped to deal with frequent drops in blood sugar. Which is why stress is put forward as a large contributing factor in insulin resistance and why imbalanced blood sugar might increase your risk of burning out. Throw lack of sleep into the mix (another system stressor) and you can really understand the vicious circle formed of stress, sleep and insulin.

Maintaining blood sugar balance and improving insulin sensitivity is therefore super important to ensure:

- Great energy levels all day long.
- Healthy mood balance.
- A regular sleep–wake cycle.
- Healthy hormone balance.
- Healthy weight management…

and to prevent burnout!

7.4 What causes blood sugar spikes and how can we prevent them?

Fear not, we can step off this rollercoaster and improve insulin sensitivity. But first we need to understand how we got on it in the first place. The key to this is understanding how the foods we eat are absorbed into the bloodstream.

Spikes in blood sugar can occur if we overeat, eat too often and/or if what we eat contains too much carbohydrate. Carbohydrates break down into glucose, whereas protein and fats are digested much slower and breakdown into amino and fatty acids. Amino and fatty acids can be converted into glucose later, but we don't need to worry about this for now. The important concept to grasp here is that that protein and fats are not capable of rapidly rising blood glucose levels in the same way that carbohydrates can.

This isn't to say that all carbohydrates are bad and that you should stop eating them, but it is important to understand how they may affect your blood sugar. Not all carbohydrates are built the same, nor will they all necessarily spike our blood sugar.

To help us understand this more, scientists created the glycaemic index (GI) and the concept of glycaemic load (GL). The index classifies foods based on their sugar content and the load calculates their potential to raise blood sugar levels based on a combination of factors:

- Their sugar content.
- How quickly and easily they are broken down and absorbed.
- How much of it you are likely to consume.

The higher the GL rating, the greater the impact on blood sugar levels and the greater the burden on your blood sugar balancing hormones.

Complex carbohydrates (like root vegetables and wholegrains), containing three or more sugar molecules, may rank higher on the GI than simple carbohydrates (like white bread and table sugar), which only contain one or two molecules. *But*, they also tend to be higher in fibre, which reduces their load. This why the GL should be relied upon more than the GI.

Fibre is a substance that cannot be digested by humans. As a result, fibrous carbohydrates take longer to digest and breakdown and will therefore rank much lower on the GL. In this way, a diet high in fibre and lower-GL foods can support healthy blood sugar balance.

High-GL foods	Low-GL foods
Chocolate, biscuits, cakes	Leafy greens and salad
Crisps	vegetables
Bread	Berries
White potatoes	Root vegetables: beetroot,
Pasta	carrots, sweet potatoes
Processed foods of any kind	Squashes, pumpkin
Fruit juices	Protein: fish, organic meat and
White rice	poultry, seeds, beans, pulses
	Healthy fats: nuts, seeds,
	avocados, olives

Other foods can also slow the digestion process down. Protein and healthy fats, for example, take longer to digest. They also increase satiety, initiating the 'stop' signal to the brain to let it know that you are full, and delaying the 'I'm hungry again' signal keeping you fuller for longer (you can read more about gut–brain signalling in Chapter 9).

One of the best regulators of insulin is exercise. We will talk about exercise as part of my Mood Boosting Method, which I introduce in Part 3.

Becky's burnout story continued

Testing of Becky's adrenal function revealed a Stage 1 burnout picture. Becky was mounting a decent stress response, but her cortisol was spiking unhelpfully at night-time. This mirrored low levels of her sleep hormone, melatonin. Her blood sugar marker HbA1C came back above optimal. I suspected dysregulated insulin was at the root cause of her evening cortisol spike, her sleep issues and brain fog. Left undealt with this could have perpetuated burnout progression.

For Becky, my priority was getting her some immediate support for her mood. As her melatonin was low and her diet was low in protein, I suspected her serotonin might be low too. With my encouragement and a GP referral, Becky was diagnosed with acute depression and prescribed an antidepressant. This proved to be super helpful for Becky. Once her mood began to lift and she felt ready, we began some gentle work to balance her blood sugar. For Becky, this meant making swaps to her coffee and chocolate after 2pm, eating three substantial, protein-rich, low-GL meals a day and having a device-free hour before bed.

At her second follow-up, Becky reported that she was now sleeping through the night, and her evening sugar cravings had completely disappeared. After six months, Becky told me she had sailed through her performance review and had ventured out on a few dates. She continues to practise sleep hygiene and to eat with blood sugar balance in mind. With her GP's support and guidance, she had started to reduce the dose of her antidepressant. Stage 2 burnout averted!

My top tips for supporting blood sugar balance

1. Balance your plate.

Ensure your plate contains a balance of protein, healthy fats, vegetables and low-glycaemic-load carbohydrates:

- Protein – delays transit time in the intestine and can mitigate the blood sugar spikes associated with consuming carbohydrates on their own. Individuals in studies who consumed protein with every meal experienced reduced sugar cravings and had less reliance on sugary snacks throughout the day.[63]

- Low-GL carbs – contain greater amounts of fibre. Fibre slows down the digestive process, keeping us fuller for longer and keeping sugar cravings at bay, and usually results in a slower release of sugar into the bloodstream.
- Healthy fats – increase satiety and are essential for wider hormone balance. Fats are also necessary to support the absorption of vitamins A, D, E and K.

If you would like a visual idea of how to make up a blood sugar balanced plate, visit the resources section on my website for a helpful visual: The Good Mood Plate.

2. Avoid blood sugar dysregulation triggers.

Avoid skipping meals, rapid eating, stimulants and highly processed foods, which can all trigger the sugar rollercoaster. Manage or offset stress where possible.

3. Eat at regular intervals and avoid snacking.

Aim to space meals at four- to five-hour intervals. This allows the gut to rest and blood sugars to normalize. Try to reduce snacking where possible. If there is to be a longer period between meals, choose a snack that features protein or healthy fats alongside low-GL carbs. Hummus on oatcakes or a portion of low-sugar fruit with a small handful of nuts are great examples of blood sugar balanced snacks.

---

[63] Astrup, Raben, and Geiker, 'The Role of Higher Protein Diets in Weight Control and Obesity-Related Comorbidities.'

Insulin and cortisol are bossy when it comes to biological function. We have already seen that our sex hormones cower to them. Similarly, our thyroid hormones are susceptible to their influence. Hypothyroidism presents with very similar symptoms to burnout, so in clinic we will always want to rule it out. Let's find out more in the next chapter.

CHAPTER 8

A BURNT-OUT THYROID?

Thyroid hormones play a key role in mental development, brain chemical regulation and metabolism. Even a small decrease in thyroid hormones can result in fatigue, mood swings, depression, brain fog and impaired cognitive function. Low thyroid hormones may also be a factor in weight gain, constipation and menstrual disturbances.

The thyroid needs a certain amount of cortisol to function effectively and is highly susceptible to stress. Both high and low levels of cortisol can impact thyroid function, making it vulnerable at any stage of burnout.

You may have been tested before and told that your thyroid hormone levels are 'normal'. But normal doesn't always mean *optimal*. Sub-optimal thyroid hormone levels could also be contributing to your symptoms.

Hannah's burnout story

We met Hannah in Chapter 1. She is our 33-year-old, stressed-out international employment lawyer. When Hannah came into clinic, she complained that she was struggling to get out of bed in the morning and only really felt like she 'got going' after lunch. Her ability to concentrate was poor and she said she was starting to lose her train of thought in big client meetings, which she felt was hindering her career progression.

Alongside the fatigue and brain fog, Hannah reported weight gain and constipation. Her mood had recently dropped, and her GP had prescribed an antidepressant that she wasn't tolerating very well. She was also taking a high-strength multi-vitamin that her friend (who was also working with a nutritionist) had recommended for her, and she was consuming a high-carbohydrate/low-protein diet.

When we suggested testing her thyroid function, Hannah was initially reluctant as her GP had already tested her thyroid stimulating hormone (TSH) levels and told her they were normal.

We'll find out whether this was true for Hannah later. For now, let's explore what the thyroid actually does.

8.1 What is the thyroid?

The thyroid is a small, butterfly-shaped endocrine gland located in the front of your neck, just below your voice box. Its main function is to regulate metabolism, which simply means the process of converting the food we eat into energy to enable the human body to function. In children, the thyroid is responsible for stimulating growth and brain development. In adults, the thyroid controls our basal metabolic rate and regulates how hard each cell is working: increasing mitochondrial volume (see Chapter 11), increasing body temperature and converting fat stores into energy. It also increases the effectiveness of a group of neurotransmitters you are now familiar with called 'catecholamines' (dopamine, noradrenaline, adrenaline), thereby activating our central nervous system to improve concentration levels. Mental clarity, motivation and focus, here we come!

The thyroid performs these essential tasks by producing and secreting the thyroid hormones:

- **Thyroxine** or **T4**, which is essentially the precursor hormone for:
- **Triiodothyronine** or **T3**, which is ten times more physiologically active than T4. Approximately 80% of T4 is converted into T3, not in the thyroid itself but in peripheral tissue, primarily in the liver and the kidneys.

If the body's demand for energy is increased – for example if you are outside on a cold day, or if you are pregnant – the thyroid will ramp up hormone production, and vice versa if less energy is needed.

The thyroid knows how much hormone to produce because – you've guessed it – it receives a signal from the brain. Specifically, our now familiar friend and master – the pituitary gland – will receive the nod from the hypothalamus that it is time to increase energy and it will secrete the signalling hormone known as TSH, which instructs the thyroid to produce more hormones. This cascade is known as the hypothalamic–pituitary–thyroid, or HPT axis.

8.2 Thyroid dysfunction

Symptoms occur when the thyroid becomes *over-* or, more commonly, *under*active; namely, producing too much thyroid hormone (*hyper*thyroidism) or not enough (*hypo*thyroidism).

Hyperthyroidism affects 1% of the population and is mainly observed in younger women. It is primarily caused by an autoimmune condition known as Graves' disease. However, hyperthyroidism can also be transient if the thyroid becomes temporarily inflamed (thyroiditis). Postpartum women, for example, can experience a temporary surge in thyroid hormones. Symptoms of hyperthyroidism include fatigue and changes in mood (irritability, anxiety, hyperactivity) alongside weight loss, increased appetite, palpitations and excessive sweating. The condition usually requires medical intervention; however, ensuring the diet is rich in immune-supporting nutrients and antioxidants is a good complementary strategy (see Chapter 10 for more on inflammation).

Hypothyroidism affects up to 5% of the population, with an estimated further 5% being undiagnosed. It is eight or nine times more common in women than men and becomes more prevalent as we age, although signs and symptoms can appear as early as in our 30s.[64]

Symptoms include:

- Fatigue, especially in the morning, that improves as the day goes on.
- Depression/low mood.
- Brain fog/inability to focus.
- Weight gain/weight-loss resistance.
- Constipation.
- Sensitivity to cold/cold extremities.
- Menstrual disturbances.
- Low libido.
- Fertility issues.

Notice how Hannah's symptoms match the first five in this list?

Hypothyroidism is also a risk factor in miscarriage. If you are planning for a baby, please do get your thyroid checked if you are experiencing any of the above symptoms.

---

[64] Chiovato, Magri, and Carlé, 'Hypothyroidism in Context: Where We've Been and Where We're Going.'

8.3 Causes of hypothyroidism

There are two primary causes of hypothyroidism: nutrient deficiency and an autoimmune condition called Hashimoto's disease.

Nutrient deficiency

Thyroid hormones comprise two nutritional building blocks that you need to be aware of:

- Tyrosine – an amino acid derived from protein (you may remember from Chapter 5 that tyrosine is also the building block for dopamine, adrenaline and noradrenaline).
- Iodine.

Worldwide, iodine deficiency is the most common cause of hypothyroidism, particularly in underdeveloped countries. In the West, governments have taken steps to mitigate deficiency through dietary fortification programmes, such as adding iodine to salt. Despite these efforts, iodine intake remains sub-optimal, with fewer of us consuming natural sources (fish and seaweed). Pregnant women are identified as particularly vulnerable to iodine deficiency.[65]

The temptation here might be to pop an iodine supplement, but I would actually urge against this: iodine surges have been linked with inducing thyroid autoimmunity and it is very easy to over supplement or supplement unnecessarily. Getting your iodine levels tested is always advisable and your practitioner will be able to advise you on a suitably accurate test with an approved lab (hint this is *not* the kind available on the internet!).

---

[65] Patriota et al., 'Prevalence of Insufficient Iodine Intake in Pregnancy Worldwide: A Systematic Review and Meta-Analysis.'

Iodine and protein are just the start of the nutritional picture. Just as we have seen so far in this book, there are many nutritional components that play a part in the creation, conversion and transportation of thyroid hormones. A deficiency in any one of the following may impact overall function:

- *Selenium* – involved in multiple stages of thyroid hormone production and utilization. Selenium also possesses antioxidant and anti-inflammatory properties; the thyroid gland has the highest selenium content per gram of tissue than anywhere else in the body, making it an essential nutrient for thyroid function.
- *Iron* – supports thyroid hormone production, conversion and receptor binding. Low iron is associated with underactive thyroid.[66]
- *Zinc* – a key immune-supporting nutrient, which also supports thyroid hormone conversion.
- *Vitamin A* – required to support thyroid hormone production and enables active thyroid hormone T3 to bind to receptor cells.

Hashimoto's

Autoimmune hypothyroidism occurs when our immune system, which usually works in our favour to fight infection, turns against us and attacks our thyroid gland. The ensuing damage means we are unable to produce sufficient thyroid hormones. The causes of thyroid autoimmunity are not yet fully understood; however, there is a body of research linking autoimmune conditions to intestinal permeability, or 'leaky

---

[66] Luo et al., 'Iron Deficiency, a Risk Factor of Thyroid Disorders in Reproductive-Age and Pregnant Women: A Systematic Review and Meta-Analysis.'

gut'.[67] Coeliac disease and non-coeliac gluten sensitivity may be a contributing factor to both the breakdown of the gut lining and Hashimoto's (see Chapter 9 for more information on the vital role of gut health).

A deficiency in immuno-supporting nutrients such as vitamin D and selenium may also be a factor in thyroid autoimmunity, alongside broader changes in hormone balance. Changes in immune function during pregnancy, for example, may induce Hashimoto's.[68] There may also be a genetic factor, with Hashimoto's hypothyroidism running in families.

The antibodies produced in this autoimmune response: *anti-thyroid peroxidase* (TPOAb) and *anti-thyroglobulin antibodies* (TgAb) can be tested in blood and are often positively detected years before any overt changes in thyroid hormone production, providing an early indication that thyroid support may be needed.

8.4 The link between burnout and hypothyroidism

Cortisol levels can influence both HPT-axis signalling and T4 to T3 conversion. A certain amount of cortisol is required to support conversion of T4 to T3 in the peripheral tissue (liver and kidneys). Where adrenal output is reduced, for example in Stage 3 of burnout, conversion may reduce, thereby reducing levels of active thyroid hormone T3.

Conversely, elevated levels of cortisol, present in the acute or prolonged phase of the stress response (think Stages 1

---

[67] Sategna-Guidetti et al., 'Autoimmune Thyroid Diseases and Coeliac Disease'; Cayres et al., 'Detection of Alterations in the Gut Microbiota and Intestinal Permeability in Patients With Hashimoto Thyroiditis'; Ilchmann-Diounou and Menard, 'Psychological Stress, Intestinal Barrier Dysfunctions, and Autoimmune Disorders: An Overview.'

[68] Świątkowska-Stodulska et al., 'Endocrine Autoimmunity in Pregnancy.'

and 2 of burnout), can suppress the release of TSH from the pituitary gland. In this scenario, the thyroid doesn't get the message to produce hormones. High levels of cortisol can also reduce conversion of T4 to T3; you're in survival mode here, don't forget, so let's slow down metabolism and store some fat around the middle! Cortisol also acts to suppress the immune system, enabling thyroid antibodies to thrive. From this, you can see the link between two small yet mighty endocrine glands: the thyroid and the adrenals. Fortunately, nurturing one will by default nurture the other.

Hannah's story continued

Testing revealed that Hannah's TSH was indeed within 'normal' range, but it was above optimal. Her active thyroid hormone T3 was low, indicating that, although she was producing some thyroid hormones, her high cortisol levels and poor diet may have been impeding her from converting it into a usable form.

Her urinary iodine levels were high, and she tested positive for thyroid antibodies, indicating Hashimoto's. We deduced that her Hashimoto's may have been triggered by the high levels of iodine in her multi-vitamin and exacerbated by cortisol-suppressed immune function and the amount of bread in her diet.

I immediately took Hannah off her multi-vitamin and asked her to eat protein with every meal. I guided Hannah on changes to her evening meal to increase thyroid- and immune-supporting nutrients and asked her to take a smoothie to work with her on the days she wasn't travelling. Finally, I asked her to trial a gluten-free diet.

Hannah came back in for her follow-up and looked like a different person. She said even her team had commented on the change in her morning energy levels (and mood!). She remarked that she had tried to eat a piece of toast the day before her appointment, and it had caused such a dip in her mood and energy that she resolved to keep gluten out of her diet for good. By her next follow-up she had agreed with her GP to come off her antidepressant medication and her constipation had improved. She told me she had sailed through her performance review and was being considered for partnership in her law firm.

8.5 How do I know if my thyroid is underactive?

As you have seen, many of the symptoms of thyroid dysfunction are non-specific – fatigue, mood imbalances, menstrual irregularities, changes in weight and constipation – meaning they may have other root causes. This is why testing really can be helpful. Thyroid dysfunction can usually be identified through blood testing. Your GP will usually offer to test TSH and T4, which is a good starting point. Unfortunately, GPs do not routinely screen the active form of thyroid hormone T3 – bonkers, right? That's the hormone doing all the work! Nor will they always offer to test thyroid antibodies.

In addition, the test ranges that are used to diagnose and treat underactive thyroid are arguably too broad and remain the subject of much debate in the clinical literature at the time of writing. Mild–moderate (or 'sub-clinical') hypothyroidism may be present when blood markers sit *within* the current normal clinical ranges – particularly when an individual is symptomatic, like Hannah. However, treatment (in the form of thyroid hormone replacement therapy) is not offered at this level despite evidence that disease onset can be delayed or prevented entirely if acted upon early enough. Fortunately, functional medicine practitioners, like me, are clinically trained to not only undertake a full thyroid screen but also to check whether your markers are *optimal* – not simply normal. They will also be able to offer dietary and lifestyle advice to support optimal thyroid function.

My top tips for supporting thyroid function

1. Consume a whole-food diet built around plant proteins, wild-caught oily fish, lean organic meat, vegetables, wholegrains and some fruit to provide access to key nutrients that support thyroid hormone production and transportation:

   - Salmon, sardines, sea vegetables and to a lesser degree eggs and dairy products provide access to *iodine*.
   - Avocado, pumpkin and sesame seeds, cashew nuts and banana provide access to the amino acid *tyrosine*.
   - Organic meat, poultry, fish, nuts, seeds, legumes and pulses are *iron*-rich foods.
   - Fresh oysters, shellfish, ginger root, lamb, nuts and sardines provide access to *zinc*.
   - Yellow- and orange-coloured vegetables (squash, pumpkin, sweet potato, carrot, nectarine, melon, papaya, peach, apricot) alongside eggs and mackerel provide access to *vitamin A*.

2. Consume five Brazil nuts a day to obtain the thyroid-supporting nutrient *selenium*.

3. Balance your blood sugar.

Keeping your blood sugar regulating hormones insulin and cortisol in check is essential for optimal thyroid function. Too much insulin and/or cortisol can suppress thyroid hormone production and conversion. Ensure each meal contains a balance of protein, healthy fats, vegetables and low-glycaemic-load carbohydrates. See Chapter 7 for more information.

4. Manage stress – see Chapter 13 for how!

5. Avoid stimulants: caffeine, sugar, artificial sweeteners and alcohol can all disrupt blood sugar balance and thyroid function.

6. Get outdoors into the sunshine for *vitamin D.* In the winter months, supplementation may be required (see Chapter 18 for more information about supplementation).

7. Identify and eliminate food intolerances that may be causing an immune reaction: gluten, lactose or casein in wheat and dairy products may exacerbate autoimmune Hashimoto's in some individuals. Trial gluten- and dairy-free diets to see if your symptoms improve.

8. Get tested. A full thyroid screen can help to identify whether your thyroid is functioning optimally and check for the presence of thyroid autoimmune antibodies. Testing can also check levels of thyroid-supporting nutrients such as iron and vitamin D.

One of the common symptoms of a burnt-out thyroid is constipation. In fact, gut symptoms are really common in burnout and other stress-induced mood disorders generally. The gut is highly sensitive to stress – and remember that digestion is one of those 'non-essential' functions that our stress response down-regulates. Specifically, raised cortisol levels inhibit the digestive system by shunting blood away from it to the brain and muscles. In burnout, digestive issues caused by repeatedly raised cortisol levels lead to increased stress and an even greater need for cortisol. Does this sound like you? If yes, it's time to listen to your 'gut feeling'. Let's explore what this means in the next chapter.

CHAPTER 9

THAT GUT FEELING: THE ROLE OF THE GUT–BRAIN AXIS

The digestive tract is the interface between us and the outside world.

Most people are aware of the digestive system's role in breaking down and absorbing the food we eat. However, the gut is also the first line of defence in the human immune system and can communicate with our brain to influence our mood and cognitive performance. The digestive tract is also home to a vast microbial ecosystem, known as the gut microbiome: an essential part of our biology that, when balanced, promotes good health and stress resilience.

Grace's burnout story

Grace was a successful business owner. Her stress was not placed upon her by a boss or a corporate environment, but was caused by the pressure she put on herself to be successful – to be the best in her industry.

Grace presented with low mood, frequent migraines and brain fog. Her bowels were loose, often urgent, and she frequently experienced painful bloating and gas. She said she had always been self-motivated and able to rely on her own drive but lately she felt like she didn't have the energy to function and that her motivation had deserted her. Despite this, Grace was still managing to eat a protein-rich diet with plenty of green vegetables – suggesting that she was consuming the building blocks she needed to help regulate her mood and energy levels – although her diet lacked colour. She confessed that she frequently 'inhaled' her food and ate when she was feeling stressed.

9.1 Stress resilience and good mental health begin in the gut

The gut is often the first port of call for a nutritionist or functional medicine practitioner investigating unexplained symptoms. It is difficult to address symptoms of burnout such as low mood, anxiety, poor sleep, fatigue and brain fog if the digestive system is not functioning properly. A stressed-out gut trying to communicate with a burnt-out brain is not the best combination!

Consider that all of the essential nutrients we have talked about so far need to be able to reach the brain and beyond to carry out their function. This means, with the exception of vitamin D, they first need to navigate the vast terrain of our digestive tract where three key processes need to occur:

1. Food digestion.
2. Nutrient absorption.
3. Waste elimination.

Digestion is a mechanical and chemical process beginning at the mouth and ending at the anus. The food we eat is propelled along the digestive tract and broken down with the help of stomach acid, digestive enzymes and bile. These chemicals are composed of, and activated by, nutrients we obtain from our diet. You see how all biochemistry in the body relies on what you eat? Even digestion itself!

The process is complex, with a high potential for dysfunction. Throw chronic stress and poor nutrition into the mix and we have the perfect storm for gut dysregulation.

9.2 Gut function and stress

Remember that, under stress, digestive function is down-regulated to enable the body to focus on survival. This is your sympathetic nervous system in action. Once the perceived threat has passed, normal (parasympathetic nervous) function is able to resume. This is completely natural and when our stress response is functioning optimally there shouldn't really be a problem. However, exposure to chronic stressors and/or being more susceptible to stress not only increases your risk of burnout but can also have a negative effect on gut function.

Some of you may have experienced nausea, vomiting or diarrhoea in response to an acutely fearful or anxious situation like public speaking or a professional exam. Maybe you have experienced chronic constipation or crippling trapped wind when you have been trying to keep all your work–life plates spinning. This is the result of your stress response firing.

It is fair to say that burnout, and indeed many other mood disorders, go hand-in-hand with poor gut function. The research tells us that if you are diagnosed with depression or generalized anxiety you are more likely to experience symptoms of IBS and vice versa.[69] But why is this? Well, I would like to introduce you to the gut–brain axis.

---

[69] Whitehead, Palsson, and Jones, 'Systematic Review of the Comorbidity of Irritable Bowel Syndrome with Other Disorders: What Are the Causes and Implications?'

9.3 The gut–brain axis

The gut is frequently referred to as our *second brain* and is home to at least 100 million neurons – the largest collection of nerve cells in the human body – a vast web known as the 'enteric nervous system'.

Despite seeming quite far apart, the brain and the gut are connected both physically and chemically – a connection known as the gut–brain axis. Originating in the brain, the *vagus nerve* connects the gut to the central nervous system and enables bidirectional messaging between the two organs. Similarly, chemical messengers produced in the gut can travel to the brain via the bloodstream and vice versa.

A healthy brain will support digestive health. However, under stress, the burnt-out brain can send unhelpful signals that disrupt digestion and the balance of our gut microbiome. Similarly, a healthy gut, with the help of our bacterial friends, will produce the brain chemicals that regulate mood, memory and attention, whereas a poorly functioning gut or imbalanced microbiome can negatively influence our mental health and be a contributing factor in burnout.

Think of the gut–brain axis as your biological broadband. In fact, let's dive into this metaphor a bit further.

Your anti-stress ethernet cable

The vagus nerve provides hard-wired communication comparable to an ethernet cable, for those of us old enough to remember what one of those is! The vagus nerve makes up approximately 80% of your parasympathetic nervous system, or your 'rest-and-digest' state. As has already been seen in Chapter 5, the parasympathetic nervous system is critical to anti-stress communication and supports healthy digestion (remembering that digestion is not a priority when the opposing *sympathetic* nervous system is firing).

Exposure to the chronic stress associated with burnout causes us to lose what is called 'vagal tone'. Poor vagal tone equals poor anti-stress communication between the gut and the brain, leaving us less resilient to stress, more susceptible to delayed emotional recovery from stressful events and ultimately burnout. Fortunately, vagal tone can be strengthened by eating the right foods and undertaking anti-stress activities such as breathwork, laughter and singing, which we discuss more in Part 3.

Your biochemical wi-fi

Not only is the gut home to the largest collection of nerve cells, it also:

- Is the largest hormone-producing organ in the body.
- Secretes the neurotransmitters serotonin, dopamine, glutamate and gamma-aminobutyric acid (GABA), which we learned in Chapter 5 are our mood-regulating chemicals. In fact, 90% of the 'happy' hormone/neurotransmitter serotonin's receptors are located in the gut, which may explain what we call our 'gut instinct', or why we 'feel' our emotions in our gut.
- Houses 70% of the human body's immune cells.

Collectively, the hormones, neurotransmitters and immune cells in your gut can be thought of as chemical messengers, which make up your gut's biochemical wi-fi. They can travel via the bloodstream to the brain and beyond, and communicate in a similar fashion to the wireless communication delivered by wi-fi: completely invisible to the naked eye and pretty damn amazing.

Myth busting

Contrary to popular belief, the gut is not a neuro-transmitter factory for the brain. Modern research has concluded that serotonin (and other neurotransmitters) produced in the gut are actually more likely to be utilized in the gut itself, supporting motility and other gut functions, or in the periphery. Even if these chemicals were to travel to the brain, they would be unable to cross what is known as the blood–brain barrier.[70] It is far more likely that our moods are regulated by neurotransmitters produced in the brain itself. See Chapter 5 for how to support neurotransmitter production in the brain.

9.4 The gut barrier: The first line of defence

The digestive system is the first line of defence in our immune system. For example, the stomach produces acid that not only aids digestion of food and the breakdown of protein into those essential amino acids, but also kills off bacteria that may have arrived from the mouth that shouldn't really be entering the small intestines.

In the small intestine, the gut wall creates a physical barrier between us and the outside world. It is designed to allow safe passage for nutrients and health-promoting chemicals through its walls, while keeping toxins, undigested food and other harmful molecules out. (Remember, the brain does not distinguish between the types of stress you face. *Physical* stressors such as sugar, processed foods, alcohol, drugs and other environmental toxins that find their way

---

[70] Bektaş et al., 'Does Serotonin in the Intestines Make You Happy?'

into your gut contribute to your overall stress burden just as much as psychological stress – and can also be a contributing factor in burnout.)

Think of the small intestine like The Wall in *Game of Thrones*, keeping the White Walkers at bay in the north so that the rest of Westeros can prosper. Like The Wall, the small intestine features many gates or 'tight junctions', which can be opened and quickly closed to allow the good guys (nutrients) through. The small intestine is monitored by your biochemical wi-fi, so that it knows exactly when to open the gates.

Much like The Wall, the gut lining, which is only one cell thick, is susceptible to damage and enemy attack. Processed, high-sugar foods, poorly digested food, alcohol, over-the-counter medication, injury and disease can all contribute to gut-lining damage, with chronic stress being enemy number one.

You may have heard of the term 'leaky gut', which essentially means increased traffic of 'bad guys' into our system as a result of cracks in the intestinal wall or faulty gates. Fortunately, patrolling the gut wall is our very own version of the Night's Watch, which can sound the alarm and raise an army of immune cells in the event of a breach. When working effectively, these immune cells can swallow invaders and begin repairing any damage.

Problems arise when our immune cells are constantly on call, dealing with stressor after stressor; paracetamol, after wine, after chocolate, after Big Mac meal – you get the picture. In this scenario, potentially harmful molecules make it past an overwhelmed Watch into Westeros (the bloodstream) and can rapidly travel to other parts of the kingdom (your body) to launch an attack.

Meanwhile, at the gut wall, the immune response is never quite resolved, leaving little time for repairs and paving the way for low levels of chronic inflammation. Chronic inflammation is another stressor that adds to your burnout burden. In susceptible individuals, an over-activated immune system fails to distinguish between the goodies and baddies, and begins to attack the wrong molecules/cells! At best this can make us sensitive to certain foods and at worst can lead to autoimmune conditions (conditions where the immune system attacks healthy tissue).

We will talk more about immunity and inflammation and its links to brain health and burnout in Chapter 10. But for now, I think you get the idea that sub-optimal gut health can have far-reaching or systemic effects in the human body, and nurturing the gut is essential to burnout recovery and prevention. I have also begun to show that the symptoms of a burnt-out gut go way beyond IBS.

Signs and symptoms of sub-optimal gut function			
Bloating	Indigestion	Brain fog	Hormone imbalance
Constipation	Offensive wind	Fatigue	Skin complaints
Diarrhoea	Reflux	Mood imbalance	Food sensitivity
Cramps	Heartburn	Sleep issues	Weight gain
IBS	Cramping	Migraine	Inflammation

The *Game of Thrones* fans among you will know that the Night's Watch is a team – a diverse bunch working together for a common cause: defence of the realm. Towards the end of the series (spoiler alert), they even allow their frenemies, the Wildlings, to join forces with them. All the better to fight the enemy. Our biochemical gut border patrol is no different: human immune cells working alongside and in partnership with a player known as the 'gut microbiome'.

9.5 The gut microbiome

A calm and healthy gut relies on a balanced and healthy microbiome. The bacteria that live alongside us, predominantly in the lower (or large) intestine, support human physiological function.

You're probably thinking, 'hang on a minute, Rach'. Haven't I just spent the last few years sanitizing all surfaces and washing my hands to the tune of 'Happy Birthday' to rid myself of germs, and now you're telling me I need them? Well, yes. It does take a bit of a shift in mindset, as we have long thought of germs as bad. But, like many things in life, there are the good, the bad and the downright ugly when it comes to microbes. What we need is an appropriate balance between good and bad – and to avoid the ugly like the literal plague!

Let me see if I can convince you as to their vitalness to health and – most importantly – burnout prevention. One of the microbiome's primary roles involves maintaining the integrity and barrier function of the gut wall, protecting the brain (and the rest of the body) from toxins that should remain in the gut.

The microbiome forms part of our biochemical wi-fi. There are strains of bacteria in the *lactobacilli* and *bifidobacterium* genera, which have been identified as exerting anti-stress, anti-anxiety and mood-protective effects when present in good amounts.[71]

---

[71] Messaoudi et al., 'Beneficial Psychological Effects of a Probiotic Formulation (Lactobacillus Helveticus R0052 and Bifidobacterium Longum R0175) in Healthy Human Volunteers'; Langkamp-Henken et al., 'Bifidobacterium Bifidum R0071 Results in a Greater Proportion of Healthy Days and a Lower Percentage of Academically Stressed Students Reporting a Day of Cold/Flu: A Randomised, Double-Blind, Placebo-Controlled Study.'

The microbiome feeds on our undigested food and in doing so helps to extract and synthesize nutrients such as B vitamins that we would not be able to produce on our own. And, while munching away, these microbes also produce health-promoting by-products such as *short-chain fatty acids*, which help to balance inflammation in the body. Nice!

These are just some of the ways in which the gut microbiome protects us from disease. We have only just scratched the surface in our human understanding of the potential of the human microbiome. It is a fascinating and ongoing area of research. Type 'gut-microbiome' into PubMed (the go-to database for published scientific research) and you will see the spike in studies and discussion on this topic over the last ten years.

Stress and the microbiome

Just as gut function can be influenced by stress, so too can the composition of our microbiome and vice versa, leading to the expansion of the term 'gut–brain axis' to the gut–brain–microbiota axis.

A pivotal animal study published in the *Journal of Physiology* in 2004 identified that the composition of your gut microbiome can affect the way your brain responds to stress.[72] Germ-free (GF) mice (these are mice that have been born without a gut microbiome and housed in a sterile environment) proved to be less resilient to stress than normal, microbiome-intact mice. The GF mice demonstrated prolonged recovery times after stress exposure and had higher levels of circulating stress hormones than their counterparts. Furthermore, when the researchers introduced probiotic bacteria into GF mice,

---

[72] Sudo et al., 'Postnatal Microbial Colonization Programs the Hypothalamic-Pituitary-Adrenal System for Stress Response in Mice.'

their resilience to the stressor improved and their reactivity to stress reduced. Fascinating stuff.

It is unsurprising, then, that researchers have observed microbial disturbances in the stool samples of humans with anxiety and depression – mood disorders that we have seen are closely linked to burnout – and shown us that improving microbial diversity can improve our resilience to these conditions.[73]

Feeding the microbiome

A healthy microbiome relies upon diversity and balance, allowing the 'good guys' to thrive while keeping the potentially harmful microbes in check. You can think of the gut microbiome as your garden: fill it with flowers and nurture it regularly and it will bloom and thrive. Abandon its flowers or, worse, don't plant any at all, and it will become overgrown and full of stubborn weeds.

We can support microbial balance by consuming *probiotic* and *prebiotic* foods. *Probiotic* foods contain live bacteria that are beneficial to health. They help to repopulate the microbiome if the good guys are in short supply. *Prebiotics* are a type of fibre that we as humans cannot digest but that our microbiome loves to eat. Prebiotics essentially feed and sustain a healthy population of 'good bacteria' in our gut. Some examples of pro- and prebiotic food sources are listed in the following box.

---

[73] Nikolova et al., 'Perturbations in Gut Microbiota Composition in Psychiatric Disorders: A Review and Meta-Analysis'; Bear et al., 'The Microbiome-Gut-Brain Axis and Resilience to Developing Anxiety or Depression under Stress.'

Probiotic foods	Prebiotic foods
Live natural (unflavoured) yoghurt	Onions
Fermented soybean products such as miso, tempeh and natto	Garlic
	Leeks
	Jerusalem artichoke
Sauerkraut	Asparagus
Kefir (soured yoghurt)	Berries
Kimchi (Korean pickle)	Bananas
Kombucha (a fermented tea drink)	Beans and other legumes
	Steel-cut oats

Two temptations present themselves if you suspect microbial imbalance:

1. Start popping a probiotic supplement.
2. Give the microbiome a good 'clean'.

I mention both of these here as there are many 'experts' out there advocating one or both approaches.

I share my thoughts on supplementation in more detail in Chapter 18. It is true that there is a lot of good research supporting probiotic supplementation in improving stress resilience and mood disorders. Probiotic supplements are broadly safe, and I recommend a blend of scientifically proven strains on my website if you want to give them a try.

However, be aware: you can have too much of a good thing. Adding in probiotics unnecessarily could upset the delicate microbial balance in the gut and exacerbate overgrowth of bacteria in some individuals, particularly if the microbes have migrated up to the small intestine (a condition known as small intestinal overgrowth, or SIBO). If you experience upper-abdominal bloating, probiotics might not be for you. Furthermore, simply adding a probiotic to repopulate the good guys in the gut will do nothing to address the overgrowth of the bad guys if you keep on feeding them with the processed, sugary foods that they love. Probiotics are not a panacea for gut health.

As for microbial cleansing, whether top-down (antimicrobial, antifungal or antiparasitic pills or potions) or bottom-up (colonic irrigations), many approaches are indiscriminate in the microbes they 'cleanse'. You risk sacrificing the good with the bad, you might not really need it and, quite frankly, it probably isn't addressing the root cause of your individual burnout!

I met someone once who enthusiastically told me they were doing a parasite cleanse and I asked them, 'oh do you have a parasite?' to which they replied, 'I have no idea.' I think my blank expression may have said it all (I could never play poker!). Also, as gross as it may seem, parasites, like many other bacteria, can live alongside us happily without causing any problems whatsoever. We don't necessarily need to go after them with the weed-killer, even if we *know* we have one.

The message here is: *test* don't *guess*, and don't *mess*, *unless* you have been advised to by a professional. Understand your personal needs and seek appropriate clinical advice. We do use probiotics and antimicrobial/-fungal/-parasitic supplements in clinic if appropriate. We also refer out for antibiotic prescriptions in some cases. The key difference is we utilize these options appropriately and effectively, based on all the clinical information and scientific evidence available to us.

Grace's story continued

Grace's stool test revealed reduced digestive function, meaning that – despite consuming some great food – she wasn't breaking it down effectively and therefore her ability to actually absorb these nutrients was diminished. We also observed markers of 'leaky gut', which might explain her symptoms of systemic inflammation (brain fog, migraine, fatigue, low mood). Also interesting in Grace's stool test was her microbiome profile. We observed a pattern of moderate dysbiosis (microbial imbalance): Grace had sub-optimal levels of mood-supportive bacterial strains, alongside an overgrowth of some sulphur-producing bacteria and a *potentially* problematic parasite.

We took a top-down (brain-to-butt) approach to support Grace with her burnt-out gut. First: getting her to slow down and eat mindfully – so that her brain got the message to initiate digestion – and to chew her food thoroughly. We supported nutrient absorption by encouraging Grace to consume bitter foods, and gut-barrier function by feeding her microbiome with polyphenol-rich foods and removing gluten. Once all this was implemented, we undertook some gentle antimicrobial work to help address the bacterial overgrowth. We judged antiparasitic work unnecessary, as her symptoms resolved. Stress management was emphasized throughout her programme, so that Grace could frequently enter her 'rest-and-digest' nervous system state. We also utilized a carefully tailored therapeutic supplement plan, staged across her programme.

Grace worked with us for six months. After just one month, Grace came beaming back into clinic and reported that she hadn't had a single migraine and she could feel her 'mojo' returning. By the four-month stage, Grace was feeling energized and she was no longer fearful of getting caught short by her bowels. At six months, the painful gas and bloating had dissipated. We then put Grace on a maintenance programme so that she could continue her gut-healing journey and, when we spoke to her after 12 months, she was happily living pain free.

My top tips for supporting gut–brain health

1. Manage stress: as we have seen, high stress levels can detrimentally affect digestive function and the composition of our microbiome. Offset stress using techniques set out in Chapter 13.

2. Stay hydrated: water is needed to produce a healthy stool and positive mood. Aim for two litres of good-quality water a day.

3. Chew food thoroughly: chewing initiates the digestive process, signalling to the brain that it is time to release digestive enzymes and letting the stomach know to produce stomach acid.

4. Consume bitter foods (rocket, artichoke, radishes, chicory, herbs, etc.), which aid digestion and can improve vagal tone.

5. Consume adequate dietary fibre: diets higher in fibre are associated with lower incidence of mood disorders and support healthy digestion in many ways:
   - Stimulating the digestive muscles to contract, supporting motility.
   - Containing prebiotics to feed the 'good' bacteria.

- Coating the gut lining, supporting barrier and immune function.
- Supporting waste elimination by binding used-up hormones (like cortisol and oestrogen) and adding bulk to the stool.

Fibre can be found in whole, unprocessed foods such as vegetables, fruit and wholegrains.

6. Space meals at four- to five-hour intervals: the digestive system needs time to rest and initiate a digestive tract cleaning process called the 'migrating motor complex' (MMC). The MMC cannot activate if we are eating all the time!

7. Try adding some live probiotic foods to your diet (see list on p. 128).

8. Reduce triggers of poor gut function:
   - *Sugar* – diets high in sugar can encourage unhelpful bacteria and yeasts/ fungi to thrive in the gut.
   - *Antacids* – many people take antacids for indigestion, which act by lowering levels of stomach acid. But stomach acid is needed for the breakdown of proteins. Incompletely digested proteins can increase inflammation and cause damage to the gut lining.
   - *Antibiotics* – while beneficial for acute infections, regular and chronic use of antibiotics can suppress the growth of beneficial bacteria.
   - *Alcohol* – alcohol is dehydrating and can contribute to gut lining damage, increasing the risk of infection and inflammation.
   - *Gluten* – gluten has been linked to damage to the tight junctions, or gates, in the gut wall and increased intestinal permeability.

Grace's story highlights how critical gut health is for burnout prevention. A gut that is leaky can contribute to inflammation and mess with our immune system. Recall that, like digestion and reproduction, repair is also down-regulated when our stress response is active. To maintain resilience in times of high stress, it is important that we look at the influence of inflammation and immune health.

CHAPTER 10

THE ROLE OF INFLAMMATION AND IMMUNE HEALTH

Has supporting your immune system ever been more important than now? I don't think so. Life changed in 2020, didn't it? Most of us set about figuring out how we could support our immune system, developing a new respect for the vital role it plays in protecting us, and how significant the affects can be when it isn't functioning at its best. A sneeze or a cough that may have previously gone unnoticed now makes you a social pariah – and if you are burnt out you may have noticed a cough or a cold or two! Burnout may also make your experience of a virus more unpleasant or prolonged. Nothing is going to zap your energy or bring your mood down quicker than the frustration of getting sick, again!

10.1 The immune system under stress

Immune function, like digestion and reproduction, is down-regulated when the stress response is initiated. There is no time for leisurely tissue repair when we are fighting for our very survival. Remember, that is what your brain thinks you are doing when you are stressed or burnt out: trying to survive in the face of threat.

Our stress hormone, cortisol, plays a key role in dampening our immune response. Cortisol is anti-inflammatory.

Consider the different stages of burnout. In Stages 1 and 2, we might observe the over-activation of the adrenals and thus excessive cortisol production. During this stage, cortisol is dampening our immune response. This is when frequent and prolonged infections can arise. Studies have shown that the more stressed-out you are the more susceptible you are to catching common colds and respiratory tract infections.[74] In 2022, a Harvard University cohort study of 55,000 volunteers, most of them women, found that high pre-pandemic stress and anxiety levels increased susceptibility to developing 'long covid' – symptoms of the COVID-19 virus that lasted beyond three months.[75]

Conversely, at Stage 3, when the body is exhausted and the adrenals are unable to keep up with the demand, insufficient cortisol is produced. This sets the scene for chronic inflammation as cortisol is no longer able to perform its vital anti-inflammatory role. Why is this relevant? Well, contemporary science has linked chronic inflammation to the rise of modern lifestyle diseases such as Alzheimer's, heart disease, diabetes and so on.[76] In fact, inflammation in the brain is put forward as one of the root causes of mood disorders and chronic inflammation is perceived by the brain as stress.[77] What a vicious cycle burnout can be. When considered in this context, it is easy to see why burnout might lead to depression or vice versa!

[74] Cohen, Tyrrell, and Smith, 'Psychological Stress and Susceptibility to the Common Cold.'

[75] Wang et al., 'Associations of Depression, Anxiety, Worry, Perceived Stress, and Loneliness Prior to Infection With Risk of Post–COVID-19 Conditions.'

[76] Furman et al., 'Chronic Inflammation in the Etiology of Disease across the Life Span.'

[77] Miller and Raison, 'The Role of Inflammation in Depression: From Evolutionary Imperative to Modern Treatment Target.'

10.2 What is inflammation?

Inflammation sits at the heart of our immune response. When we get injured or infected, inflammation is part of a healthy immune response. Inflammation supports the elimination of toxins and damaged cells from the body, fights invading microbes and repairs damaged tissue. However, inflammation that is inappropriate or unresolved can damage healthy tissue and exacerbate burnout.

Symptoms such as fatigue, brain fog, anxiety, depression, IBS, weight gain, hormone imbalance, joint pain, migraines, food intolerances and skin complaints are all indicators that inflammation may be imbalanced.

At tissue level, inflammation is controlled by a group of hormones called 'eicosanoids'. Some of these hormones are *pro*-inflammatory, meaning they initiate or increase inflammation; and some are *anti*-inflammatory, meaning they reduce or resolve inflammation. These hormones must operate in balance with one another to ensure a normal inflammatory response.

A simple example of how inflammation works is to imagine you have cut your finger. Your body responds by releasing pro-inflammatory eicosanoids. These chemicals trigger blood vessel dilation, which enables white blood cells and vital nutrients to reach the damaged area. You may notice that your finger becomes red, swollen or inflamed. This is your inflammatory immune response getting to work at repairing the skin and tackling any potential germs. In response to inflammation, healthy tissue releases anti-inflammatory eicosanoids that prevent the inflammation from spreading and halt the immune response once the cut has healed.

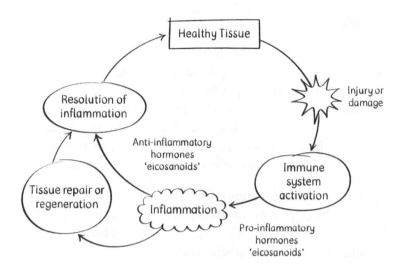

An insufficient pro-inflammatory response inhibits repair and microbial defence, whereas an insufficient anti-inflammatory response enables inflammation to persist, unresolved. Even low levels of inappropriate inflammation can be detrimental to health.

As we have already seen, chronic stress alongside dysregulated adrenal function and inappropriate cortisol production (high or low levels) can impact the inflammatory response. However, other diet and lifestyle factors, commonly observed in burnout, can also inhibit the production of anti-inflammatory chemicals.

10.3 Essential fatty acid balance

Our inflammation-balancing hormones, eicosanoids, are made from special fats known as 'essential fatty acids', or EFAs. You may have heard of some of the most famous ones: *omega-6* and *omega-3*. They are considered essential because they cannot be synthesized by the body and must, therefore, be consumed in your diet.

An ideal ratio of omega-6 to omega-3 is 4:1; however, modern Western diets have evolved to a ratio that is closer to 20:1. This EFA balance is unhelpful for inflammation, as omega-6 foods tend to be pro-inflammatory whereas omega-3 foods tend to be anti-inflammatory. Mood disorders such as anxiety and depression have been linked to a poor omega-3:6 ratio, which is similarly unhelpful in burnout.

Why has the balance skewed?

Well, the best source of omega-3 is, hands down, oily fish. It contains the most biologically active types of omega-3 (Eicosapentaenoic acid, or EPA, and Docosahexaenoic acid, or DHA). Historically, fish would have formed a big part of our diet, particularly if we lived near a river or the sea. But with the Industrial Revolution, the growth of the food industry and most of us heading into cities for work, the popularity (and availability) of fresh, and particularly oily, fish has dwindled. Many of us have grown up on battered white fish, sourced from the freezer in 'finger form' or from the chippy – not a salmon fillet or smoked mackerel in sight!

Simultaneously, our oceans became increasingly more polluted and fish were over-farmed, making fish an unpopular and increasingly unsustainable food source. This led some to seek out plant-based sources of omega-3, such as seeds (flax, chia, pumpkin) and sea vegetables. Sounds good, right? We could all do with eating more plants.

The only real downside is that these plant foods do not contain those active forms of omega-3: EPA and DHA. The types of omega-3 found in plants are less biologically active and require conversion to EPA and DHA once inside the human body. Unfortunately, we humans aren't that efficient at converting plant-derived omega-3s into EPA and DHA. And when you are burnt out, your body is already working overtime to achieve basic function – you don't need to give it more work to do. Feeding yourself foods that don't require this extra work is definitely preferable. In the wild, fish feed on nutrient-dense grasses and algae. They do the conversion to EPA and DHA for us. This is what makes oily fish such a good source of omega-3, especially when you are burnt out.

If you really struggle to eat enough oily fish – by which I mean salmon, mackerel, sardines or herring – three to four times a week, or you are vegan, then supplementation may be a consideration for you (see Chapter 18 for more on this).

Revisiting Carly's burnout story

Remember Carly, the chief engineer from Chapter 6? As well as struggling with hormone havoc, Carly also reported frequent infections and joint aches. Carly's diet was lacking in colour and any kind of fish. She was relying on microwave meals and convenience food, grabbed in between meetings at work or after the children's bath and bedtime.

Recall that testing had revealed Stage 2 burnout: high cortisol levels, which were likely suppressing her immune function. Blood testing also identified a vitamin D deficiency, raised hsCRP (a marker of inflammation) and a poor omega-3:6 ratio.

Carly supplemented with vitamin D, C, omega-3 fish oil and other immune-supporting nutrients in the short term. She also began a programme of active relaxation techniques to calm her nervous system. When she felt able to make dietary change, she gradually added oily fish, rainbow-coloured vegetables and other foods to support her immune function and inflammation balance. At her second follow-up, Carly reported that she had not suffered from any infections in the time she had been working with me and her joint pain had reduced by 50%.

The role of processed foods

Alongside this decline in eating really good sources of omega-3 (or choosing omega-3 foods that we cannot convert very well), contemporary Western diets rely heavily on meat, dairy and processed foods, all of which feature higher levels of omega-6. The majority of our burnout clients will be leaning on fast, convenient, omega-6-rich foods to sustain themselves as they are too tired to cook or even think about meal planning. Don't forget, we are biologically programmed to grab whatever we can, to quickly mobilize energy under stress (remember cortisol's role in the burnout sugar rollercoaster in Chapter 7?). However, it is highly inconvenient for us that those same foods promote inflammation, which the brain views as stress, and therefore increase the overall burnout burden.

Omega-6 is prevalent in many processed foods, predominantly due to the industry's use of vegetable oils. I don't think I am alone in thinking that the term 'vegetable oil' is particularly deceptive. If the term refers to 'vegetable' or any type of plant, surely it must be healthy? The truth is that most fats in liquid form, such as those extracted from nuts and seeds, are highly unstable. Refining them – through the application of heat and pressure and the addition of other chemicals – damages and denatures them. It alters their chemical structures and strips out their beneficial nutrients, ultimately making these liquid fats more pro-inflammatory to humans and unhelpful for burnout.

This doesn't mean you need to avoid nut and seed oils all together. Instead, look for oils that have been minimally processed, by which I mean that the oil has been extracted from the plant by mechanical means, without the application of heat. You are looking for cold-pressed nut and seed oils here. They are best used on food after cooking or as a salad dressing so as not to damage them with heat.

A quick word on red meat

Animal fats and their products, such as eggs and dairy, are pro-inflammatory if consumed in excess. Modern farming techniques mean that most farm animals are grain fed; their diets are therefore high in omega-6 and low in omega-3, tipping the inflammation balance unfavourably. Depending on where in the world you are reading this book (farming regulations differ from country to country) these animals may also be pumped full of synthetic growth hormones and antibiotic drugs. Crikey! Not good for them and definitely not good for us.

Conversely, animals that are free to roam and are naturally grass fed tend to be higher in omega-3 fats. Organic egg yolks, for example, are an excellent source of DHA, a type of omega-3 that promotes brain health. So, my top tip when it comes to animal products is to buy local, organic and higher-welfare animal produce from a butcher or a farm shop. Better for your health, better for the environment and better to be supporting local businesses.

Inflammatory foods/lifestyle factors	Anti-inflammatory foods
Animal fats	Wild fish and seafood
	Flaxseed and chia seeds
Animal products, e.g. eggs and dairy	Sea vegetables
	Nuts and seeds

Hydrogenated fats (margarine, vegetable oils, processed foods)	Cold-pressed seed oils, e.g. flaxseeds, sesame and pumpkin
Sugar	
Alcohol	Green and brightly coloured vegetables
Stimulants (caffeine, nicotine)	
Stress	Fruit, e.g. berries
Excessive exercise	Wholegrains (brown rice, oats)
Frequent infections	Organic eggs
Injury	Organic animal produce

10.4 Other immuno-supportive nutrients

The immune system doesn't just rely on essential fatty acids and inflammation balance to function effectively. There are many other complex processes at work, and it is important to mention some other key nutrients that we associate with immune function. These are linked to optimum nutrition and burnout prevention/recovery.

Antioxidants

Antioxidants perform a key role in mopping up the potentially harmful by-products of inflammation, such as *free radicals* or *reactive oxygen species*, aka ROS. Left unchecked, these chemicals can be damaging to human tissue and consequently detrimental to health. Excessive amounts of free radicals and ROS have been linked to many chronic diseases, including cognitive decline, major depressive disorder and cancer.

Some nutrients, like vitamins C, E and beta-carotene (a plant derived from vitamin A) can act as antioxidants in their own right. Other nutrients, such as the minerals selenium and zinc, are crucial for synthesizing other chemicals that can act as antioxidants, glutathione being the most noteworthy. Many other micro-nutrients found in brightly coloured plant foods, such as carotenoids, flavonoids, phenols and polyphenols, are also thought to possess antioxidant properties. This is why we really should think about eating a rainbow every day for immune and mental health.

Remember our sleep hormone, melatonin? This also acts as an antioxidant, helping to protect our brains from inflammation. There is emerging research that lower melatonin is linked to cognitive decline, Alzheimer's and dementia.[78] Supporting melatonin levels is important not only for our moods but also our long-term brain health.

Vitamin C

As well as acting as an antioxidant, vitamin C contributes to the cellular function of both the innate and adaptive immune system. Vitamin C deficiency is associated with an increased risk of catching a winter cold or other respiratory tract infection. Conversely, frequent infections can also induce vitamin C deficiency, when demand for vitamin C's antioxidant potential is higher. Remember also that the adrenals are a large consumer of vitamin C. All things considered, it is hardly any wonder that vitamin C is depleted when we are burnt out.

Food sources of vitamin C go beyond lemons and limes. Green veggies, strawberries, pineapple and other brightly coloured veg are great sources. Supplementation may also be a consideration in times of chronic stress and / or burnout: see Chapter 18.

---

[78] Cardinali et al., 'Melatonin Therapy in Patients with Alzheimer's Disease.'

Vitamin D

Vitamin D is a group of fat-soluble steroid compounds:

- Cholecalciferol (or vitamin D3), synthesized in the skin following sun exposure and naturally occurring at low levels in certain foods, such as oily fish, eggs, liver and butter.
- Ergocalciferol (or vitamin D2), a plant-derived form used to fortify foods in some European countries.

Vitamin D's most well-known function is to regulate bone metabolism and the concentration of calcium in the bloodstream. However, vitamin D is also an immuno-modulator, which helps us to control infections and reduce inflammation. It was thrust into the spotlight as a result of the COVID-19 pandemic, with research inversely linking vitamin D status to infection rates and disease severity.[79] Vitamin D supplementation appeared to offer a protective effect against the virus, especially in women.[80]

But vitamin D status and viral infections were known to be linked long before the pandemic. Consider that viruses tend to be more prolific in the winter, so much so that it is even referred to as the 'cold and flu season'. At the same time of year, sunlight is at a premium and vitamin D levels are lower. Throw into the mix studies that show that adults who report a recent cough, cold or other respiratory tract infection are more likely to have insufficient blood levels of

[79] Kaufman et al., 'SARS-CoV-2 Positivity Rates Associated with Circulating 25-Hydroxyvitamin D Levels'; Maghbooli et al., 'Vitamin D Sufficiency, a Serum 25-Hydroxyvitamin D at Least 30 Ng/ML Reduced Risk for Adverse Clinical Outcomes in Patients with COVID-19 Infection.'
[80] Louca et al., 'Modest Effects of Dietary Supplements during the COVID-19 Pandemic: Insights from 445 850 Users of the COVID-19 Symptom Study App.'

vitamin D, and I think the link is obvious.[81] Interestingly, there may also be a link with mood disorders such as seasonal affective disorder (or SAD), as dopamine and serotonin rely on vitamin D for synthesis.

In clinic, one of the first questions we ask a potential client who is struggling with the symptoms of burnout is: do you usually catch a winter cold? If the answer is 'yes', we will want to check their vitamin D status. The same applies if low mood or motivation is a main symptom.

The UK's latitudinal position makes it virtually impossible for its inhabitants to synthesize vitamin D in the skin between October and April. As food sources alone are also unlikely to provide sufficient amounts, supplementation might be necessary to achieve optimal vitamin D levels. See Chapter 18 for more information.

10.5 Inflammation and the brain

Just like the gut, the brain is similarly protected from its external environment by a wall of cells known as the blood–brain barrier. This being the case, you might well be wondering how inflammation in the rest of the body could possibly affect the brain and the central nervous system if there is a physical barrier.

Well, firstly, just like the gut wall, the blood–brain barrier is susceptible to damage and can become leaky. A leaky brain allows toxins and other potentially harmful biochemicals to gain access to our highly sensitive central nervous system. When this happens, an invasion is recognized by specialist immune cells in the brain and an inflammatory response

---

[81] Ginde, Mansbach, and Camargo, 'Association Between Serum 25-Hydroxyvitamin D Level and Upper Respiratory Tract Infection in the Third National Health and Nutrition Examination Survey.'

is launched. This is why it is super important to support blood–brain barrier function by supplying the brain with fats from oily fish nuts and seeds.

Secondly, certain immuno-modulating chemicals are capable of crossing a robust blood–brain barrier. This isn't a problem in and of itself: we want the immune system to be able to access and support the brain. What is important to consider is that when pro-inflammatory biochemicals cross over into the brain, they are capable of initiating the production of similar pro-inflammatory chemicals in the central nervous system, thereby increasing inflammation in the brain.[82]

One such pro-inflammatory chemical capable of crossing the blood–brain barrier is interleukin-6 (IL-6). IL-6 is a reliable biomarker of systemic inflammation (meaning we can test levels to ascertain whether there is widespread inflammation in the body). In a study of 500 volunteers aged 30–54, researchers discovered that higher levels of circulating IL-6 were associated with poorer outcomes in tests of mental executive function and attention/working memory.[83] The same research group also discovered that central inflammation was associated with reduced grey matter volume in the hippocampus and prefrontal cortex areas of the brain.[84]

---

[82] Varatharaj and Galea, 'The Blood-Brain Barrier in Systemic Inflammation.'
[83] Marsland et al., 'Interleukin-6 Covaries Inversely with Cognitive Performance among Middle-Aged Community Volunteers.'
[84] Marsland et al., 'Interleukin-6 Covaries Inversely with Hippocampal Grey Matter Volume in Middle-Aged Adults.'

My top tips for supporting inflammation balance and immune function

1. Consume foods rich in omega-3 such as fish, flaxseed, chia seeds and pumpkin seeds and their cold-pressed oils, and sea vegetables. Most supermarkets sell samphire, seaweed and other sea vegetables. You can also source them in powdered form to stir into smoothies or sprinkle on salads.

2. Include some sources of omega-6 alongside omega-3 foods. Sunflower and sesame seeds, as well as wholegrains such as brown rice and oats, provide access to essential omega-6 fats, helping you to achieve a healthy ratio of omega-6 to omega-3. Sunflower and sesame oils should only be consumed if they are virgin or cold-pressed. Most shop-bought sunflower and sesame oil has been refined, diminishing the beneficial properties of these seeds. Read the labels carefully.

3. Cook with olive oil. Most fats in liquid form are unstable. Heating the oils of nuts and seeds can damage the essential fats contained in them, promoting inflammation when consumed. Cooking with olive oil is preferable as the monounsaturated fats in olive oil can withstand higher temperatures before becoming damaged.

4. Reduce consumption of farmed animal fats/products. Choose instead organic, grass-fed animal products.

5. Increase antioxidant rich/supportive foods such as brightly coloured fruits and vegetables, herbs and

spices such as peppers, tomatoes, sweet potatoes, courgettes, aubergines and berries. Ginger and turmeric are fantastic anti-inflammatory and anti-oxidant foods that are relatively cheap, readily available and can be added liberally to your diet. Think ginger teas and home-made curries.

6. Get some sunshine to boost your vitamin D.

7. Support gut barrier health – see Chapter 9.

8. Reduce pro-inflammatory foods/lifestyle factors such as alcohol, smoking, sugar and excessive exercise.

I hope you are still with me. We have covered a lot of ground, discussing some pretty big biological systems and their organs on our journey to understanding what imbalances may be driving the symptoms of burnout and/or being caused by stress. Most of them you have probably heard of before. The terms 'hormones', 'gut' and 'inflammation' are familiar to most of us, even if you didn't exactly know what they were before.

But before we move on to Part 3 and look at 'what to do about it', I want you to be aware of two critical burnout-preventing biochemical processes that you probably haven't heard of before. I call them your 'burnout M&Ms'.

CHAPTER 11

YOUR BURNOUT M&MS

OK, don't get too excited, neither of your burnout M&Ms involves chocolate or peanuts. They stand for 'methylation' and 'mitochondria'. Ooooh (tumbleweed)… stick with me.

Why are they worth mentioning? Well, burnout is going to affect your energy and it's going to affect your mood. Without mitochondria you can't make energy and without methylation you can't produce the brain chemicals that regulate your mood. In fact, there is an awful lot you can't do, biochemically speaking, without your M&Ms.

You'll never see them; mitochondria are microscopic organelles and methylation is a hidden biochemical process. But once you know about them, you can nurture them to become your burnout-beating friends.

11.1 Mitochondria: Our energy engine rooms

Mitochondria are at the centre of all human energy production at a cellular level.

With any machine, optimum energy output relies on an efficient metabolic engine. Human beings are no different: every single cell within our body contains an engine room, known as the mitochondrion. This is where energy is produced. It is hardly surprising that a poorly functioning engine could lead to symptoms of low energy and fatigue and ultimately contribute to burnout.

Mitochondria offer a fantastic example for me to highlight to you how optimal biological function relies on optimal nutrition and how poor nutrition can lead to malfunction.

Mitochondria convert carbohydrates, protein and fats from the food we eat into the energy required to undertake all biochemical processes in the body. In order to carry out this task the mitochondria require various nutrients as helpers or 'co-factors', such as magnesium, B-vitamins and iron. We have seen these nutrients crop up a lot in this book, as they are also required to support hormone and mood balance. Unfortunately, these helper nutrients are highly susceptible to depletion by stress. A diet that is low in these supporting nutrients and/or where these nutrients are being poorly absorbed can result in inefficient energy production and therefore fatigue.

Mitochondria are also essential for stress and reproductive hormone production. Without optimal mitochondrial function, we cannot produce cortisol and so we cannot mount our stress response!

Here are some other things you need to know about mitochondria.

Free radicals and mitochondrial damage

Mitochondria are susceptible to damage. When burning fuel to generate heat, potentially toxic fumes are also produced. This is also the case with human cellular energy production. When we produce energy, we also create potentially dangerous chemical by-products called 'reactive oxygen species' (ROS) – or 'free radicals' as they are often referred to in the media. Free radicals are highly reactive little buggers and, if they are not neutralized, they race around wreaking biochemical havoc; damaging tissue, cells and our mitochondria. They are the proverbial spanners in our engine works!

We met free radicals in Chapter 10 as they are produced as part of our inflammatory response against infection. Free radicals are also produced in response to physiologic stress and excessive exercise. However, free radicals are not unique to our internal environment: we are also exposed to them from the outside world. Sources of environmental ROS include:

- Inhaled chemicals:
  - Industrial pollution.
  - Exhaust fumes.
  - Smoking.
  - Pollen.
- Food, specifically:
  - Heated or chemically treated unsaturated fats (you might find these in processed foods, labelled as hydrogenated fats/oils, but you can also inadvertently generate ROS yourself by cooking with oils. More about this in Chapter 10).
  - Burnt food.
  - Cured meats.
- UV radiation.
- Certain medications.

Neutralizing free radicals is the job of antioxidants and, as we saw in the previous chapter, our antioxidant status relies on optimal nutrient levels – vitamins C, E and A and the minerals zinc and selenium, to name a few. If your diet is low in fruit and veg (and if you are stressed out, the research tells us it probably is) your antioxidant capacity might be reduced, increasing your susceptibility to free radical damage.[85]

---

[85] El Ansari, Adetunji, and Oskrochi, 'Food and Mental Health: Relationship between Food and Perceived Stress and Depressive Symptoms among University Students in the United Kingdom.'

Damaged mitochondria are unable to efficiently produce energy. In order to protect the mitochondria from external damage it is important to ensure the cell walls are robust. Cell membranes are made up of a fatty bi-layer, the building blocks of which come from – you've guessed it – fats from our diet. (Another shout out to grab an avocado or eat some oily fish, ladies!)

I think you are getting the picture here: insufficient nutrients equals insufficient biochemical raw materials, and insufficient raw materials paves the way for functional imbalance and poor energy production.

Engines under stress

Stress can impact the function of mitochondria. Research tells us that exposure to chronic stress decreases mitochondrial energy production and causes mitochondria to swell.[86] Stress can also detrimentally affect mitochondrial DNA and antioxidant capacity and increase the production of free radicals. Yikes, not good!

Consuming antioxidants can modulate the effect of chronic stress on mitochondrial function and engaging in moderate (not excessive) exercise also protects mitochondrial health.[87] So we can see once again how a functional approach can support mitochondrial function and prevent a key symptom of burnout.

---

[86] Picard and McEwen, 'Psychological Stress and Mitochondria: A Systematic Review.'
[87] Sorriento, Di Vaia, and Iaccarino, 'Physical Exercise: A Novel Tool to Protect Mitochondrial Health.'

Revisiting Carly's burnout story... again

We met Carly in Chapters 6 and 10. Carly was 'tired and wired' when she came into my clinic. I suspected her mitochondria may not be functioning optimally and needed some TLC. Let's look at the clues to see if this stacks up:

- Carly was stressed and in a high-cortisol state, which can suppress mitochondrial function and increase free radical production.
- Carly was fighting frequent infections and her inflammation was imbalanced, which may have increased free radical production.
- Carly's diet was low in antioxidants and protective fats, making her mitochondria vulnerable to free radical damage.
- Carly's sex hormones were low – mitochondria are needed to make these hormones.
- Carly lacked the energy she needed to perform at her best – mitochondria are at the heart of all cellular energy production.
- Carly's energy levels normalized when she took steps to manage stress, addressed her inflammation balance and increased antioxidants in her diet.

Pretty strong clinical evidence, wouldn't you agree? In Carly's case, testing revealed 'oxidate stress', which put simply is a disturbance in the balance between free radical production and her antioxidant capacity. It also revealed that levels of her master antioxidant, glutathione, were low. Antioxidant and mitochondrial support were definitely indicated in Carly's case.

Carly's story highlights that there is often no single root cause at the heart of burnout, and that we often need to dig deep to understand what's really going on.

Carly presented with a web of stress-driven functional imbalances, which were unique to her. This warranted highly personalized support that the traditional approach (an antidepressant in her case) would not have been able to address. This is the beauty of functional medicine.

My top tips for supporting mitochondrial function

1. Consume foods rich in the energy-production co-factors magnesium, B vitamins and iron. These can be found in dark, leafy greens, mushrooms, eggs and organic meat.

2. Eat plenty of rainbow-coloured fruits and vegetables, which are rich in the antioxidant vitamins C and E, selenium and zinc, in order to ward off any free radical damage.

3. Consume a balance of monounsaturated fats from avocado and olive oils as well as essential fatty acids such as omega-3 from oily fish and omega-6 from sunflower seeds.

4. Manage stress – you will see this feature in all my Top Tip sections. This is why I have dedicated a whole chapter (Chapter 13) to restoration and stress-management tools and techniques. However, managing stress also extends to reducing or removing dietary stressors like sugar and alcohol, which deplete us of the energy-building nutrients we need to keep the engine running.

5. Engage in moderate exercise – see Chapter 15 for more.

11.2 Methylation: The hidden cycle at the root cause of burnout?

Methylation is a ubiquitous biochemical process that is happening right now in your body; in fact, it has occurred billions of times while you have been reading this sentence. It is the process of donating, or adding, a 'methyl group' to a molecule in order to make it biochemically active.[88] Also known as 'one-carbon metabolism', methylation is the simple, yet essential, process behind many of the bodily functions that I have mentioned so far:

- Neurotransmitter synthesis and metabolism.
- Hormone metabolism.
- Detoxification.
- Energy production.
- Immune function.

It also plays a vital role in DNA synthesis and repair, and gene expression/suppression.

Stress can inhibit methylation and this has been linked to several symptoms of burnout, including:

- Insufficient sleep.
- Chronic fatigue.
- Mood imbalances.
- Hormone imbalances.
- Infertility.

As with all the other biological processes I have described in this book, methylation is no different in that it requires

---

[88] Chemistry lesson in the small print for those of you who are feeling extra geeky: a methyl group is composed of one carbon atom bound to three hydrogen atoms. In chemical notation it is written like this: CH_3. These one-carbon units are how methylation came to be nicknamed 'one-carbon metabolism'.

optimal nutrient status for effective function. The process is heavily dependent on the following nutritional components:

1. **Methionine:** an essential amino acid (meaning we cannot produce it in the body and must therefore obtain it from protein consumed in the diet). Methionine is the start of the methylation cycle that directly and indirectly produces other important organic compounds such as:
   - S-Adenosylmethionine (SAMe) – a universal methyl donor.
   - Glutathione – our master antioxidant.
   - Homocysteine – a toxic amino acid by-product of methylation, which must either be detoxified or remethylated into methionine with the help of…
2. **Vitamin B12,** or methylcobalamin (the active or methylated form of vitamin B12).
3. **Folate,** or 5-methyltetrahydrofolate (5-MTHF – the active or methylated form of folate).

'Folate' (or vitamin B9) is a generic term used to describe both the naturally occurring folate found in plant foods and folic acid, the synthetic form used to fortify foods and found in supplements. Folate does not arrive in the body in an active form and must undergo its own methylation process to activate it. Folate is essential to DNA synthesis – we cannot make DNA without it. This is one of the reasons why folic acid is often recommended to pregnant women. Methylated folate is also essential for neurotransmitter synthesis.

We can see the paradox that methylation requires methylated compounds to function! This is why the methylation process happens in cycles (five, in fact), with substances constantly re- and de-methylating themselves in order to keep the chain alive. Other dietary co-factors are involved, including B2, B3, B6, zinc, magnesium, choline and betaine (TMG).

A deficiency or sub-optimal level of any of these nutrients may hinder methylation.

Why is methylation so important in burnout and mental health?

Methylation is the process that converts the amino acids phenylalanine, tyrosine and tryptophan into noradrenaline, dopamine, serotonin and melatonin; and tyrosine into thyroid hormones. So let me be clear: without methylation, you cannot produce the chemicals required in the first step of your stress response (noradrenaline and consequently adrenaline). Without methylation, you cannot produce the chemicals that keep you happy, give you motivation and help you sleep (serotonin, melatonin and dopamine). Without methylation, you cannot produce the hormones that supercharge your nervous system (thyroid hormones).

In summary, without methylation, you cannot beat burnout.

Becky's burnout story, revisited

Remember Becky from Chapter 7? Becky was depressed and struggling to sleep. She presented with Stage 1 burnout. I suspected that Becky might be struggling to methylate. Why?

Becky's vegetarian diet appeared to lack the building blocks for methylation. It was:

- Low in protein.
- Naturally lower in vitamin B12.
- Lacking in folate-rich green vegetables.

Blood testing confirmed sub-optimal folate and B12 levels. She also had low levels of melatonin, which, along with serotonin, require methylation for their production. Finally, hormone testing revealed sluggish Phase 2 detoxification in the liver, indicative of sub-optimal methylation.

Once Becky added the methylation building blocks back in her diet, she started to feel better and was able to reduce her antidepressant medication.

For Becky, uncovering this invisible root cause was invaluable not only in her recovery but also in preventing her burnout from escalating further.

My top tips for supporting methylation

1. Ensure the diet contains plenty of folate-rich foods: broccoli, Brussels sprouts, leafy greens, peas, chickpeas and kidney beans.

2. Also ensure adequate levels of B12-rich foods: meat, fish, dairy and eggs.

3. Ensure adequate sleep – check out the tips in Chapter 13.

4. Practise stress-management techniques such as yoga and Tai Chi, which may have a positive im-pact on methylation. See Chapter 13 for more tips.

5. Get tested. Blood testing can assess levels of active B12, folate and homocysteine (the toxic by-product of the methionine cycle) to evaluate whether additional methylation support might be required.

Right at the start, I said that burnout was a very individual experience. Over the course of the last few chapters, you have seen how the life experiences of different women brought them to burnout, and how functional testing revealed biochemical imbalances in their nervous system, their hormones, their gut, their immune function and in their M&Ms – all of which perpetuate a burnt-out state. You also witnessed, through these women's stories, how a personalized approach to their diet and lifestyle was helpful for them. But, in all of this, we must not forget that there are factors that predispose us to burnout: an inherited stress-resilience level or ability to cope, handed to you by the genetic lottery.

CHAPTER 12

YOUR GENES

It was previously thought that our genes decided our fate. We were born with a unique genetic code, one set inherited from our mother and one from our father. While it is true that our genetic sequence is both unique and fixed, what we didn't understand back then was that genes can be turned on and off. What is more, environmental factors such as our diet and lifestyle can influence whether genes are activated or not. More fascinating still, our gene expression can be influenced not just by our own lifestyle, but also the lifestyles of our parents and our grandparents before us. Mind blown? Mine was too.

Epigenetics is the science that has illuminated the concept that gene expression can be altered by environmental factors. If a mother experienced stress during pregnancy, this can influence the health outcomes for the child through gene expression alteration. It is the same if she smoked heavily, drank alcohol or consumed a nutrient-depleted diet while pregnant. The genetic code itself remains unaltered, but what is switched on or off could be.

But these effects can also occur before pregnancy. One of the starkest illustrations of this is to be found in research on descendants of Holocaust survivors. In these studies, the descendants – who had not experienced the horrors of concentration camps themselves – were more likely to have reduced resilience to stress and demonstrate hyper-vigilance or fearful behaviour.[89] This is an example of stress being passed down and experienced by the next generation, due to epigenetic alterations to gene expression triggered by environmental factors.

12.1 What is nutrigenomics and what are SNPs?

The emergence of epigenetics has given rise to a further area of science known as 'nutrigenomics', which seeks to establish what effect food and nutrients can have on gene expression.

Single nucleic polymorphisms, also known as SNPs, are variations on the genetic code that may either offer a protective effect or increase susceptibility to disease. They are compared to a 'wild type', which simply means the genotype most commonly found at that position on the human genome. Nutrigenomic testing in functional medicine focuses on identifying SNPs to enable diet and lifestyle optimization. This is the ultimate in health personalization.

Yet it is important to remember two things:

1. Possessing a gene variation that makes us more susceptible to a particular health condition does not mean we are destined to become ill. If the internal environment is good, these genes may never be expressed.
2. Likewise, having 'strong' genes does not make us invincible. Under the right environmental conditions

---

[89] Yehuda et al., 'Holocaust Exposure Induced Intergenerational Effects on FKBP5 Methylation'; Dashorst et al., 'Intergenerational Consequences of the Holocaust on Offspring Mental Health: A Systematic Review of Associated Factors and Mechanisms.'

(stress, poor diet, anti-nutrients and so on), we can still suffer from burnout and beyond.

12.2 Genetic SNPs that can influence mood

The following is a list of the genes that might be influencing both your mood and your ability to cope with stress, and why. Importantly, these are all genes that can be up- or down-regulated by environmental (diet and lifestyle) factors.

- FKB5B: this is your stress-resilience gene. It controls your response to cortisol. Variations in this can predispose you to hyper-vigilance. It is also involved in the tryptophan steal (see Chapter 5), reducing the availability of serotonin in the brain.
- CRHR1: this gene encodes for the corticotropin-releasing hormone receptor, and determines HPA-axis functionality. Variations can amplify your experience of stress and your perception of fear.
- NYP: this gene encodes for the molecule neuropeptide Y, which protects us against stress-derived mood disorders like anxiety and depression and supports cognitive function under pressure.
- OXTR: this gene encodes for the 'cuddle hormone', oxytocin's, receptor expression, which modulates the fear centre in our brain.
- BDNF (Val66MET): encodes our ability to synthesize the neuroplasticity-enhancing molecule BDNF. Chronic stress down-regulates this gene.
- DRD2 and DRD4: encode for our dopamine receptors.
- DBH: encodes for the enzyme that converts dopamine to the precursor stress-alert hormone, noradrenaline.

- PNMT: encodes for the enzyme that converts noradrenaline to adrenaline.
- COMT: determines how well we metabolize both dopamine and oestrogen.
- TPH1 and TPH2: encode for the enzymes that convert tryptophan to serotonin.
- HTTLPR: encodes for the serotonin-transporter molecule.
- HTR1A and HTR2A: encode for our serotonin receptors.
- MAOB: determines how well we metabolize serotonin.
- MTHFR: encodes how well we are able to synthesize methyl-folate, required for methylation (see Chapter 11).
- GABRA2: encodes for GABA-receptor activity. Variations may reduce receptor expression and sensitivity to GABA and its sedative effects.

This list is not exhaustive, but simply an illustration of the complexity at play. If you are interested in finding out more, Dr Ben Lynch's book *Dirty Genes* is a great read.[90]

---

[90] Lynch, *Dirty Genes: A Breakthrough Program to Treat the Root Cause of Illness and Optimize Your Health.*

PART 3

WHAT TO DO ABOUT IT?

Now we have covered all the possible imbalances that could be going on behind the scenes, I am sure you are ready to discover how you can tackle burnout naturally. Maybe you have even skipped to this part, because you just want to find out what to do to feel better. I get it.

In this section, I am going to introduce you to my Mood Boosting Method. It could easily have been called my 'stress-busting, resilience-increasing, fatigue-fighting and burnout-banishing method', but I thought that all sounded a bit too wordy! The word 'mood' means 'a conscious state of mind' and refers to a prevailing emotion. It describes the way we *feel*. When I think about burnout and the way that feels, I know I want to feel differently: happier, calmer, more energized, positive, motivated, able to relax, well rested. And so, my Mood Boosting Method was created with this in mind.

It looks like this:

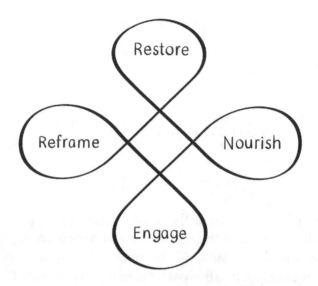

The method has been designed to bring together the research and evidence on how to combat fatigue and emotional overwhelm naturally, under four distinct headings: Restore, Nourish, Engage and Reframe. Although the next few chapters discuss these steps in that order, you do not need to read or action them in a strict sequence.

The method is flexible, recognizing that each reader has arrived at this point with their own unique needs. It may be that one step is calling to you more than the others. It is really important that you tune into that inner voice and take yourself to the chapter that you feel you need the most, first.

In practice, when a client is that exhausted, anxious and depressed, they are unable to comprehend or take on a huge amount of change. They might need to start simple, building gradually towards taking on more challenging changes as they start to feel better.

This book is no different. You won't find anything massively complex in what follows. You can build upon and revisit the information in your own time.

CHAPTER 13

RESTORE: THROUGH REST AND RELAXATION

Out of all the stages of my Mood Boosting Method, this is arguably the most important step. If you are arriving at this book exhausted or at Stage 3 of burnout, then this is the step that you're going to want to start with.

Rest and relaxation are vitally important for mood stability, although many of us fail to recognize or prioritize this.

Ironically, it is also the step that you are most likely to skimp on if you are at Stages 1 or 2 of burnout! If that is you, you may already be telling yourself one of the following:

- I don't have time to rest! Resting isn't going to get my 'to do' list done!
- I can't relax. It's just not me and I don't know how.
- Sit still and meditate – are you freaking kidding me?
- I'll sleep when I'm dead. (Yes, you sure will – sooner than you think if you're not careful!)

I've heard it all before... and I've said it all before too! Getting clients to manage their stress is one of the biggest challenges we face in clinic.

When we are stressed out (and maybe even when we are not) we do not prioritize our health and we do not put ourselves first. We carry on doing all the things we feel we *should* be doing: the societal expectations and self-imposed standards of who and what we should be. But let me tell you: stress isn't cool. Being busy is not a badge of honour. If you need a reminder of the long-term consequences of chronic stress, head back to Chapter 3.

There are three elements to stress management:

1. Managing (and reducing where possible) the sources of stress (stressors).
2. Adjusting our psychological response to stressors, helping our brain to reclassify what it should deem stressful.
3. Managing and offsetting our physiological response to stress.

The first step involves identifying all the things in our lives that we view as stressful and then classifying them into controllable vs uncontrollable, avoidable vs unavoidable. If they are controllable or avoidable, we can say 'no', delegate or ask for help. Not everything has to be done by you, nor do some things have to be done at all. If the stressor is food or lifestyle (controllable) then this is something you can work on in Chapters 14 and 15 (the 'Nourish' and 'Engage' steps of my Mood Boosting Method).

Adjusting our psychological response to stress is an involved process and can take time, which is why I have dedicated Step 4: Reframe to doing just this.

For now, I want to make this important point: there are some stressors that we cannot avoid and nor would we want to. Sometimes, delegating or saying 'no' just isn't possible. Instead, we have to find a way to offset unavoidable stress.

This section is all about managing and offsetting our physiological response to stress through rest and relaxation.

13.1 Sleep

The first thing you are going to do is sleep! Sleep is vitally important time for your body to repair and your brain to decompress, both of which are essential for keeping you resilient. Sleep is the antidote to our stress hormone, cortisol, and counteracts its metabolic effects in the body. If you don't believe me, then watching sleep expert Matthew Walker's Ted Talk will definitely focus the mind (see the Resources section at the back of this book for the link to this video).

The stress–sleep–mood circle can be a vicious one. Feeling anxious can disrupt sleep, which can lead to low mood. In one study, a chronic sleep deficit of six hours in just one week increased levels of the stress hormones adrenaline, noradrenaline and cortisol by 50–80%![91] Whatever stage of burnout you are at, you probably have an increased need for sleep.

Practising sleep hygiene can help you prepare for a good night's sleep and support positive mental health. Winding down can help signal to your brain that it is time for bed and begin the process of retraining your internal rhythms. (Remember that cortisol is a circadian hormone and is supposed to be raised in the morning and low in the evening.) Reading a book or taking a bath can help. Using Epsom salts (magnesium sulphate) in your bath may offer additional mood-boosting benefits: magnesium plays a vital role in brain function and mood, and low levels are associated with an increased risk of depression.

For optimal sleep conditions, the Institute for Functional Medicine suggests that you should keep your bedroom

---

[91] Samel Alexander, Vejvoda Martin, and Maass Hartmut, 'Sleep Deficit and Stress Hormones in Helicopter Pilots on 7-Day Duty for Emergency Medical Services - PubMed.'

clean, cool and dark. You should also ensure your pillow and mattress are comfortable and that the room is quiet.[92]

Conversely, using media devices such as mobile phones and iPads in bed can negatively impact sleep. A small study found that refraining from mobile phone use 30 minutes before bedtime improved mood as well as sleep duration and quality and working memory.[93]

You should also avoid the notorious sleep disrupter – alcohol. Alcohol is often used to help unwind after a stressful day and many of us consume more than we intended in an attempt to beat the blues. However, binge drinking is associated with increased incidence of depression and anxiety. Alcohol also disrupts sleeps quality, which is a risk factor for mood disorders (more about alcohol in Chapter 14).[94]

Sugar and eating late can also disrupt sleep. If you are actively digesting food, this is not conducive for sleep. Also consider that your blood sugar hormones, insulin and cortisol, are working away to ensure your blood sugar is stabilized after a big meal. What you don't want is a cortisol spike either before bed or while you are asleep. Generally, finishing eating at least two hours before bed is advisable. That said, if you are genuinely hungry before bed, hummus and oatcakes make a great evening snack. Chickpeas are sometimes called 'nature's Prozac'. They contain the essential amino acid tryptophan, which is the precursor for the sleep hormone melatonin. The carbohydrates in the

[92] IFM, 'Good Sleep Hygiene May Help Protect Against Infectious Diseases | The Institute for Functional Medicine.'
[93] He et al., 'Effect of Restricting Bedtime Mobile Phone Use on Sleep, Arousal, Mood, and Working Memory: A Randomized Pilot Trial.'
[94] Chueh, Guilleminault, and Lin, 'Alcohol Consumption as a Moderator of Anxiety and Sleep Quality.'

oatcakes help with tryptophan absorption, ensuring it can reach the brain more easily.

If, after implementing a healthy night-time routine, you are still struggling to drop off, a natural supplement might help. See Chapter 18 for my suggestions.

13.2 Active relaxation and mindfulness

OK, so getting plenty of rest is key for restoration. The other thing that you need to be thinking about is finding time in your day for active relaxation. (Hint: I don't mean flaking out in front of Netflix... although obviously there is a time and a place for this too.) The key word here is *active*. I don't mean physically active. Instead, I mean you should be consciously engaging in relaxation, not mentally escaping somewhere else. The science tells us that an average of ten minutes of active relaxation every day is enough to offset daily life stress![95] Wow, that's all. Ten minutes!

When we consciously relax, we are activating our 'rest-and-digest' (parasympathetic) nervous system, which counteracts our stressed-out sympathetic nervous system. If we are facing stressors all day long (work, poor diet, the news, social media, negative thoughts), the brain cannot activate the off switch and this is when a chronically stressed state can ensue, creating the perfect environment for maladaptation and disease. However, by tapping into the parasympathetic nervous system – even for a short amount of time – we are essentially breaking the circuit of the stress loop, letting the brain know you are safe and prompting it to reinstate healthy bodily function.

---

[95] Chang et al., 'Effects of Abdominal Breathing on Anxiety, Blood Pressure, Peripheral Skin Temperature and Saturation Oxygen of Pregnant Women in Preterm Labor'; Ma et al., 'The Effect of Diaphragmatic Breathing on Attention, Negative Affect and Stress in Healthy Adults.'

So, what does active relaxation actually entail? Well, there many different options but they all involve an element of *mindfulness*.

What is mindfulness?

Mindfulness is a stress-management technique designed to improve your mood and overall wellbeing. It is defined as 'the awareness that arises by paying attention on purpose, in the present moment, and non-judgementally'.[96] The origins of mindfulness lie with the teachings of the Buddha; however, the modern practice has been adapted to a set of non-religious tools and techniques. There has been an explosion of scientific research into the health benefits of mindful practices, ever since John Kabat-Zinn developed the first evidence-based mindfulness course 'Mindfulness Based Stress Reduction' in 1979. The research highlights the benefits of mindfulness to employee mental health, in that it can reduce occupational exhaustion and improve personal achievement – both dimensions of burnout.[97]

Mindful practices are varied and take time to learn. The mind is a muscle that needs to be trained in much the same way as any other. The key is to find what works for you. Some take longer than others to master the practices. If you are time poor, then maybe start with some breathwork or a short meditation. I've listed some active relaxation practices below, along with an explanation of why each is beneficial for offsetting stress and boosting your mood.

Yoga: yoga is well known for its mindful elements. Particularly helpful restorative practices include 'yin', which

---

[96] Kabat-Zinn, *Full Catastrophe Living, Revised Edition: How to Cope with Stress, Pain and Illness Using Mindfulness Meditation, xxxvii.*
[97] Janssen et al., 'Effects of Mindfulness-Based Stress Reduction on Employees' Mental Health: A Systematic Review.'

involves holding floor-based poses for longer, and 'yoga nidra', which is almost like a yogic-sleep. Very relaxing!

Breathwork: another mindful technique, which you will tap into if you practise yoga, is breathwork or *pranayama*. This tool is particularly great if you don't have time to get to a yoga class. It's free and takes as little as ten minutes to carry out. There are many different types of breathing techniques. Some fire you up and get you energized, while others help you feel balanced and calm. Some may even help you sleep.

If you have never engaged in breathwork before then I encourage you to begin by taking my one-minute breathwork challenge. Find a quiet place at home or at work, close your eyes and breathe in deeply through the nose to the count of six. Feel your lungs expand and allow the breath to get right down to your belly. Exhale in the same steady way to the count of six. Continue until you have completed five rounds of this, by which time you will have been breathing mindfully for one minute. Well done! Now next time you might expand this to two minutes and upwards until you are able to complete ten minutes' active relaxation.

This technique is a balancing breath and can be used to both calm and focus you. It can literally be practised anywhere – at your desk, on the train… even on the loo. (I've hidden in the ladies' before now and completed a few rounds to calm me down. And while I am confessing, I have also used this technique to help me through bikini waxes and trips to the hygienist! It definitely helps.)

There are too many breathing techniques to cover here, but there are some great resources online if and when you are ready to explore. James Nestor's book *Breath* is a fabulous read and will expand your knowledge – see the Resources section at the back of this book.

Meditation: meditation is a mindful practice that has been shown to reduce stress and improve mental health. Meditation does take time to perfect, and I am the first to admit that I have struggled to master the art. As a novice, your best bet is to join a guided meditation group and let someone else steer you on your meditation journey. Although I don't advocate jumping online first thing in the morning, it is not hard to find influencers or wellbeing professionals offering free morning meditations that you can join in with (just don't get sucked into scrolling!). Alternatively, there are some great meditation apps out there that enable you to build your meditation practice up gradually at a time that suits you. The main thing is to find a time of day that works for you and set a reminder on your phone to meditate.

Tea drinking: whole-leaf and herbal teas contain stress-relieving compounds, and the practice of tea drinking can be mindful. If you have ever been to one of my wellbeing events, we almost always begin with a tea ceremony. It is a welcoming gesture but also helps participants to feel grounded and present. It taps into the ancient Chinese ritual of tea drinking, where tea was historically drunk as a health tonic and always consumed communally. Since tea has been commoditized, we have lost some of the sanctity and ritual that used to be associated with tea drinking. Today, China is the only nation where tea is still hand-picked; tea harvested in this way is whole-leaf and retains higher nutrient levels.

Whole-leaf tea contain many phytochemicals (bioactive compounds found in plants), such as:

- Tea polyphenols, which act as antioxidants in the body and provide an excellent fuel source for the good bacteria in our gut.
- Alkaloids, e.g. caffeine.
- Vitamins.
- Minerals.
- L-theanine.

L-theanine is a unique amino acid that has an anti-stress effect in the body. It can slow the release of caffeine, supports cortisol removal from the body and is able to cross the blood–brain barrier. In the brain, it enhances both serotonin and dopamine, thereby positively affecting our mood and our motivation. A recent study in the journal *Nutrients* found that L-theanine was able to alleviate stress-related symptoms of depression and anxiety.[98]

As well as whole-leaf tea, other teas can support stress relief:

- Chamomile is consumed throughout the world for its calming properties. In clinical trials, chamomile was able to reduce anxiety, improve overall wellbeing and improve sleep quality.[99]
- Peppermint tea contains a compound called 'rosmarinic acid', which keeps our calming neurotransmitter GABA in play for longer. This creates a relaxing, anti-anxiety effect – similar to alcohol but without the side effects!

13.3 Taking the pressure out of self-care

As well as *active* relaxation, there are many other ways we can relax. Frankly, if you are at Stage 3 of burnout, and/or super anxious, then sitting with your thoughts and meditating might not be helpful right now – and that is OK. You don't need me to tell you that taking yourself off for a massage or escaping in a good book is also relaxing. For me, if I'm feeling particularly low or overwhelmed, I need my duvet and I need Disney. That is my (literal) comfort

---

[98] Hidese et al., 'Effects of L-Theanine Administration on Stress-Related Symptoms and Cognitive Functions in Healthy Adults: A Randomized Controlled Trial.'

[99] Chang and Chen, 'Effects of an Intervention with Drinking Chamomile Tea on Sleep Quality and Depression in Sleep Disturbed Postnatal Women: A Randomized Controlled Trial.'

blanket, which helps me to zone out and self-soothe. So don't worry if active relaxation isn't for you straight away. For now, the main thing is to be kind to yourself.

The purpose of the mindfulness section is to give you a set of scientifically proven tools and techniques to prevent burnout and help you offset stress. It is not intended as a big stick for you to beat yourself up with or feel guilty about.

Unfortunately, the concept of self-care, while well intentioned, has mutated into yet another social pressure. One more thing that we need to strive to be perfect at, alongside having the perfect body and age-defying skin. In that context, self-care is the opposite of relaxing. It's stressful and anxiety inducing, one more thing on the to-do list – and when we don't manage to tick it off, we feel like failures.

Well, I am here to tell you that self-care is not something that you *should* do, it is something you *can* do – if and when you choose – that may help. If self-care does bring up unpleasant feelings (like guilt or feeling that you don't deserve to relax) then undertaking some mindset work might be helpful – see Chapter 16 for more on this.

CHAPTER 14

NOURISH: THE BRAIN AND THE WHOLE BODY

If you are feeling anything like how I felt when I burnt out, then I am guessing that this chapter might fill you with trepidation. The last thing you may feel like doing right now is changing your diet. Maybe you're living off takeaways because you just can't face your fridge or going to the supermarket. Cooking from scratch? That's for energetic people who have slept.

You might already be aware that the foods you are eating aren't helpful and are probably perpetuating the misery you feel. If you are aware – great. This is the first step towards change.

I remember saying to my doctor, when I first went to her with signs of burnout, 'It isn't rocket science, is it? Eat good, feel good.' I knew this advice was sound, but I just couldn't seem to break out of the cycle I found myself in.

It can all feel quite overwhelming, especially when we are bombarded with information about the 'right' and 'wrong' things to eat: it's on the TV and all over social media and the internet. Then there are those around you who want to help by forcing onto you *their* opinion of what you should be eating. Wherever we turn, there is an 'expert' telling us what to do. But remember: there is only one of you, and your needs are unique. You are your own expert. My role, and my aim for this book, is to arm you with the information you need to discover what *your own* body and mind need to feel better.

We are going to take it slow. I am not going to ask you to give anything up. All I am going to ask is for you to make some small adjustments and build up from there, as and when you feel ready.

14.1 Hydrate

A nice and easy place to begin is to consider your water intake. It is no secret that human health relies on staying hydrated: water is needed for life. You can survive for weeks without food, but only a matter of days without water (three, maximum). Your hydration status can also influence your mood. Mild dehydration can significantly increase negative feelings such as anger, confusion or depression. Increasing water intake, on the other hand, can reduce feelings of anxiety.

Increasing your water intake is a straightforward and inexpensive change to help tackle the symptoms of burnout. The first step could be as simple as filling a large glass in the evening, leaving it somewhere visible when you go to bed and drinking it as soon as you rise. That first morning water intake before you do anything else serves several purposes: firstly, and perhaps most importantly, it represents a positive and manageable action that you are taking to tackle overwhelm head on. Secondly, that single morning glass instantly increases your overall water intake, whatever your starting point is, and finally, it sets you up for a Good Mood Day – firing up both the body and brain.

When I ask even the most overwhelmed and change-fearful clients, 'could you just drink a glass of water?' they all say, 'yes' – they can cope with this.

Over time, once this morning routine is embedded, begin to find other times of day to increase your water intake. Always drink from glass or a stainless-steel bottle *not* plastic (remember those EDCs from Chapter 6?) and ideally filter your water to remove any potentially brain-toxic chemicals. Water can be drunk either hot or cold; you can add fruit or vegetable slices to give natural flavour, or try a commercially prepared herbal tea. However you drink it, all water intake contributes to your overall level of hydration.

14.2 Setting the right foundations

Let's turn our attention to diet, and begin the process of flooding the brain with mood-boosting and fatigue-fighting nutrients. In particular, we need to replenish the nutrients that are depleted with stress (magnesium, B vitamins and vitamin C).

The basic premise of personalized nutrition and functional medicine is that we are all unique and therefore there is no single 'diet' or way of eating that can be universally recommended to protect us all from burnout or mental health disorders. However, if you have been paying attention throughout this book, I am sure you have realized the important role that optimal nutrition plays in biological function – and how poor nutrition can contribute to reduced stress resilience, fatigue, mood dysregulation and burnout.

In reverse, a healthy diet can protect you from these conditions. In 2013, the SMILES study was the first clinical trial to prove that dietary change can have a positive effect on mood disorders. In this study, a phenomenal 33% of drug-resistant participants in the intervention group achieved complete remission from depression in just 12 weeks when following a healthy diet![100]

---

[100] Jacka et al., 'A Randomised Controlled Trial of Dietary Improvement for Adults with Major Depression (the 'SMILES' Trial).'

In my clinic, we work on five brain-nourishing foundations and then personalize them depending on the individual's needs. Here are my top five dietary basics when it comes to nourishing your body and mind for burnout resilience and overall mental health.

Eat whole foods

By this, I mean foods without a label. These foods should be predominantly fresh and plant-based, complemented with a small quantity of fish and meat. When deciding which meat or fish to buy, first consider your budget and then buy the highest quality that you can afford. Understand where your meat comes from and what it has eaten. Favour grass-fed, wild-caught and organic animal and fish products. Spending slightly more on slightly less should help you to strike the right balance.

Minimize processed foods

This goes hand-in-hand with my first tip to eat whole food. Processed foods containing refined fats and sugars are notorious mood disrupters and are unhelpful when it comes to feeling happy and calm. They perpetuate stress in the body. So gradually start to reduce these foods.

Eat the rainbow

Compiling a plate of food that is brightly coloured is not only pleasing to the eye – your brain will thank you too. Consuming diversely coloured foods helps provide access to weird and wonderful stress-busting and fatigue-fighting micronutrients, such as flavonoids and plant phenols, which are beneficial to mental health.

Include low-glycaemic-index foods

Now is not the time for ditching the carbs – we need fibre to help us digest our food effectively. We also need carbs to help protein reach the brain, without which the brain cannot produce those mood-regulating chemicals we talked about in Chapter 5.

But the carbs you select can influence your mood. Refined flours in pasta and bread can disrupt our blood sugar balance, which is unhelpful for our mental health. Swap white rice and pasta for wholegrain or wild varieties, or even a pseudo grain like quinoa.

Follow a Mediterranean eating pattern

The Mediterranean eating pattern features plenty of vegetables and fish, occasional meat, and healthy fats from olive oil, avocado and nuts. Although there is no universal anti-burnout diet, the Mediterranean eating pattern is a good place to start (find out why in Chapter 17).

14.3 How to make changes to your diet

Change isn't always easy. It's important to take it slow and steady when recovering from burnout. You are going to focus your attention and make changes, one at a time, to each of these meals, in this order:

1. Breakfast.
2. Dinner (that is, your evening meal – also known as 'tea' to those up north).
3. Lunch (your midday meal).
4. Snacks.

Take them one at a time, and only move on to the next one when you feel comfortable that you have adopted the changes. Most importantly, take your time and be kind to yourself.

Breakfast

If you focus on just one meal each day, let it be breakfast. Why? The first meal of the day can really set you up for what I like to call a 'Good Mood Day'. Or it can send you off on the burnout sugar rollercoaster – the internal highway to Stress City. It might sound like I am being glib here, but seriously: breakfast is the most important meal of the day for keeping you resilient to stress. Don't skip it or delay too long before eating it. I want you to aim to eat before 10 a.m. each day.

Remember that if you put off breakfast, you are increasing the risk of a drop in blood sugar. Having read this book, you now know that this places the body under stress and will result in the brain signalling to the adrenal glands to produce your stress hormone, cortisol, in an effort to bring things back to normal. Cortisol is an appetite stimulant and can seriously affect your food choices.

You may recognize this in yourself. You might not feel hungry when you first get up, so you put off breakfast. This in itself isn't problematic. But if you then dive into the day, running on empty, and get to 12 p.m. and suddenly feel starving... trust me, nothing is going to send you out to Gregg's for a sandwich and a cake quicker than a cortisol spike! We are trying to avoid this situation by ensuring you eat breakfast.

OK, so Step 1 is to eat breakfast; now, what to eat?

I encourage you to eat a protein-rich breakfast. Protein will furnish the system with those amino acid building blocks that you need to regulate your mood and maintain healthy brain chemistry, protecting you from burnout. One of the easiest ways to get protein in first thing is eggs. They are quick and versatile. If you have more time (say, at the weekend), you may consider fish as a protein-rich breakfast (think smoked salmon, grilled mackerel, kippers). Always serve your eggs (or fish) with some vegetables like mushrooms, kale, spinach, tomatoes or peppers. These will ensure you access the co-factor nutrients required for neurotransmitter synthesis.

If you are taking breakfast to work with you, you are going to want something portable.

Perhaps my favourite way to start the day is with a mood-boosting smoothie. Their beauty is in their portability and their nutrient density. You can really pack a lot into your morning meal with a smoothie and you can disguise the taste and texture of vegetables in them too – suitable for even the most veggie-averse individuals. The trick is not to overload them with high-sugar fruits (like mango and banana). Ensure balance by including sources of protein like seeds and nut butters, and healthy fats like avocado. I have included some recipe ideas at the back of the book, and you can download my smoothie builder guide on the website to create your own.

Equally transportable and easy to 'prep-ahead' are overnight oats or chia pudding. Adding low-sugar fruits (berries, apple, pear), nuts and/or seeds will increase the nutrient density and – in the case of nuts and seeds – the protein content. But do me a favour and bin those instant porridge pots. Not only are the flavoured versions loaded with sugar, but they are also devoid of any protein and may contribute to blood sugar dysregulation and sub-optimal brain function. Not what you need heading into that meeting with a new client.

What about granola? It depends. Not all granolas are built the same. The trick is to look at their ingredients. First test: can you understand them all? If 'yes', you can evaluate how natural the ingredients are. Secondly, assess their protein-to-carbohydrate ratio. You are looking for a ratio of 1:4 or less. Most are 1:6 or more.

Recipe ideas covering everything I've mentioned here are included at the back of this book. Spend at least a week nailing breakfast and just breakfast.

Dinner

Now, on to dinner. You might be wondering why I have skipped lunch and moved straight on to your evening meal. There is a reason for this: you are more likely to have control over when and what you eat in the evening as you are probably at home. You are also more likely to have access to cooking facilities than at work (depending on where you work). Finally, if you can get into a routine of preparing healthy meals in the evening, you can also work towards preparing leftovers that you can then take for lunch the next day. Happy days.

OK, I can hear the deep intake of breath here, because you suspect I am going to ask you to cook from scratch. This is only partly true. I am going to ask you to prepare meals wherever possible using whole-food ingredients. You are aiming to veer away from meals that arrive as if by magic on the doorstep (takeaways) or that are 'ready' to just heat up in the oven or microwave. (I'm talking about mass-produced ready meals here. If you have some meals ready to heat up that you know have been home cooked using fabulous ingredients, then absolutely use them.)

What I'm *not* suggesting here is that you avoid convenience all together. When you are in the throes of overwhelm, healthful convenience can be super helpful to taking back some control. So, by all means, utilize microwavable rice and pulses sachets and pre-chopped veg. Recipe box subscriptions are also a good shout when you are feeling burnout, as they take the pressure off meal planning, recipe curation and even shopping! The main thing is that you keep it *simple* and *manageable*, so that you can begin to feed your body with those fatigue-fighting nutrients.

On your plate, you are aiming for roughly:

- One third of your plate made up of protein (a palm-sized portion), for example organic meat or poultry, wild fish, eggs, lentils, beans, tofu or tempeh.
- A small amount of healthy fat (a thumb-sized portion), for example avocado, nuts, seeds or olive oil.
- A fist-sized portion of complex carbs, for example rice, root vegetables, quinoa, wholegrain pasta/noodles (add a little more if you have exercised pre-dinner).
- Two to three great big handfuls of mixed veg, one of which should be green.

I've included some recipe inspiration for meals that can all be doubled up to create leftovers in the back. You will also find some recipe book suggestions in the Resources section. Amelia Freer's book *Simply Good for You* is one of the best I've seen for creating simple meals that aren't overwhelming when you are feeling burnt out.

Also in the recipe section at the back of the book you will find some suggestions for healthy desserts (under the 'Snacks' heading).

Lunch

Wherever possible, lunch can be leftovers so that you aren't tempted to pop to the supermarket and grab a soggy sandwich on your lunch break. That said, if you work in the city, you might have more choice for healthy grab-and-go lunch options. If that's you then great. Look out for options with the same proportions you aimed for at dinner.

The other option is to prep ahead. Many of the lunch and dinner (and even breakfast) recipes at the back of the book can be prepared in advance, stored in the fridge and then taken as a packed lunch to eat cold or reheat. Ask yourself whether you genuinely have time for this, though. What I *don't* want you to do is dive into this and end up getting meal-prep fatigue. This can lead you to revert to old habits and then feelings of failure or guilt. To avoid burnout, we want to take things off our plate, not pile more on. So be honest with yourself.

Snacking

To snack or not to snack? The research on this is conflicting at times. My advice would be to be guided by your symptoms. If you find yourself exhausted in Stage 3 burnout, it is going to be super important to reduce the demand on your stress axis. I would therefore suggest eating small, manageable meals every three hours until you start to feel a little better. I've included some snack ideas at the back.

Once you have more energy, or if you are closer to Stage 1 burnout, I suggest spacing meals every four to five hours and making them more substantial and balanced for blood sugar. This will naturally mean that you need to snack a lot less. This also enables what is called the 'migrating motor complex' to sweep the digestive tract clean (it cannot do this if you are digesting food all the time). Once your meals become more balanced, you should also notice that you have more stable energy throughout the day, and reduced mood swings and cravings. If the gap between meals is going to be longer than six or seven hours (maybe you are going to an exercise class after work or need to feed the kids), then I advocate having a snack at the mid-way point to avoid any potential drops in blood sugar.

What should your overall eating schedule look like? Something like this:

9 a.m. – breakfast

1 p.m. – lunch

4 p.m. – snack

7 p.m. – dinner

14.4 My Top Mood Foods

Over the years, I have come to fondly refer to certain foods as my favourite 'mood foods'. They feature nutrients that help us to manage or prevent the symptoms of burnout. I want to share them with you here along with why I think they are so beneficial. You will note that they also feature in my recipe suggestions in the back of this book.

Avocados

Avocados are a great mental health food. They are rich in the monounsaturated fats that our brains need to function at their best, as well as other mood-boosting nutrients such as folate and magnesium, which are often depleted in burnout. Folate supports cell function in the cognition centre of our brain – the hippocampus. Increasing folate in the diet can reduce the risk of depression.[101] And magnesium, also known as 'nature's tranquiliser', has been shown to have a positive effect on symptoms of anxiety.[102]

Avocados feature in my smoothie recipes *The Mood Booster* and *The Green Burnout Buster.*

Oily fish (or chia seeds)

Oily fish is an excellent source of omega-3, an essential fatty acid that the body cannot produce and so must be sourced from the diet. There is a wealth of research highlighting the beneficial effect of omega-3 in burnout-related mood disorders: major depressive disorder and generalized anxiety.[103]

If you're vegan, you may need an omega-3 supplement (see Chapter 18). Chia seeds are a moderate dietary source of omega-3. In addition, they are a source of fibre, required to feed the 'good bacteria' in our gut. As we saw in Chapter 9, keeping a healthy balance of bacteria supports positive gut–brain signalling, and scientists believe that this explains why a diet high in fibrous foods – like chia – can reduce the risk of depression and alleviate symptoms of anxiety.[104] Try my *Chia Pudding* recipe for a grab-and-go breakfast.

---

[101] Beydoun et al., 'Serum Folate, Vitamin B-12, and Homocysteine and Their Association with Depressive Symptoms among U.S. Adults.'

[102] Boyle, Lawton, and Dye, 'The Effects of Magnesium Supplementation on Subjective Anxiety and Stress – A Systematic Review.'

[103] Larrieu and Layé, 'Food for Mood: Relevance of Nutritional Omega-3 Fatty Acids for Depression and Anxiety.'

[104] Foster, Rinaman, and Cryan, 'Stress & the Gut–Brain Axis: Regulation by the Microbiome'; Taylor and Holscher, 'A Review of Dietary and Microbial Connections to Depression, Anxiety, and Stress.'

Broccoli

Broccoli is a girl's best friend. It is part of the brassica family, which helps us to detoxify excess and used-up hormones in the liver, particularly oestrogen. Broccoli contains folate, which supports the methylation process, and helps channel tryptophan down the right chemical pathway (when stress can send it the wrong way) to make our happy hormone, serotonin.

Try my *Baked Salmon & Broccoli* recipe.

Quinoa

Quinoa is a source of low-glycaemic index (GI) carbohydrate. The research indicates that consumption of high-GI foods such as white bread, white rice and pasta increases the risk of stress-induced mood disorders like depression. On the other hand, those consuming higher quality/low-GI carbohydrates are 30% less likely to develop depression.[105] Check out my *Roasted Mediterranean Vegetables & Quinoa Salad* at the back of the book.

Berries

Berries are a rich source of antioxidants, required by the brain to ward off damage from toxins and other potentially harmful molecules. Polyphenols are a particularly potent type of antioxidant found in berries that help keep the brain plastic and resilient to stress.[106]

I've used berries in my *Mood Booster* smoothie, my *Fruits of the Forest Overnight Oats* and my *Chia Pudding*.

---

[105] Gangwisch et al., 'High Glycemic Index Diet as a Risk Factor for Depression: Analyses from the Women's Health Initiative.'
[106] Huang et al., 'Linking What We Eat to Our Mood: A Review of Diet, Dietary Antioxidants, and Depression.'

Brazil nuts

Brazil nuts contain mental-health-supportive micronutrients; for example, 'ellagic acid', a bioactive compound that can exert an antidepressant effect, and selenium, a resilience-enhancing mineral.[107]

Dark chocolate

Dark chocolate (over 70% cacao) can stimulate the release of the feel-good neurotransmitter dopamine, and the 'cuddle hormone' oxytocin. Who doesn't feel better after a hug? Dark chocolate is also a source of iron, which helps to deliver oxygen to the brain and regulate the chemical pathways involved in mood and behaviour.

Tip: eat a handful of Brazil nuts and a few squares of dark chocolate together as the perfect mood-boosting mid-afternoon snack.

Peppers

Brightly coloured vegetables like peppers are an excellent source of vitamin C. Vitamin C is required for the synthesis of the mood-regulating neurotransmitters dopamine and serotonin, and chronic stress depletes our stores of this vitamin. Diets containing high amounts of vitamin C have been associated with elevated mood.[108]

Peppers are the shining star of my *Speedy Roasted Red Pepper Soup*.

---

[107] Bedel et al., 'The Antidepressant-like Activity of Ellagic Acid and Its Effect on Hippocampal Brain Derived Neurotrophic Factor Levels in Mouse Depression Models.'

[108] Pullar et al., 'High Vitamin C Status Is Associated with Elevated Mood in Male Tertiary Students.'

Sweet potato

Sweet potato is a rich source of the plant form of vitamin A: beta-carotene. Vitamin A plays a key role in brain and immune function. It has been shown in the research to improve depression and fatigue.[109] Check out my *Sweet Potato Mash* or even add cooked and cooled sweet potato to a smoothie!

Chickpeas

Chickpeas are sometimes called 'nature's Prozac'. They contain the essential amino acid tryptophan – the precursor for the happy hormone, serotonin, and the sleep hormone, melatonin. Hummus spread onto oatcakes makes a great evening snack. The carbohydrates in oatcakes help with tryptophan absorption, ensuring it can reach the brain more easily.[110]

Chickpeas are the star ingredient of my *Moroccan-style Stew*.

As well as foods, there are also certain herbs, spices and drinks that are worth a mention for their mood-enhancing effect.

Saffron

In clinical trials investigating the efficacy of saffron supplementation in mild-moderately depressed patients, researchers consistently found that saffron was effective at reducing symptoms of depression compared to a placebo. Furthermore, the therapeutic effect of saffron

---

[109] Bitarafan et al., 'Effect of Vitamin A Supplementation on Fatigue and Depression in Multiple Sclerosis Patients: A Double-Blind Placebo-Controlled Clinical Trial.'

[110] Spring, 'Recent Research on the Behavioral Effects of Tryptophan and Carbohydrate.'

was equal to that of traditional antidepressants such as fluoxetine, imipramine and citalopram in mild-moderate depression.[111]

Turmeric

A meta-analysis of six clinical trials involving 377 patients with depression concluded that curcumin, the active ingredient in turmeric, was clinically effective at reducing the symptoms of depression and anxiety.[112] Piperine, a compound found in black pepper, can increase the bioavailability of curcumin by 2,000%.[113]

Oregano

In-vitro research revealed that oregano extracts were able to inhibit the reuptake of neurotransmitters serotonin, dopamine and noradrenaline (a similar mechanism of action to most modern antidepressants). The same study also observed increased levels of serotonin in the brains of rats and improved depressive and anxious behaviour in mice that had been given oregano extracts.[114]

Green tea

Drinking green tea for health isn't new, but increasing evidence supports its use for modulating mental health. A recent clinical trial published in the journal *Nutrients* found that L-theanine, a unique amino acid present in green tea,

---

[111] Tóth et al., 'The Efficacy of Saffron in the Treatment of Mild to Moderate Depression: A Meta-Analysis.'

[112] Ng et al., 'Clinical Use of Curcumin in Depression: A Meta-Analysis.'

[113] Shoba et al., 'Influence of Piperine on the Pharmacokinetics of Curcumin in Animals and Human Volunteers.'

[114] Mechan et al., 'Monoamine Reuptake Inhibition and Mood-Enhancing Potential of a Specified Oregano Extract.'

was able to reduce stress-related symptoms of depression and anxiety in otherwise healthy adults.[115]

Spotlight on: Matcha green tea

Matcha is a type of green tea, grown in the dark to enhance its caffeine and L-theanine content. Matcha and other green teas also contain a compound called ECGC (epigallocatechin gallate), a potent, tea-specific antioxidant that may help to reduce inflammation in the brain. Researchers speculate that these anti-inflammatory compounds reach the brain by modulating our gut microbiome – fascinating![116]

The health benefits of matcha tea have piqued the interest of scientists. Studies of this tea have discovered that matcha can increase attention, speed and a type of long-term memory called 'episodic' memory.[117] This type of memory relates to specific episodes in your life, like your first day at school or your first kiss! Hypothetically, this is due to the enhanced ECGC and L-theanine content.

Matcha contains less caffeine than coffee and the L-theanine helps to slow the caffeine release. So, if you get the jitters with coffee, green tea or matcha might be the mood-boosting and stress-relieving drink for you!

---

[115] Hidese et al., 'Effects of L-Theanine Administration on Stress-Related Symptoms and Cognitive Functions in Healthy Adults: A Randomized Controlled Trial.'

[116] Unno et al., 'Anti-Stress Effects of Drinking Green Tea with Lowered Caffeine and Enriched Theanine, Epigallocatechin and Arginine on Psychosocial Stress Induced Adrenal Hypertrophy in Mice.'

[117] Dietz, Dekker, and Piqueras-Fiszman, 'An Intervention Study on the Effect of Matcha Tea, in Drink and Snack Bar Formats, on Mood and Cognitive Performance.'

14.5 Notorious mood disrupters

There are certain foods that are notorious mood disrupters and are unhelpful when it comes to feeling happy, calm and resilient to stress.

Top of that list has got to be:

Refined sugar

Research shows that the more sugar we eat, the more likely we are to become depressed.[118] So, although it might feel good in the moment, it won't help in the long run.

Refined flours (in pasta and white bread)

These are basically sugar in disguise, as they get converted into sugar when we eat them. (During the milling process, white/refined flour has all the fibre stripped from it so there is nothing to slow absorption into the bloodstream.) Sugar in whatever form can disrupt our blood sugar balance, which is unhelpful for our mental health.

Artificial sweeteners

Many people believe these are the healthy alternative to sugar; however, research shows they produce the same response as sugar in the body – increased insulin.[119] What's more, recent research suggests that artificial sweeteners may also increase the risk of anxiety – a classic Stage 2

---

[118] Westover and Marangell, 'A Cross-National Relationship between Sugar Consumption and Major Depression?'; Hu, Cheng, and Jiang, 'Sugar-Sweetened Beverages Consumption and the Risk of Depression: A Meta-Analysis of Observational Studies.'
[119] Pepino et al., 'Sucralose Affects Glycemic and Hormonal Responses to an Oral Glucose Load.'

burnout symptom.[120] Scientists observed that mice that drank water containing aspartame, an artificial sweetener commonly found in diet drinks and food, exhibited pronounced anxiety-like behaviours in a variety of maze tests. Aspartame exposure also produced changes in gene expression in the amygdala (remember – that's the brain region that regulates anxiety and fear), and down-regulated the calming neurotransmitter GABA.[121] If you are already feeling tired and wired, I would encourage you to step away from the sugar-free/diet/zero drinks that are being marketed to you as healthy alternatives. I suspect that time and more research will show us they are not helpful at all for burnout prevention and mental health in general.

Refined fats: vegetable oils

These can promote inflammation, which has been linked to many chronic diseases including depression.[122]

Alcohol

Alcohol is a known depressant. Many of us use alcohol to relax; however, alcohol disrupts sleep quality, which is a risk factor for mood disorders. It also depletes us of all of those vital nutrients that keep us resilient to stress.[123] So,

---

[120] Choudhary and Lee, 'Neurophysiological Symptoms and Aspartame: What Is the Connection?'

[121] Jones et al., 'Transgenerational Transmission of Aspartame-Induced Anxiety and Changes in Glutamate-GABA Signaling and Gene Expression in the Amygdala.'

[122] Miller and Raison, 'The Role of Inflammation in Depression: From Evolutionary Imperative to Modern Treatment Target.'

[123] Lieber, 'The Influence of Alcohol on Nutritional Status'; Nourse, Adamshick, and Stoltzfus, 'College Binge Drinking and Its Association with Depression and Anxiety: A Prospective Observational Study'; Chueh, Guilleminault, and Lin, 'Alcohol Consumption as a Moderator of Anxiety and Sleep Quality.'

while it might relax us in the moment, in the long run it primes our brains to be more fearful, hyper-vigilant and vulnerable to burnout.

Unfortunately, we live in a society where alcohol is socially accepted; I would even go so far as to say *expected*. Name any other drug – because that is what alcohol is – that we feel the need to justify reducing our consumption of or abstaining from?

If you said to a friend, 'I'm not going to snort coke any more', they would probably say, 'Good idea, think of your health, how can I help?' Tell the same friend, 'I'm not drinking tonight', and they respond incredulously with, 'Why?! What's wrong with you?' or, and this one really pisses me off, 'Stop being a bore and have a drink.'

Like I said right at the outset of this chapter, I am not going to ask you to give anything up. But it would be remiss of me not to highlight how much alcohol can accelerate the road to burnout and impede recovery. Only you know how much this relates to you. Please do seek help if you need it. Also know that the tide is turning: most bars now offer delicious non-alcoholic alternatives for when you are ready to venture back out.

Gluten?

Hmmm, this isn't as clear-cut. Some studies show that eliminating gluten from your diet can alleviate anxiety and reduce depression, whereas other studies show no impact.[124] In clinic, we are guided by symptoms and testing. If there is any indication of leaky gut or autoimmunity then we do

---

[124] Häuser et al., 'Anxiety and Depression in Adult Patients with Celiac Disease on a Gluten-Free Diet'; Addolorato et al., 'Anxiety but Not Depression Decreases in Coeliac Patients after One-Year Gluten-Free Diet: A Longitudinal Study.'

take gluten out, because the research is more definitive for these conditions.[125] Remember Hannah from Chapter 8? She noticed an instant crash in her energy levels after she ate toast, having eliminated it for four weeks; gluten wasn't serving her body well.

At the outset, I said I wasn't going to ask you to give anything up. That said, the easiest way to tell whether gluten is a problem for you is by reducing or eliminating it from your diet for a short period of time, ideally four weeks. If you feel better without it, great. Similarly, if you notice your symptoms are exacerbated when you reintroduce it, this is a sure sign that gluten might not be helpful in your burnout journey.

A gluten-free diet is problematic in itself as the 'industry' has developed many heavily processed alternatives, which may increase exposure to other mood disrupters (sugar, artificial sweeteners, refined oils). It is perhaps more helpful to suggest that you include more *naturally* gluten-free foods, so that you don't fall into that trap.

Foods that contain gluten	Foods that are naturally gluten free
Wheat, barley, rye, spelt Bulgar wheat, couscous, pasta Bread, biscuits, cake Soy sauce	Corn, gram flour (chickpea), nut flours (chestnut, almond) Buckwheat, rice, quinoa, pulses (peas, beans, lentils) Tamari (naturally gluten-free soy sauce)

---

[125] Fasano, 'Zonulin, Regulation of Tight Junctions, and Autoimmune Diseases'; Fasano, 'All Disease Begins in the (Leaky) Gut: Role of Zonulin-Mediated Gut Permeability in the Pathogenesis of Some Chronic Inflammatory Diseases.'

Coffee?

Is coffee bad for me? The answer to this is – you've guessed it – it depends. Coffee has been demonized as being a stressor due to its caffeine content. However, most research on caffeine's effect on stress has not been conducted on coffee itself but on caffeine extracts. Caffeine, extracted from coffee and used in trials at concentrated levels, can indeed raise cortisol levels; however, the limited research into coffee itself makes the answer inconclusive.[126]

What we do know is that coffee is so much more than caffeine. It actually contains polyphenols, which may be beneficial to some. Similarly, tea, which contains less caffeine, also contains other therapeutic properties that have actually been shown to lower cortisol.[127]

Caffeine tolerance and metabolism is regulated by genes known as CYP1A2 and ADORA2A. Variations on these genes can mean you are less able to process caffeine well. We can test for this in clinic, but you probably already know the answer from your own experiences with caffeine. If one cup of coffee drunk hours before bed keeps you awake and gives you the jitters, then coffee probably isn't for you. If you can drink it and sleep like a baby, you may be able to enjoy a moderate amount.

Ultimately, all stimulants have the capacity to activate the stress response. It may be best to enjoy one or two cups of coffee or matcha in the morning and then swap to herbal teas in the afternoon for their calming effect.

---

[126] Clark and Landolt, 'Coffee, Caffeine, and Sleep: A Systematic Review of Epidemiological Studies and Randomized Controlled Trials.'

[127] Hidese et al., 'Effects of L-Theanine Administration on Stress-Related Symptoms and Cognitive Functions in Healthy Adults: A Randomized Controlled Trial.'

CHAPTER 15

ENGAGE: IN PHYSICAL ACTIVITIES AND HOBBIES

If you have been overworked and stressed out for some time, it is likely that you may have disengaged. Disengaged socially from friends and family, disengaged physically from the activities that you know keep you well and boost your mood, and disengaged from yourself, your personal interests and the things that bring you joy.

This part of my Mood Boosting Method is about re-engaging in physical activity, social connection and generally having fun.

15.1 Get active

Nothing is going to give your mood an instant boost like some exercise. There is scientific evidence that physical activity of all types can relieve stress, anxiety and depression.[128] So, whether you are a runner, a weightlifter or a yogi, you can boost your mood by keeping active.

The evidence on the positive connection between exercise and mental wellbeing and stress-resilience is abundant. Not only can exercise improve your mood, it can increase the volume of those areas of your brain (the hippocampus and the prefrontal cortex) that support cognition and executive

---

[128] Sharma, Madaan, and Petty, 'Exercise for Mental Health.'

function, and help to down-regulate your response to stress.[129]

One of my favourite things to recommend when I talk about the protective effects of exercise on the brain is a fabulous Ted Talk by neuroscientist Wendy Suzuki. It's called 'The brain-changing benefits of exercise'. In this talk, Wendy talks about how exercise is beneficial for your mood and memory – not just in the short term but also in the longer term, helping protect us from mood disorders and cognitive decline. You can find a link to this video in the Resources section of this book. It only takes 15 minutes to watch, and I promise by the end you are going to feel inspired to get up and move your butt!

The main thing here is not to overdo it and to start slowly! For some of you this might actually mean doing less exercise, not more. Simultaneously, training for a marathon while trying to develop increased stress resilience simply isn't going to work. Remember that exercise is a controllable stressor on the system. It will activate the HPA-axis and produce cortisol. So, while we are trying to nurture the adrenals and the stress response, take it easy!

Here is what I recommend:

Walking

Burnout recovery: whenever you feel up to it.

Burnout prevention: up to seven days a week.

Assuming you are able-bodied, walking is one of the easiest and most instant steps you can take to support burnout prevention and recovery. Just get out of the house and into

---

[129] Wilckens et al., 'Exercise Interventions Preserve Hippocampal Volume: A Meta-Analysis.'

the fresh air, even if just for five minutes, as soon you feel able to. It's just about making a start, without placing any pressure or expectation on yourself. More about walking below.

Yoga

Burnout recovery: up to two days a week.

Burnout prevention: up to seven days a week.

When considering how to structure your exercise regime for reducing stress and keeping burnout at bay, I would – without doubt – begin with yoga. Practising yoga can increase levels of the calming neurotransmitter gamma-aminobutyric acid (GABA), helping us to relax and switch off from negative thoughts and emotions.[130] In studies, yoga has been shown to have a cortisol- and inflammation-lowering effect, while at the same time increasing endorphins and BDNF.[131] It is a mindful practice that is reported to positively modulate the sympathetic nervous system and the HPA-axis (our psychological and physiological response to stress).[132]

There are many different types of yoga. Try a variety until you find the practice for you. For restorative purposes it may be better to try slower, more mindful practices like yin and hatha yoga, rather than the fast-paced ashtanga or hot-and-sweaty Bikram yoga, until you are feeling more resilient. Given the variety, you can easily incorporate gentle yoga into your daily routine without stressing the system.

---

[130] Streeter et al., 'Effects of Yoga versus Walking on Mood, Anxiety, and Brain GABA Levels: A Randomized Controlled MRS Study.'

[131] Tolahunase, Sagar, and Dada, 'Impact of Yoga and Meditation on Cellular Aging in Apparently Healthy Individuals: A Prospective, Open-Label Single-Arm Exploratory Study.'

[132] Pascoe, Thompson, and Ski, 'Yoga, Mindfulness-Based Stress Reduction and Stress-Related Physiological Measures: A Meta-Analysis.'

Strength training

Burnout recovery: up to two days a week.

Burnout prevention: up to four days a week (allowing for rest days and depending on your other training).

Strength training is another great way of busting some stress. I'm not sure of anything that feels more empowering than lifting weights and feeling strong. It challenges your muscles but is less of a stress on the system than cardiovascular work (unless you are lifting ridiculously heavy weights, in which case you need to calm it down). Maintaining muscle mass is also super important for us ladies as we age, so not only are you preventing burnout you are also preparing yourself for menopause and reducing your risk of osteoporosis in later life.

Research supports resistance, or strength, training as a mood-boosting activity. Studies report that training at low-to-moderate intensity with weights has an anti-anxiety effect.[133] Similarly, a meta-analysis of 33 clinical trials reported that resistance training significantly reduced depressive symptoms among adults, regardless of their overall health status.[134]

Don't get me wrong: lifting weights can be daunting at first. I 100% advocate finding yourself a good personal trainer who can support and guide you, while respecting your need to balance training with restoration.

Remember that yoga and other bodyweight exercises can also be classed as strength training. So if you are mixing up some restorative *and* more challenging yoga sessions, then you are also ticking the strength box.

---

[133] Strickland and Smith, 'The Anxiolytic Effects of Resistance Exercise.'

[134] Gordon et al., 'Association of Efficacy of Resistance Exercise Training With Depressive Symptoms: Meta-Analysis and Meta-Regression Analysis of Randomized Clinical Trials.'

Aerobic

Burnout recovery: zero to two days a week.

Burnout prevention: two to four days a week.

Aerobic exercise is thought to improve your mood by increasing blood circulation in the brain and positively impacting the HPA-axis. Just 30 minutes of moderate exercise such as jogging, swimming, cycling or dancing can improve your mental health and cognitive function.[135] Even a brisk walk or half an hour of gardening can help.

High-intensity interval training (HIIT)/running

Burnout recovery: zero.

Burnout prevention: zero to three days a week.

Running is thought to be the archetypal stress buster. To an extent, this is true. We ran as cave women, mainly when we were hunting or running away from a predator. Nowadays, we associate the endorphin release, or the 'runner's high', with making us feel good and reducing stress upon completing a good run. If this sounds like you, great.

My only word of caution is that running is a high-intensity exercise that is quite stressful on the system. If you are experiencing all-day fatigue and a high level of stress, then I recommend cutting back on the running.

HIIT is a good compromise and can feel equally as rewarding (who hasn't felt Joe Wickes' energy – love his workouts!). But in general, anything high intensity should be approached in moderation, and avoided in times of chronic stress or burnout.

---

[135] Guszkowska, 'Effects of Exercise on Anxiety, Depression and Mood.'

Not sure if you are doing too much? The trick is to see how you feel *after* exercise. Do you feel energized and is that energy sustained? Or do you feel tired and sleepy within a couple of hours of exercise? The latter suggests the balance isn't quite right and you could do with reducing the amount of exercise you are undertaking and/or swapping intensive cardiovascular activity for strength-based activities such as yoga or weight training. Once you are feeling more resilient you can start adding the running back in again.

15.2 Get outside

Wherever you live, try to get outside into nature where possible.

Nature walks or bike rides

Not only does walking or cycling in nature fit the bill for getting active, getting outdoors in the fresh air is also beneficial in other ways. If you live in a built-up city, getting out into the countryside provides valuable relief for the brain (and the whole body) that is working hard to protect you from environmental pollutants, and sends some lovely clean oxygen to the brain.

Walking or cycling in nature can also be a great way to gain perspective and appreciate the simple things in life. Did you know that when you listen to birds tweeting or observe the changing colours of the seasons you are engaging in mindfulness? Mindfulness has proven stress-relieving and mental health benefits.[136] (More about mindfulness in Chapter 13.)

---

[136] Janssen et al., 'Effects of Mindfulness-Based Stress Reduction on Employees' Mental Health: A Systematic Review.'

For pet lovers, having a dog not only motivates you to get out and actually go for a walk daily, but it also usually inspires connection with others – even if it's just a 'hello' from a fellow dog walker. It helps us feel less alone and socially isolated, which are both stressors on the system. I am constantly remarking to friends about how no one talked to me on walks until I got a dog.

There is so much that can be achieved from just going for a walk or jumping on your bike.

Blue space

My favourite place to be is either on or besides the water. I don't think I was alone in taking up paddle boarding during lockdown. We also own an inflatable kayak and when we go on holiday we sail (like, actual yachts – I still can't believe we learned how to do this!). I realize these are all quite active pastimes and being active is not everyone's idea of fun; however, the research on blue spaces supports their positive impact on mental health.[137] So even if you just go and sit by the water and take it all in, this could help you to de-stress.

15.3 Hobbies and other activities to make you feel engaged

Hobbies

Reconnect with old hobbies. What was it you always used to enjoy doing and no longer make the time for? It could be as simple as playing a musical instrument, or maybe you are a bit arty? Maybe you like a good old-fashioned home-improvement project (pick something *small* if you are burnt

---

[137] Gascon et al., 'Outdoor Blue Spaces, Human Health and Well-Being: A Systematic Review of Quantitative Studies.'

out – don't go knocking down walls!). Completing projects or doing something creative, like learning a new song or painting a new picture, can give us a feeling of satisfaction and contentment, firing our happy hormone, serotonin.

Laugh

Laughter is the best medicine, right? Who hasn't felt better after a good giggle or one of those amazing laughing fits where you just Can't. Stop. Laughing! And if that isn't proof enough, it is also backed up by science.

Remember our anti-stress ethernet cable from Chapter 9? The vagus nerve passes directly through our diaphragm. When we laugh, the diaphragm contracts and pushes air out of our lungs, both of which physically massage our vagus nerve. This in turn improves vagal tone and helps to increase our resilience to stress.

An American study found that laughing at humorous movies reduced circulating cortisol levels and improved memory function.[138] Laughter has also been shown to increase levels of the brain cell growth chemical BDNF, and to improve subjective happiness and relieve occupational stress.[139]

---

[138] Bains et al., 'Humors Effect on Short-Term Memory in Healthy and Diabetic Older Adults.'

[139] Cheng et al., 'Incongruent Expression of Brain-Derived Neurotrophic Factor and Cortisol in Schizophrenia: Results from a Randomized Controlled Trial of Laughter Intervention'; Lee and Lee, 'The Effects of Laughter Therapy for the Relief of Employment-Stress in Korean Student Nurses by Assessing Psychological Stress Salivary Cortisol and Subjective Happiness.'

Sing

The vibrations created when we sing can also stimulate the vagus nerve. This is me giving you permission to put on your favourite song, grab the hairbrush and make like Katy Perry and ROAR, or Taylor Swift and 'Shake it Off' (just my suggestions – I'm sure you're way cooler than me!). Or, if you are feeling really brave, you could take your 'gift' public. Research tells us that singing in groups can improve our mood and immune function, while reducing stress and circulating cortisol.[140]

Cry

OK, so crying isn't perhaps your normal idea of fun; however, it is an activity that can relieve stress and improve your mood. Conversely, holding your emotions inside – known as 'repressive coping' – has been associated with poor mental health outcomes, hypertension and chronic disease.[141] As women we often suppress tears because we don't want to be seen as weak or labelled 'emotional' compared to our male colleagues. But crying can be an important release and actually healthier than keeping everything bottled up.

Crying allows us to physically release stress and emotional pain – tears contain stress hormones. Crying also stimulates the production of endorphins and oxytocin, letting the brain know that we are safe so it can stop the stress response and allow internal balance to be restored.[142]

---

[140] Fancourt et al., 'Singing Modulates Mood, Stress, Cortisol, Cytokine and Neuropeptide Activity in Cancer Patients and Carers.'

[141] Mund and Mitte, 'The Costs of Repression: A Meta-Analysis on the Relation between Repressive Coping and Somatic Diseases.'

[142] Sharman et al., 'Using Crying to Cope: Physiological Responses to Stress Following Tears of Sadness.'

Crying is sometimes easier said than done. If you are feeling particularly blocked, seek out an activity that will help you along. Maybe it's a heart-warming, slightly sad movie that just gets you every time. For me it's *Marley and Me*. I defy anyone not to cry at the end of that film (well, maybe if you're a cat person). It actually makes me laugh *and* cry so is a double stress reliever. If I know I need a good release, I set aside a Sunday afternoon, curl up on the couch with my box of tissues and get ready to sob.

Tip: I wouldn't watch/read anything too heavy, scary or 'real life'. You don't want to overwhelm yourself more by facing further distress. The idea here is escapism and release; to activate the parasympathetic nervous system – not a tense, stress-activating, two-hour recreation of the battle of Dunkirk or worse...

15.4 Social connection

When thinking about improving your resilience to stress, it is important to re-engage with your social network. Or, if you don't feel like you have much in the way of family and friends, then start seeking ways of establishing new support networks – whether that is getting professional help or finding new ways to connect with other human beings socially.

Think back to prehistoric times, which is where your stress response has evolved from. The key to survival was about being part of a tribe, a group, where you could feel safe and part of something bigger than yourself. If you faced a bear attack, you would be more likely to survive it as part of a group than if you tried to fight it off alone.

Modern research shows us that social connection is just as important today as it was then. Humans perform better in the face of both acute and chronic stress if they have a strong support network than if they try to deal with it alone. This can be as simple as talking to someone, whether a friend or a therapist, about what is going on. The simple act of talking helps reduce feelings of isolation and physiologically lowers the stress burden on the body.[143]

Find whatever works for you. If you don't have much family, or your friends have all disappeared while you have been pursuing your career, then you need to get creative. The answer can be as simple as attending business networking events or joining a book club. When I worked away from home, I joined a running club. It was only an hour a week, but it was contact with other human beings, doing something I enjoyed. One woman I spoke to recently, who had retired and just moved to an area where she didn't really know anyone, posted on a local Facebook group, explaining her situation and asking if anyone wanted to join a 'ladies-that-lunch' group. She was inundated with responses. I heard a similar story about a movie club – for women who wanted company when they watched a film. They all go for a chat afterwards. Where did I hear these stories? From a book club I joined at a health food café! (Books and great food – what a combination!)

Be brave and find your tribe. They are out there waiting for you, I promise.

15.5 When to disengage: The social media drain

Disengaging from activities that bring you down is just as important as engaging in activity that makes you feel good. This requires a good, hard look at your life to identify what (and maybe even who) isn't serving you and your mental health.

---

[143] Seeman et al., 'Social Relationships, Gender, and Allostatic Load across Two Age Cohorts.'

Undoubtedly, one of the biggest drains on our time and our mental health is the amount of time we spend glued to screens – our phones, our laptops, the TV. In this technological and instant age, we have the world at our fingertips. This is fabulous for productivity, yet overwhelming for our brain. It is information overload, and while our brains are amazingly adaptive, we might actually be frying our brain cells.

Picture, if you can, a time before mobile phones – when news was conveyed by letters, telegrams and newspapers (I know, I sound like a dinosaur – bear with me). Back then, we received distressing news *once*. We registered it in our mind, and our body began the process of dealing with that information. Coping, adapting and eventually completing the stress cycle.

Now imagine you are getting that same piece of information over and over again, on repeat. It could be an incessant WhatsApp chat, or a stream of retweet notifications. Your phone constantly 'pinging' away. Or you turn on the news and the latest war or economic crisis is being relayed to you on multiple channels, on the hour, every hour. Remember way back at the beginning of the book we said that maladaptive states occur following *repeated hits on the stress response*, and/or when the stress response is *prolonged*. This is what is happening with information overload. You are feeding burnout.

If you know you are spending way too much time scrolling on social media or watching the news, this might be contributing to your feelings of overwhelm, which undoubtedly won't be helping your mood.

Set boundaries:

- Pick a time of day to watch the news/check your social media and stick to it. Find out what you need to know, or engage with your followers, and then switch off.

- Turn off notifications.
- Take weekly digital detoxes where you (shock horror) turn your phone off!

This can apply to any behaviour you are engaging in that is not serving you well. Identify yours and disengage.

CHAPTER 16

REFRAME: NEGATIVE THOUGHTS AND LIMITING BELIEFS

The final step in my Mood Boosting Method is 'Reframe'. This step is all about identifying any limiting beliefs that may be holding you back and catching and reframing negative thought patterns. It is about developing a stress-resilient mindset; helping you to feel more in control.

Recall Chapter 1, when we said that feeling stressed out is not just about the threat or stressor itself but also your *perception* of it? Some of us are hyper-vigilant: nervously anticipating a stressful situation before one even exists. And some of us are hyper-responders: perceiving even the mildest of incidents as life-threatening. Both these dispositions repeatedly activate the stress response and can accelerate the path to burnout.

Alternatively, a hyper-vigilant or hyper-responsive state may arise as a *result* of burnout! Remember that chronic stress can decrease the size of the rational, cognitive parts of our brain, like the prefrontal cortex, while increasing the volume of more primitive areas, like the amygdala. This makes us less resilient to stress and more vulnerable to being controlled by the monkey mind.

Either way, we need to take back the reins to reduce the risk of burnout happening again in the future. Reframing is a technique that uses the conscious parts of our brain to reprogramme the subconscious parts. It's about giving the primitive circuitry in your brain new information about the reality of your world, to replace the old; reclassifying threat and your ability to cope with it. Reframing is a common feature of many psychotherapeutic and coaching approaches including, for example, cognitive behavioural therapy (CBT) and neurolinguistic programming (NLP).

Like anything worth doing, reframing takes time and practice. Your brain is a muscle, and it requires strength training just like the rest of your body does. You wouldn't take up running and expect to run a marathon on day one, so be kind to yourself at the beginning. This may be something you work on for the rest of your life, and that's OK. Life is about the journey.

There is a reason why this is the last step in my Mood Boosting Method: reframing is a powerful personal development technique that can improve resilience, support effective performance and enable you to fulfil your career potential. As such, it can form an important part of burnout prevention or regression limitation. However, if you are arriving at this book tired, wired and on the verge of burnout, commencing some personal development work is hardly going to be the first thing you will feel like doing. My advice would be to undertake the suggestions in the 'Restore' and 'Nourish' sections (Chapters 13 and 14, respectively) and come back to this section once you are feeling brighter and more energized. Your brain needs to rest and refuel.

It is also important to acknowledge the severity of your negative thoughts and feelings here. If in doubt, seek the help of your GP or a psychotherapist.

16.1 Limiting beliefs

Limiting beliefs are the convictions that we hold about ourselves or the world around us that we believe, falsely, to be true. They hinder us from taking opportunities and reaching our full potential. Left unchecked, they can perpetuate a negative state of mind and hyper-vigilance to stress.

Some examples of limiting beliefs might be:

- 'I thrive on stress.'
- 'I'm not good sleeper.'
- 'I'm too tired to make a change.'
- 'I can't get through the day without chocolate.'
- 'I can't relax without wine.'

But they can also run deeper to:

- 'I'm not good enough.'
- 'I don't deserve to be happy.'
- 'I'm never going to succeed.'

Limiting beliefs develop throughout our lifetime as a result of our upbringing, education and life experiences. Often these beliefs are not consciously known to us and identifying them might require the support of a therapist, coach or counsellor.

Once known to you, you can work on developing alternative beliefs that serve you better. For example:

- 'I am enough.'
- 'I can do anything I set my mind to.'
- 'Success is within me.'
- 'Stress doesn't serve me.'
- 'There are lots of ways I can relax.'

Check out my website www.re-nutrition.co.uk for a simple belief-change exercise that you can undertake at home.

16.2 Check your language

Consider the language you use generally and towards yourself. Is it negative? Are you programming yourself to feel bad because of the words you choose?

For example, you might frequently say things like:

- 'I am *terrible* for eating chocolate when I am feeling low', or
- 'I'm a *sucker* for working late.'

When you use language like this, your subconscious mind and belief system are getting the message that you are a terrible person and a sucker. Woah… that is not going to help your mood.

Consider saying instead:

- 'I am *great* at reaching for the biscuits in the afternoon!'
- 'I am *fantastic* at getting work done.'

Now you are telling yourself you are great and fantastic. I don't know about you, but I feel better already!

Another tip for lifting your mood with language is to enhance the good and diffuse the bad. So many of us, when asked how we are feeling, will reply 'not bad' when we are actually feeling OK or even good. Try saying, 'I feel amazing' or 'fabulous'. It might sound ridiculous, but using enhanced positive language like this can actually make us feel a little better – even when our mood doesn't quite match the words.

Diffusing or downgrading negative language can also take the edge off. So for example, you might usually say, 'this lockdown is *dreadful*; I am having a *horrendous* time'. Consider saying instead, 'this lockdown is challenging and is testing me at times'. Can you see how this has downgraded the negative language and thereby diffused its effect on your mood?

16.3 Breaking negative thought patterns

In his book *The Big Leap*, Gay Hendricks says that worry is only really useful if it is about something we can immediately change or have control over. He advocates that we shouldn't pay any attention to negative thought patterns as they can spiral out of control and are not, generally, based in reality. His two-part test to establish whether a thought is worth paying attention to is:

1. Is it a real possibility?
2. Can you do anything about it to make a positive difference?[144]

Using this test, worrying about whether you have packed your laptop for your presentation today is classed as a worthwhile thought. But worrying about whether you are good enough to deliver it, or predicting that everyone will laugh at you, is not!

Important note: all this said, it is still OK to feel overwhelmed, anxious or low. These feelings are normal, and identifying and acknowledging them is important. What I am offering are just simple tools to put you back in the driving seat and help you to cope.

If you do find yourself in a negative thought spiral, change your state. It takes 15 minutes to change neurological pathways. Get up and go for a 15-minute walk or do an

---

[144] Hendricks, *The Big Leap: Conquer Your Hidden Fear and Take Life to the Next Level*.

alternative distracting activity for the same amount of time. Notice how your thoughts have changed when you return.

16.4 Practising gratitude

One of the best tools for reframing negative thoughts and beliefs is practising gratitude. Focussing on what you have instead of what you don't have. So, if your day is weighing heavily on you, take a step back and consider three things you are grateful for. It can be quite handy to have a notebook by the side of your bed so you can write down what you feel grateful for before bed and/or first thing in the morning. It is a great way of clearing the brain of the daily negativity or taking your thoughts away from a bad night's sleep.

Gratitude journaling has been shown to lower stress levels and help create a positive mindset.[145] In her book *Exploratory Writing*, Alison Jones highlights that putting pen to paper is an often-overlooked tool for processing our thoughts and feelings.[146] She proposes that the psychological benefits to exploratory writing for wellbeing include:

- Increased mental resilience (we feel able to take ownership of a stressful experience when we write about it).
- Sense-making – utilizing free writing to make sense of our thoughts and feelings and stressful events.
- Self-coaching – helping ourselves to view these thoughts, feelings and events differently.
- Mindfulness (and all the benefits that come from this, which we discussed in Chapter 15).

---

[145] Emmons and McCullough, 'Counting Blessings versus Burdens: An Experimental Investigation of Gratitude and Subjective Well-Being in Daily Life.'

[146] Jones, *Exploratory Writing: Everyday Magic for Life and Work.*

16.5 Finding space for quiet reflection/introspection

Sometimes in life we need a perspective check. I think many of us will agree that the first lockdown during the COVID-19 pandemic was a chance for many of us to step back and think about what was important to us. A worldwide reframe that was completely out of our hands.

In the pandemic, the metaphorical space for reflection was gifted to us. Similarly, when you contemplate or contribute to something bigger than yourself, it enables you to step out of your own head, gain perspective and reframe your thoughts. It has been shown that giving up your time to help others is an excellent mood booster.[147] Now, I'm not suggesting that you go out volunteering and pile even more commitments on your plate when you are already stressed out, but maybe consider it in the future when you are feeling better. It would also tick the 'Engage' box, too.

For now, think simple. Here are some of my favourite simple activities to engage in that support reflective thinking and a sense of perspective.

Watch the sunrise/sunset

There is something so comforting and certain about observing the daily rhythm of the sun. It's also a really mindful activity that can be quite restorative as well as affording you some valuable time to reframe your thoughts. I'm actually writing this section of the book on a rustic balcony in Vietri sul Mar, Italy. It's 6:55 a.m. on a warm and breezy October morning. The sun is rising over the mountains ahead. Sometimes the sun goes behind a cloud and the light dims. After a time, she re-emerges, seemingly stronger than before.

---

[147] Huo et al., 'Volunteering, Self-Perceptions of Aging, and Mental Health in Later Life.'

Stargaze

I challenge you to find a greater perspective-giver than looking out at the night sky. My husband engaged in this new hobby during the first lockdown and his enthusiasm was infectious – so I began to join in. I even gifted him a telescope for his birthday in 2020. You obviously don't need a telescope to stargaze, though. Just head outside and look up. There are so many positives for your mental health: you are outside in the fresh air, you are contemplating something larger than yourself, and you are taking a mindful moment just for you. The whole activity activates that parasympathetic nervous system, enabling you to offset stress.

Spend time in a sacred space

OK, I'm not especially religious, but I notice that every time I am in a church – for whatever reason – that it is strangely comforting. Despite worship being a seemingly communal type of activity to engage in, it can be a solitary experience and offer the time and space to think about life beyond yourself. And it doesn't even have to be worship, in the traditional sense. For example:

- At a wedding or a funeral service, there is always time for individual prayer. Whether you pray to a God or not, this time can be invaluable to spend reflecting and reframing your thoughts.
- I like to visit churches and temples when I am travelling, to appreciate the architecture, culture and history of a place. Sometimes, while I am there, I will light a candle and think about those in need or that I have lost. It allows me to turn my thoughts towards others and also provides me with a moment to grieve, which many of us rarely allow ourselves the time to do.

Whatever your beliefs or religious persuasion, the concept of spirituality is familiar to many of us. It is a weighty feeling that can carry us through and help us to prevent burnout. It is a belief that we can make a change and reap the professional and personal rewards. Spirituality has been shown to increase resilience to stress, especially as we age.[148]

[148] Manning et al., 'Spiritual Resilience: Understanding the Protection and Promotion of Well-Being in the Later Life.'

PART 4

WHAT TO DO NEXT?

I am hoping by now that you can see how transformative a functional approach to burnout can be. Maybe, like I was, you are hungry for more.

The temptation now might be to do some online research of your own. Before you know it, you are down a rabbit hole of misinformation: following a trendy diet, taking *the* magic burnout pill (supplement) and ordering some dodgy test that promises to tell you all the foods you should cut out of your diet. Please *don't do it*!

I've lost count of the number of ladies I have spoken to who have cut out foods *that they read online* that they shouldn't be eating; or are taking a supplement *that they read online* would solve all their problems; or who ordered allergy or intolerance tests *that they found online* and got sucked into buying and later found out weren't scientifically sound. Then they are left wondering why their symptoms got worse or came back.

If this is you, don't worry. You're certainly not the first and you won't be the last. This next section is designed to help you on the next stage of your burnout journey, and to cut through the noise you'll find online.

- In Chapter 17, I comment on some of the latest diet trends and whether or not they may be helpful for burnout.
- In Chapter 18, I discuss supplementation.
- In Chapter 19, I talk about scientifically validated testing that might be helpful.

Finally, at the back of the book, you will find the Resources section, which will guide you to trusted books and websites you can visit if you want to read more. You're welcome!

CHAPTER 17

DIET TRENDS

There are many diet trends out there and so much information – available at our fingertips – telling us how we should or shouldn't eat. Cut out fats, or cut out carbs, ditch meat or only eat between the hours of two and six p.m. So, I'm just going to spend a little bit of time cutting through the noise for you from a burnout and broader mental health perspective.

First, I come back to the point I made right at the outset of this book: we are all different and therefore a one-size-fits-all approach is highly unlikely to be the right one for you. So why do all these trendy diets emerge? Well, because they worked for one or more individuals at a certain time in their life. They also usually centre on our obsession for weight loss or being thin. But this doesn't mean that it will work for everyone or that it is *the* best diet for our health – or for burnout prevention and mental health more broadly.

Let's consider some of these fad diets one at a time.

Low-carb, or keto diet

Pros: the benefits of this diet centre around its focus on healthy fats, which as a population we have been avoiding for the last half a century in the misguided belief that fat makes us fat. A ketogenic diet provides access to lovely monounsaturated fats in the form of nuts, seeds and avocados, alongside polyunsaturated fats from oily fish. If done correctly, this eating pattern will also provide access to sufficient protein from high-quality meat and eggs.

Cons: this diet can be sorely lacking in micronutrient diversity. Low-carb diets are inherently lower in fruit and vegetables – increasing the risk of vitamin and mineral deficiency. This also makes for a low-fibre eating pattern – and we have seen that fibre from plants is vital food for our gut microbes and essential for positive mental health.

To fast or not to fast?

Pros: intermittent fasting, or time-restricted eating (TRE), is the only dietary pattern that has been scientifically proven to elongate your life. Wow! This must be good, right?

How does it work? TRE involves having a fixed time-window for eating and an equal or longer period of fasting, usually overnight. The benefits of intermittent fasting begin when we fast for 13–15 hours. During this time period we will start to produce growth hormone, which promotes fat burning and slows down the ageing process. Fasting can also support blood sugar balance, weight loss, gut health (by providing digestive respite), mood and brain function, hormone balance, reduced inflammation and enhanced immune function (accelerate healing and repair) – all amazing for burnout prevention – *but…*

Cons: fasting, or any type of calorie restriction, is perceived by your brain as stress. If you are already anxious, exhausted and emotionally overwhelmed – and I am guessing you are as you are reading this book – fasting is literally *the last* thing you should be doing right now. If you are feeling in optimal health, then great – you could give this a go and reap the rewards.

In clinic, we see women who are completely frazzled, yet obsessed with losing weight. They declare they have been calorie counting or fasting (in other words, piling restriction and stress onto an already exhausted plate) and – lo and behold – it hasn't worked. They may also be exacerbating an underactive thyroid. (Head in hands moment for us.) Why do we do this to ourselves, ladies?

Here is my tough love for you: almost all the biological or physiological processes I have described in this book that can influence your ability to cope with stress or affect your mood, will also affect your ability to lose weight. So, if you don't address these imbalances *first*, the weight isn't coming off. You need to be healthy and resilient to stress to achieve your optimal weight. It will come, but weight loss at the expense of your mental health is not cricket, is it? Fasting can come later, when you are feeling good and maintaining a healthy lifestyle. And maybe by then your weight – or the number on the scales – will seem less important anyway.

Vegetarian/vegan

Pros: plants, plants, plants. If you take anything away from this book, it will be the realization of how amazing plants are for energizing our bodies, fuelling our brains and building resilience to stress. A plant-based diet (that is, a diet made up predominantly of plants) is to be exulted, for sure.

There are also health benefits of being plant based that ripple beyond us as individuals. The production and consumption of mass-produced meat is undoubtedly a major contributor to climate change. A plant-based diet is therefore healthier for the environment too.

Cons: unfortunately, the vegan/vegetarian trend has spawned an industry of highly processed meat alternatives containing many of the mood disrupters mentioned in this book. The result? Many (but certainly not all) of those who have elected to follow a vegan diet are actually consuming very few real plants and eating a highly processed 'beige diet' (think bread, pasta, processed soy meat-alternatives), which is undoubtedly unhelpful for optimal brain function and energy.

A vegan diet in particular is likely to be higher in carbohydrates and lower in protein – a ratio that we have seen is unhelpful for maintaining balanced moods. It is quite tricky for a vegan to consume sufficient protein. Here are some truths:

- There is some protein in grains and pulses, but on their own they are not complete proteins; that is, they do not contain all of the essential amino acids.
- Complete proteins can be found in some plant-based foods, such as edamame beans and quinoa, but crucially the mood-regulating building blocks like tryptophan are only found in trace amounts.
- One of the best plant-based sources of protein is tempeh – a traditional Indonesian food derived from fermented soy beans.

Supplemental protein may be helpful for vegans, although plant-based protein powders can also be highly processed so choosing the right one is key. Select powders that contain just the protein source, for example pea or hemp powder. You can find a list of the best sources of protein, alongside my protein powder recommendations, on the website.

Omitting animal or animal-derived protein may also result in B-vitamin and choline insufficiency, as many of our B vitamins are found in abundance in meat, fish, eggs and dairy. Many vegans are aware that they may need to supplement with B12 to avoid becoming deficient, as this nutrient simply cannot be obtained from plants. However, many are not aware that other B vitamins, essential for positive mental health (choline, folate, B2, B6 and so on), are present at lower levels in plants and may also require supplementary support.

If you are vegan and considering B vitamin supplementation, I would urge caution around seeking private vitamin injections. B12 injections are used by the medical profession for those with a condition called 'pernicious anaemia', which simply means these individuals lack the ability to absorb vitamin B12 from their food. Injections are helpful for them to get B12 directly into the bloodstream, bypassing the digestive system. However, B12 injections are increasingly being offered privately, targeting the vegan (and burnout) trend. It is worrying because these injections are often self-prescribed, and the doses are given without any knowledge of specific need or current levels. In clinic, I have seen vegan clients' blood tests come back with extremely high levels of B12 and comparably low levels of folate and B6.

B vitamins work synergistically with each other and are best supplemented together in what is known as a complex. They are also, in most cases, best supplemented in their active, methylated form. If you head over to the website, you can see my recommendations for a B-vitamin supplement.

In conclusion, based purely on the evidence, and with my nutrition hat on: while plants are amazing (and we should all be eating more of them), a diet without animal protein is not exactly ideal for optimal mental health and burnout prevention.

It is, however, important to acknowledge that veganism/vegetarianism isn't just a diet – it is a movement. People choose this lifestyle for reasons that go way beyond health; there are moral, religious and cultural factors involved here. In clinic, it is a sensitive path to tread. Here, like there, I can merely present the evidence as it stands and enable my clients – and you the reader – to decide how you balance your health with your broader values. It is such a personal choice.

For me personally, I square my health/love of animals/environmental circle by spending more and eating less meat and fish. I choose local, free range and organic, and I ask *a lot* of questions. I want to understand the provenance of my food: how and where the animals were raised, the diet they were fed and even the slaughtering process (gulp). I have been lucky to find local butchers who pride themselves on respecting the animal's whole life cycle. This is important to me. With fish, I look for wild-caught and sustainable.

Looking to the future, there are some amazing entrepreneurs out there who are seeking to create healthier, plant-based alternatives from real veg without all the additives and artificial ingredients. Hopefully, this will enable access to healthy, affordable, planet-friendly alternatives.

The Mediterranean eating pattern (MEP)

The MEP first rose to prominence in the 1950s, when research led by Dr Ancel Keys highlighted that individuals living in the Mediterranean region had lower incidence of coronary heart disease.[149] Since then, the MEP has been extensively researched by scientists trying to understand its wider application in mental health.[150]

We know that depression and burnout are similar, often co-occurring, conditions – especially at Stage 3 of burnout.

---

[149] Keys and Grande, 'Role of Dietary Fat in Human Nutrition. III. Diet and the Epidemiology of Coronary Heart Disease.'

[150] Sánchez-Villegas et al., 'Preventing the Recurrence of Depression with a Mediterranean Diet Supplemented with Extra-Virgin Olive Oil. The PREDI-DEP Trial: Study Protocol.'

Clinical trials report that consuming a modified Mediterranean diet significantly improved depressive symptoms
compared to controls.[151] Similarly, a study that followed
volunteers over a ten-year period observed that a Mediterranean diet reduced the risk of depression.[152] In particular,
participants who consumed nuts and fruit and who avoided
fast/fried food had lower incidence of depression.

Like depression, burnout also presents with symptoms such
as brain fog, forgetfulness, fatigue and weight gain. Research
suggests that the MEP is also effective at improving delayed
recall, working memory and global cognition, and may be
beneficial for weight loss and fatigue.[153] Taken together,
the MEP sounds like a good foundational framework for
protecting us from burnout.

Typically, the characteristics of the Mediterranean eating
pattern are as follows:

- Plant based: abundant in fruits, vegetables, wholegrains, beans, nuts and seeds.
- Minimally processed, locally grown, seasonally
  fresh foods.
- Moderate amounts of fish (depending on proximity
  to the coast).
- Red meat and eggs are consumed occasionally and
  in small amounts.

---

[151] Jacka et al., 'A Randomised Controlled Trial of Dietary Improvement for
Adults with Major Depression (the 'SMILES' Trial).'
[152] Fresán et al., 'Does the MIND Diet Decrease Depression Risk? A
Comparison with Mediterranean Diet in the SUN Cohort.'
[153] Loughrey et al., 'The Impact of the Mediterranean Diet on the Cognitive
Functioning of Healthy Older Adults: A Systematic Review and Meta-
Analysis'; Bendall et al., 'Central Obesity and the Mediterranean Diet: A
Systematic Review of Intervention Trials'; Baguley et al., 'Mediterranean-
Style Dietary Pattern Improves Cancer-Related Fatigue and Quality of Life
in Men with Prostate Cancer Treated with Androgen Deprivation Therapy: A
Pilot Randomised Control Trial.'

- Olive oil is the primary source of fat and total intake is moderate to high (30–40% of total energy intake).
- Low-to-moderate dairy intake – mainly cheese and yoghurt.
- Herbs and spices are used instead of salt to add flavour to foods.
- Fresh fruits and/or nuts are the typical daily dessert.
- Red wine is consumed in low-to-moderate amounts with meals.[154]

However, it is important to note that there is no single MEP: each of the 18 countries that border the Mediterranean Sea has its own definition of an MEP.

What these eating patterns have in common, though, is a focus on high-quality food choices and limiting processed, refined, manufactured and fast food.

---

[154] Boucher, 'Mediterranean Eating Pattern.'

CHAPTER 18

SUPPORTING YOUR JOURNEY WITH SUPPLEMENTS

One of the topics I get asked about the most is supplements. The questions usually come from two opposing camps:

1. The Dubious Daisies who will ask: 'Do I really need to take this supplement? I've read I can get all the nutrients I need from food?'
2. The Instant Izzys who will ask: 'Can you recommend a supplement to help me to sleep/improve my mood/lose weight/make the sun always shine?'

Izzy, I hate to disappoint you, but long-term optimal health isn't to be found in a bottle of pills. If you have picked up this book hoping to discover a single magic bullet, then I am sorry to tell you there is no quick fix (and it would be a very short book!). Instead, making small changes step by step and fully understanding your personal needs is the key.

That being said, I recognize that change is challenging – especially when you are feeling burnt out. Finding the motivation and energy to change can be tough. It can feel like a vicious circle. In this scenario, supplements can be very helpful indeed.

We use supplements therapeutically in clinic, where we are clinically trained and constantly reviewing the evidence base (clinical trials, not Dr Google – I see you, Izzy!) to understand which doses and formulations may be beneficial for supporting stress, fatigue and low mood.

Testing may reveal nutrient depletions or imbalances where supplements in the short term may be beneficial. Dietary choices may lead to some supplements being required longer term. We generally advocate a food-first approach; however, we do suggest supplements where there is clear evidence to support their use.

This goes some way to addressing Daisy's questions; however, there are also circumstances beyond identified therapeutic need where supplements may prove more broadly helpful. Unfortunately, since the Industrial Revolution and the introduction of mass farming techniques, the soil quality is not what it was. This affects the nutrient density of our food. If we lived in a perfect environment where all our food was natural and wild, like in hunter-gatherer times, then I would say, 'yes, you are probably right, Daisy – we can get all the nutrients we need from food.' Unfortunately, that is not the case – especially if you are living in the West and are mainly consuming mass-produced food, made for our convenience, from nutrient-depleted soil. For the vast majority of us, some supplementation may be helpful to close the environmental gap.

Then there are nutrients that we cannot necessarily obtain from our food. Vitamin D is the prime example of this. Some individuals may have a higher need for certain nutrients for various reasons including, but not limited to, their genetics, digestion/absorption issues, high nutrient utilization (for example in times of stress), illness or the dietary pattern they follow.

I have summarized here some supplements that may be broadly helpful and explained why. For brand recommendations and discount codes, head over to the website.

Vitamin D

I talked about vitamin D in Chapter 11. Suffice to say that we cannot synthesize enough vitamin D during the winter months and a supplement is essential. How much? I advocate a 'test, don't guess' approach. Vitamin D can be tested using a simple finger-prick blood test and then supplemental levels calculated appropriately. You might find this website helpful to understanding your personal requirements: www.grassrootshealth.net/project/dcalculator/. Alternatively, get in touch with us and we can help.

Vitamin C

When we think of vitamin C, we often think of immune function. It is true that vitamin C does play a key role in helping protect us from, and fighting off, infection. Vitamin C is also a powerful antioxidant, which helps the liver rid the body of internal and external toxins. What may surprise you to learn is that the adrenal glands and the brain feature some of the highest concentration of vitamin C receptors in the body and require sufficient vitamin C for optimal function.

Vitamin C is a water-soluble vitamin and is transient in nature. It cannot be stored in the body, and unused vitamin C will be excreted in urine – it is a 'use-it-or-lose-it' nutrient. We need to be consuming sufficient amounts every single day, alongside sufficient water to maximize absorption. This is true even if you are already in optimal health.

Now let's consider if you are at any stage of burnout. Your need for vitamin C is considerably higher, as your adrenals are working overtime to produce stress hormones. You may also be experiencing frequent infections due to stress. Your body is crying out for vitamin C. At the same time (and I'm taking a shot in the dark here) the nutrient density of your diet has probably dropped off through lack of time, energy and motivation.

A vitamin-C supplement may be helpful in this scenario. Look for a high strength (500mg–1g), slow-release formulation.

Magnesium

Stress can also deplete magnesium and if you are experiencing sleep or energy issues it may be worth considering a supplement. Magnesium also supports inhibitory and calming neurotransmitters like GABA and can dampen the cortisol response. In research, magnesium supplementation significantly reduced cortisol levels and decreased symptoms of anxiety and depression.[155]

Magnesium is best delivered into the body when bound to another molecule. Consequently, you will find various forms of magnesium available to buy. Different forms have different benefits. I have highlighted some of them below so that you can begin to navigate your way around:

Magnesium glycinate – hands down this is my favourite combination to use for anyone who is stressed and struggling with their mood. The glycine molecule that the magnesium is bound to is an amino acid, which also has inhibitory properties, so it is great for calming the nervous system. It is also one of the best tolerated formulations: if you have IBS this might be the best option for you.

Magnesium citrate – also a great option. Like magnesium, citric acid is a key nutrient in energy production and consequently might be the most suitable option for helping

---

[155] Tarleton and Littenberg, 'Magnesium Intake and Depression in Adults'; Abbasi et al., 'The Effect of Magnesium Supplementation on Primary Insomnia in Elderly: A Double-Blind Placebo-Controlled Clinical Trial.'

you with fatigue/emotional exhaustion. It may also be helpful if you experience constipation. Unfortunately, this formulation can cause stomach upsets in sensitive individuals and may not be well tolerated by those with IBS.

Magnesium malate – there is some evidence that malic acid can be helpful with pain relief.[156] We get great results in clinic with those who experience headaches/menstrual migraines or any kind of joint or muscle aches.

Magnesium oxide – cheap but poorly absorbed. I wouldn't waste your money on this one.

Generally, I would recommend taking your magnesium supplement in the evening, away from food and ideally one hour before bed to support sleep.

B vitamin-complex

Like magnesium and vitamin C, stress depletes us of our B vitamins. Except for B12, many B vitamins also fall into the 'use-them-or-lose-them' category, like vitamin C. Vitamin B supplementation may be especially important for those following a plant-based diet. The key is to find an appropriate dose for your personal needs and to ensure that the vitamins are delivered in their active, methylated form wherever possible.

Fish Oil

If you struggle to consume enough oily fish (three to four portions a week) then an oily fish supplement may be beneficial. For vegans, a plant-based alternative is highly

---

[156] Abraham and Flechas, 'Management of Fibromyalgia: Rationale for the Use of Magnesium and Malic Acid.'

recommended. There is a wealth of research supporting omega-3 supplementation to support mental health.[157]

Adaptogenic plants

Adapt-a-what-now? Adaptogens may improve your resilience to stressful situations, helping you to adapt and cope. They are unique in that they are effective in high- or low-cortisol situations. Hyper-responsive? They help calm things down. Hypo-responsive, they help gee things up.

Ashwagandha *(Withania somnifera)* is an evergreen plant found growing in the Middle East, India and Africa, sometimes also referred to as 'winter cherry' or 'Indian ginseng'. It has been used for centuries in Ayurvedic medicine and modern research supports its effect in reducing anxiety and improving insomnia. It has been shown to have a cortisol levelling effect and might therefore be helpful for those who identify themselves as being in 'wired' stages of burnout.[158]

Rhodiola (*Rhodiola rosea*) is a hardy plant that grows in remote, cold and mountainous regions of Europe and Asia. That it can survive (and thrive) in these extreme conditions tells you something about this plant's resilience. Rhodiola root has been used in traditional medicine for centuries to treat fatigue and mood disorders. Modern science is beginning to catch up and support its use, particularly for stress, exhaustion and depression – in other words, Stage 3, or 'tired', burnout.

One 12-week study showed that rhodiola was effective at improving the symptoms of burnout: reducing emotional exhaustion, depersonalization and anhedonia (the loss of

[157] Larrieu and Layé, 'Food for Mood: Relevance of Nutritional Omega-3 Fatty Acids for Depression and Anxiety.'
[158] Pratte et al., 'An Alternative Treatment for Anxiety: A Systematic Review of Human Trial Results Reported for the Ayurvedic Herb Ashwagandha.'

interest associated with a depressed mood), with significant improvements reported after just one week of use.[159] Similarly, rhodiola demonstrates potential for reducing fatigue, improving cognitive function and exerting an antidepressant effect.[160]

L-theanine is a unique amino acid found in tea that has been shown to have an anti-stress, calming effect. Concentrated extracts in supplemental form have been shown to be useful at calming the stress axis and supporting restful sleep. This might be a great supplement to take in the evening before bed.

Remember that the supplement industry is unregulated – and you really do get what you pay for. Cheap high-street supplements often contain fillers and ineffective doses and formulations.

Seek professional advice from a *clinically trained* healthcare professional[161] – especially if you are on medication, as supplements can interact. If in doubt, 'test, don't guess'. Which brings me nicely on to our next chapter, all about testing.

---

[159] Kasper and Dienel, 'Multicenter, Open-Label, Exploratory Clinical Trial with Rhodiola Rosea Extract in Patients Suffering from Burnout Symptoms.'

[160] Olsson, von Schéele, and Panossian, 'A Randomised, Double-Blind, Placebo-Controlled, Parallel-Group Study of the Standardised Extract Shr-5 of the Roots of Rhodiola Rosea in the Treatment of Subjects with Stress-Related Fatigue'; Ma et al., 'Rhodiola Rosea L. Improves Learning and Memory Function: Preclinical Evidence and Possible Mechanisms'; Mao et al., 'Rhodiola Rosea versus Sertraline for Major Depressive Disorder: A Randomized Placebo-Controlled Trial.'

[161] Clue: this isn't your life coach, massage therapist, gran, dog walker, hairdresser, nail technician or sister from another mister. It's a GP, dietician, nutritional therapist or functional medicine practitioner. Although be prepared for blank looks if you start asking your doc about ashwagandha!

CHAPTER 19

FUNCTIONAL AND NUTRIGENOMIC TESTING

Reaching the end of this book and having implemented my Mood Boosting Method, you may find yourself in one of two camps:

1. I did everything you said and some of my symptoms have improved – but I'm still experiencing XYZ.
2. I did everything you said and I'm feeling great – but I want to learn more about myself and my unique needs.

In both these scenarios, I would recommend that you seek out and work with a functional medicine practitioner. In a clinic, you are going to get a blend of scientific evidence and clinical intuition that a book simply cannot replicate. Most importantly, you will be getting person-centred advice that is as unique as you are.

Functional medicine practitioners work by taking a full health history so they can understand your journey to date. They also utilize functional and genetic testing to help identify both antecedents and mediators of your symptoms.

Testing is about getting to the root cause of your symptoms. It's about understanding what is happening in your body that might be driving your health concerns.

If you just can't understand why you feel so exhausted or why you just can't switch off your thoughts, or how these feelings might be connected to your depressed mood, brain fog and insomnia, testing could be the answer.

Testing helps to pinpoint the root causes of your symptoms, enabling dietary, lifestyle and supplement advice to be truly personalized to you. Testing can also help you to achieve effective results, fast.

The tests we use in clinic are state of the art and carried out by approved private laboratories. The tests are simple to carry out and can be done in the comfort of your own home. With the exception of certain blood tests, you can collect the samples yourself and post them to the lab. If you require a blood draw, a nurse can visit your home to take this for you, or you can visit a phlebotomy service near you.

Blood testing

As with any health concern, if you are feeling tired, wired or emotionally overwhelmed, checking the basics should always be the first port of call.

The comprehensive blood screen we undertake evaluates the key nutrients involved in the production of your mood-regulating brain chemicals and energy, such as iron, vitamin B12, folate, vitamin D and magnesium. The test also includes a comprehensive assessment of liver and kidney function, cholesterol levels, blood sugar levels, inflammation and red and white blood cell count. You can get most of these markers tested by your GP, but it is rare that he/she will be able to order all of these markers as one panel.

Hormone testing

Your hormones can play havoc with your mood. When you work and play in the fast lane, this can take its toll on how well your hormones function. Balanced hormones are key to successful communication in the body. Mixed-up chemical messaging equals mental (and physical) chaos and confusion.

The hormone test we offer assesses sex and stress hormones (and their by-products, or 'metabolites') in urine over a 24-hour period. This gives us a much better picture of what's going on than a snapshot of hormones in a single blood test. We can also test stress hormones in saliva.

This test might be useful if you are experiencing any of the following symptoms: emotional overwhelm, nervous tension, stress, anxiety, fatigue, insomnia, low mood or depression, mood swings, weight gain or an inability to lose weight, PMS, heavy, painful or irregular periods, polycystic ovary syndrome (PCOS), difficulty concentrating or brain fog, low motivation or drive, lack of energy, low libido, frequent colds or infections or IBS.

Thyroid testing

Let's not forget about the thyroid. Thyroid hormones play a key role in mental development, brain chemical regulation and metabolism. Even a small decrease in thyroid hormones can result in fatigue, mood swings, depression, brain fog and impaired cognitive function. Low thyroid hormones may also be a factor in weight gain, constipation and menstrual disturbances.

You may have been tested before and told that your thyroid hormone levels are 'normal'. But normal doesn't always mean optimal – and sub-optimal thyroid hormone levels could be contributing to your symptoms.

The thyroid screen we offer is a comprehensive assessment of thyroid function. In particular the test looks at levels of:

- Free T3 – the most metabolically active thyroid hormone, low levels of which are associated with depression.
- Thyroid antibodies – chemicals that impair thyroid function.

Both of these are markers are not routinely screened by the NHS.

This test might be useful if you are experiencing any of the following symptoms: fatigue, low mood or depression, mood swings, difficulty concentrating or brain fog, weight gain or an inability to lose weight, lack of energy, constipation, PMS, menstrual irregularities or cold extremities.

Gut testing

Your gut is often dubbed your 'second brain': home to the largest collection of nerve cells in the human body and a vast microbial ecosystem, known as the gut microbiome. Together they create a physical and chemical connection with the brain known as the gut–brain axis.

A healthy gut, with the help of our bacterial friends, will produce the brain chemicals that regulate mood, memory and attention. Similarly, a healthy brain will support digestive health. Conversely, a poorly functioning gut can negatively influence our mental and cognitive health; and, under stress, the brain can send unhelpful signals that disrupt digestion and microbial balance. This goes someway to explain why when we are feeling anxious, depressed or emotionally overwhelmed, we may also experience unexplained digestive symptoms such as constipation, diarrhoea, bloating and IBS.

The gut test we offer provides a comprehensive picture of gut function, including insights into digestion, inflammation, immune function and gut-barrier health. The test also assesses microbial diversity and the presence of unhelpful bacteria, yeasts and parasites.

This test might be useful if you are experiencing any of the following symptoms: stress, anxiety, fatigue/exhaustion, low mood or depression, mood swings, difficulty concentrating or brain fog, insomnia/sleep disturbances, digestive issues, bloating, IBS, constipation or diarrhoea, food sensitivity/intolerance, weight gain or an inability to lose weight, inflammation, migraine, skin issues or frequent colds or infections

Organic acids testing

If only we could get into that brain of yours and find out what's really going on. Well, unfortunately, the only way we can (currently) measure accurate mood-regulating brain chemicals is by, erm, cutting into the brain. Well obviously, that isn't feasible.

Fortunately, scientists have developed the next best thing: measuring levels of brain chemical metabolites in urine. This is known as 'organic acid testing', or OAT. The hormone test we use in clinic covers some of these, or we can run a standalone OAT panel.

Although it can only really tell us what is going on on the periphery, organic acid testing gives us a reasonable indication of what *might* be going on in the brain. This information can be overlayed with clinical mood symptoms and, for best results, a nervous-system DNA profile.

Nutrigenomic (DNA) testing

If you want the ultimate in personalized advice, DNA testing is for you.

Whereas the functional tests we offer assess the environmental factors driving your health issues, there may also be a genetic influence. In fact, your unique health presentation is most likely to be a combination of your genetic predisposition and the way you live your life.

Nutrigenomics is the scientific study of the effect of food and nutrients on gene expression. Certain nutrients have been shown to modulate specific genetic pathways that regulate our mood, energy levels and hormones.

Various DNA test panels are available.

My final piece of advice regarding testing is to find the right practitioner. If that is me or my team, then great. If not, then no worries – I am simply happy to have been involved in the start of your functional medicine journey.

You can find a practitioner by using the search function on the Institute for Functional Medicine's website: www.ifm.org/find-a-practitioner/.

FINAL THOUGHTS

Thank you for taking the time to read this book – and congratulations on beginning your journey towards better mental health. As you can probably tell, burnout is a subject that is close to my heart. It is my hope that, having read this book, you are now more informed about burnout, why it happens and what you can do about it.

I'd like to leave you with some final thoughts and reminders about burnout.

Burnout arises from exposure to chronic stress. Stress is a fact of life and it isn't new. We have been dealing with stress since the dawn of humankind. But modern stress is not the same as hunter-gatherer stress; it can be excessive and it can be persistent. The source of stress has shifted away from the plains of prehistory and into the workplace; and the impact of stress has drastically changed. The cost of chronic stress on our health and on the global economy is a human crisis of epic proportions.

To recap: not all stress is bad. Your stress response is a healthy part of your biology, designed to keep you safe. It is most useful when it is rapidly mobilized and rapidly terminated. Problems arise when the stress is chronic, either due to the frequency or the duration of the stressor, relative to your level of resilience. My Mood Boosting Method is designed to help you to manage chronic stress and increase your level of stress resilience, both of which will help you to prevent burnout.

But this knowledge is useless if you do not develop a level of self-awareness about your own stress levels. First, you have to recognize that you are stressed and understand that stress is not just psychological but physical too. Your brain does not distinguish between deadlines, irate bosses and persistent pressure, any more than it distinguishes between alcohol, takeaways and excessive exercise. It is all the same to the brain and it will respond accordingly. Identifying your personal stress triggers is super important.

You now know that burnout manifests itself in many different ways. This is largely due to your stress hormone cortisol's ability to modulate your nervous, reproductive, metabolic, digestive and immune systems. Common symptomology includes emotional exhaustion, occupational cynicism and reduced personal achievement. If you have ever experienced burnout, you will probably recognize yourself in this definition – I know I do. But you might be experiencing symptoms of chronic stress that extend way beyond feeling 'tired and wired' – such as insomnia, brain fog, depressed mood, irregular periods, weight gain, sugar cravings, IBS, frequent infections, migraines and joint pain. An awareness of your symptom combination is essential. Remember, symptoms are warning signals from the brain to get you to change your behaviour. Burnout does not have to be inevitable.

My Mood Boosting Method is not a quick fix. Managing stress and developing stress resilience through diet and lifestyle change takes time and repetition. It is about establishing and reinforcing new habits and enabling the brain to rewire itself for the better. Nor is burnout necessarily a once in a lifetime experience that, once tackled, will never return.

Burnout recovery and prevention is more likely be an ongoing journey. This is certainly true for me. I'm always on the lookout for signs and symptoms that I might be heading back towards burnout again. When I notice something, I take a step back and revisit the principles I have set out in this book. I check in with myself; how am I feeling? what am I thinking? I ask myself:

- Am I getting enough sleep and am I making enough time to actively relax?
- Am I nourishing my body with the right foods to build resilience or has the balanced tipped in favour of mood disrupters?
- Am I overdoing it on the exercise front and do I need to calm this down?
- Are old thought patterns creeping back in that I need to reframe?

I'm not perfect and I don't always get it right. (I felt the signs and symptoms of burnout creeping up on me as I was writing this book – what a huge irony that would have been!)

But I'm more aware of my stressors and mood disrupters now. I've learned to recognize the warning signs and symptoms that indicate to me that I might be heading down that road again. Finally, I'm also more informed about my personal diet and lifestyle needs when it comes to managing stress and bolstering my resilience levels. I know how to turn my ship around.

As I mentioned right at the outset: burnout is an entirely unique experience. Your genetics, your life experience and your current health will all determine if and how you experience burnout. Similarly, there is no one-sized approach to preventing it. Take what feels right for you from this book and leave the rest.

Remember that, despite widespread recognition as an occupational syndrome, burnout is not classed as a medical condition. This means that many of you who visit your GP with this group of symptoms will not come away with a formal diagnosis of burnout. Please do not be disheartened by this. You do not need the label to seek and receive help for stress or your mental health.

I expect you might feel drawn to the functional medicine approach, having learned how transformative it is. I'm excited for you. But this does not mean that traditional medicine should be disregarded in reaching your burnout solution. Functional medicine is better thought of as a *complementary* partner to traditional medicine, rather than an alternative.

Consider how well this joined-up approach worked for Carly: it enabled her to get to the root cause of her symptoms, make tailored diet and lifestyle changes and access prescription body-identical HRT from the NHS. All of this enabled her to shake the crippling fatigue and emotional overwhelm of burnout.

The same can be said for Becky, who needed support from her GP for her depression. Once she started to feel better we could begin tackling the root cause of her low mood (poor methylation and nutrient status), while balancing her blood sugar to combat her Stage 1 burnout.

In the USA, functional medicine is more widespread than in the UK. Many patients can access both the medical (disease diagnostics, drugs) and the functional (testing, personalized diet and lifestyle advice) support they need through their insurance – often under the same roof. It is not a perfect healthcare system, but it is my hope that one day we can replicate this unified approach here in the UK.

For the time being, I hope you find the right combination of support for you. Trust your instincts and be your own health advocate. Most importantly, be kind to yourself. The road to burnout recovery is not a race.

Good luck on your journey – and if you want to learn more, head over to our website. We would love to help.

RECIPES

A few key principles apply to all the following recipes. A source of protein is always present. Sometimes there is also a source of healthy fat. The recipes are all balanced to avoid the burnout sugar rollercoaster and bursting with micronutrients to support stress resilience. Unless specified, all recipes serve one person but can be multiplied to serve the whole family.

Breakfast

The old adage of breakfast being the most important meal of the day holds true when it comes to recovering from burnout. If balanced correctly it can really make the difference between a Good Mood Day and a ride on the burnout sugar rollercoaster.

Smoothies

All these recipes require a form of blender. A bullet blender is realistically going to be the easiest and most stress-free way to make these smoothies. For all the recipes listed below, simply add all the ingredients to the blender and blitz for approximately 30 seconds. Once made, the smoothies can be stored in the fridge for up to three hours and/or transported to the office. If consuming immediately, add 1–2 cubes of ice to the blender before blending (not necessary if you are using frozen ingredients or planning to chill them in the fridge).

Time saving tip: place all the dry ingredients in the blending cup the night before but don't add the wet ingredients until you are ready to blend. Add them in the morning and blitz: breakfast in under 60 seconds.

The Mood Booster

- ⅓ of an avocado
- Large handful of mixed (frozen) berries (a summer or forest fruits mix works nicely)
- Large handful of green veg (e.g. spinach, cabbage, kale, cucumber, broccoli)
- 250ml almond milk
- Teaspoon of almond butter*
- Heaped tablespoon of protein powder**

*Alternatively, use a tablespoon of ground almonds or a handful of raw almonds and blend these before you add the other ingredients.

** Organic whey powder or plant-based alternative.

Tip: you can cut the remaining avocado into a further two-thirds and freeze. It can be added straight to the blender from the freezer.

The Green Burnout Buster

- ½ apple
- Juice of 1 lime
- 7cm chunk of cucumber (roughly chopped)
- 4–6 chunks of frozen pineapple
- 1 handful of kale
- Tablespoon of mixed seeds
- Tablespoon of flaxseed
- ⅓ avocado
- 250–300ml filtered water

Apple Pie

- ½ apple
- Pinch (¼ teaspoon) of cinnamon
- 1 teaspoon of almond butter
- ¼ raw courgette, peeled and roughly chopped
- 1 handful of kale
- 250–300ml almond milk

Virgin Colada

- Small banana
- 4–5 (frozen) pineapple chunks
- Handful of spinach
- 200ml coconut milk
- Heaped tablespoon of protein powder

Choose your own adventure – create your own

There are endless combinations of smoothie. To support burnout recovery and sustained energy throughout the day you just need to keep a few key principles in mind:

- You need a liquid base (water, milk etc.).
- Always include 1–3 types of veg to maximize the nutrient density.
- Use low-sugar fruit to up the flavour (apple, pear, berries, citrus). Always ensure there is more veg than fruit.
- Always consider where your protein is coming from and don't leave it out (nuts, seeds, protein powder).
- Add in some healthy fats (avocado, nuts, seeds).
- Add fresh herbs and spices to up the nutritional and taste ante.

For a nice colourful guide to making your own burnout-beating smoothie, head over to the book resources section on the website: www.re-nutrition.co.uk.

Eggs your way

How do you like your eggs in the morning? Eggs are brilliant protein source to begin the day with. My personal favourite is Eggs Florentine, but the main thing is: you have them *your* way. Select organic eggs for increased nutrient density. Remember, stress depletes the body of nutrients – choosing organic eggs is a really simple, stress-free way to support replenishment.

Use two large organic eggs or three medium organic eggs and serve:

- Scrambled with smoked salmon and rocket, or
- Poached with smashed avocado on a slice of sourdough toast, or
- Boiled served with griddled asparagus, or
- In an omelette with mixed veggies, or
- Baked in a vegetable frittata, or
- With a side of kimchi (my current favourite gut-friendly addition to any egg dish).

Naked Eggs Florentine

This is my speedy way of recreating Eggs Florentine without the gluten of an English muffin and the hassle of making a hollandaise sauce. If you're out and someone is making it for you, then feel free to have the original version! There are plenty of cafés now that can make this gluten or dairy free if that's your thing.

- Small knob of butter
- 1–2 shallots, diced

- 2 large handfuls of spinach
- 6–8 mushrooms, sliced
- 2 large organic eggs
- A small wedge of lemon

Method: in a small frying pan, melt the butter and add the shallots. When they take colour, add the mushrooms. In a separate pan, add some boiling water and poach the eggs (three minutes is the sweet spot for a runny yolk). With one minute to go, add the spinach to the shallots/mushrooms frying pan and stir to wilt. Season and add a squeeze of lemon juice to taste. Serve the eggs on top of your spinach mixture.

Tip: eggs are not just a breakfast ingredient. They can be used any time of day to add protein to a meal or snack.

Grab and go breakfast options

Fruits of the Forest Overnight Oats

- Heaped tablespoon of protein powder (unflavoured, chocolate or vanilla works best)
- Handful of mixed berries
- 100ml milk of choice (I use unsweetened almond milk)
- 50g rolled oats

Method: in a blender, blitz the protein powder, berries and milk. In a bowl or portable food container, add the oats and the blended mixture and stir. Add a little more milk if it looks too thick. Leave overnight in the fridge and then 'grab and go' in the morning.

Tip: I'm using protein powder to enhance the protein-to-carbohydrate ratio of this breakfast. If you don't have any to hand, leave it out and add a tablespoon of mixed nuts when serving.

Chia Pudding

- 50g chia seeds
- 200ml coconut milk
- 1 tablespoon pure maple syrup
- ½ vanilla pod
- Your choice of fruit, nuts or seeds to serve

Method: cut the vanilla pod in half and remove the black vanilla seeds. Discard the pod. Mix together the chia seeds, coconut milk, maple syrup and vanilla in a bowl and leave to soak overnight. The chia seeds will absorb the milk and expand to form a rice-pudding consistency. Add your choice of topping. A raspberry compote with flaked almonds is nice, or just some blueberries.

Something for the weekend

Bakewell Protein Pancakes

- 25g ground almonds
- 20g rolled oats
- 1 medium egg
- 45ml unsweetened almond milk
- 1 teaspoon of honey
- ½ teaspoon of baking powder
- Coconut oil
- Large handful of cherries
- Optional tablespoon of Greek or almond yoghurt
- Optional 1 large square of 85% cacao chocolate, grated

Method: add the ground almonds, oats, egg, milk, honey and baking powder to a blending cup and blend. Melt a teaspoon of coconut oil in a frying pan and pour in the batter to create small pancakes. Stack the cooked pancakes and top with the cherries and your optional additional toppings.

Tips: leave out the honey to make a more savoury pancake. Use alternative ground nuts as your base for variety. Get creative with the toppings – the combinations are endless!

Lunch and dinner

I have combined this section simply because there is no set time of day for you to try these meals. Wherever possible these recipes can be doubled up or batch cooked so that you have leftovers for the next day. This is going to save you time and stress while you are recovering from burnout or looking for a nourishing meal on the go.

These meals are intentionally simple yet nutritionally robust, to help you build resilience without the overwhelm. When you are feeling more energetic and motivated, take a look at some of the recipe books I have included in the Resources section at the back of the book for a more expansive set of ideas.

Speedy Roasted Red Pepper Soup

I love a red pepper soup but can barely find the time to roast the peppers myself. Plus, traditional recipes lack protein. This is my time-saving version, with a secret protein ingredient! Ready in ten minutes, with leftovers. Oh, and I like mine fiery!

(Serves 2)

- 2–3 pre-roasted red peppers (the kind you buy in a jar)
- 2–3 ripe tomatoes, quartered
- 1 x 400g tin (240g drained weight) of cannellini beans, drained and rinsed
- 1 garlic clove, crushed
- 400ml vegetable stock (cold not hot)

- Optional half a red chilli, deseeded
- To serve (optional): swirl of extra virgin olive oil/ freshly ground black pepper/crème fraiche/chilli flakes

Method: add all the ingredients to a blender and blend. Adjust the consistency by adding more water if necessary. Transfer the cold mixture to a saucepan and heat to serve. Season with black pepper.

Coconut Chicken Noodle Soup

- 2 organic chicken thighs
- 80g soba (buckwheat) noodles (uncooked)
- 3cm piece of ginger, peeled and grated or finely chopped
- 2 spring onions, chopped, greens and white separated
- 1 lime, zested and cut in half
- 200ml chicken stock
- 400ml coconut milk
- 1 pak choi, chopped
- 1 tablespoon of tamari
- Coconut oil

Method: season the chicken thighs and fry in some coconut oil for 3–4 minutes each side, or until cooked through. Set aside to rest and then slice. Cook the soba noodles according to the packet instructions and set aside. To make the broth, add the white spring onions, ginger, lime zest, chicken stock and coconut milk to a pan. Bring to a simmer and add the pak choi. Once wilted, add the cooked noodles, the tamari and a squeeze of lime juice to taste. Serve with the sliced chicken thighs and green spring onions on top.

Roasted Mediterranean Vegetables and Quinoa Salad

(Serves 2)

- 1 red onion
- 1 red pepper
- 1 courgette
- 1 garlic clove
- 1 tablespoon of oregano
- Chilli flakes (optional)
- Olive oil
- 12 plum tomatoes (halved)
- 100g quinoa
- ½ lemon
- 1 tablespoon of red wine vinegar
- 1 tablespoon of extra-virgin olive oil
- 12 green olives, halved
- Thumb-sized piece of feta cheese (optional)
- Fresh basil, torn

Method: dice the onion, pepper and courgette into small bite-size pieces. Crush the garlic in a press and add to a roasting tray with the diced vegetables. Drizzle in olive oil, chilli flakes and oregano and stir. Roast for 15 minutes at 180°C (160°C fan, gas mark 4). Stir in the tomatoes and roast for a further five minutes. Meanwhile, add the quinoa to a pan and cover with 200ml of boiling water. Simmer until all the water is absorbed. Fluff up with a fork and stir in the extra-virgin olive oil, red wine vinegar and a squeeze of lemon juice. Combine all the cooked ingredients and the olives together. Top with a few basil leaves. Crumble in the feta.

Can be served hot or allowed to cool and taken as a packed lunch.

Baked Salmon and Broccoli with Sweet Potato Mash

(Serves 2)

- 2 salmon fillets
- 300g tenderstem broccoli
- Olive oil
- ½ organic stock cube
- 2 medium or 1 large sweet potato

Method: preheat the oven to 200°C (180°C fan, gas mark 6). Line a baking tray with greaseproof paper and lay the salmon fillets to one side. Season and add a drizzle of olive oil. Place the broccoli in the same tray on the opposite side. Season and rub with olive oil. Bake in the oven for 20 minutes.

Meanwhile, peel and chop the potato into cubes. Add to a pan with the stock cube and cover with boiling water. Simmer for 15 minutes or until soft. Once the potato is cooked, drain the water and mash the potato. Season with salt and pepper and serve alongside the baked salmon and roasted broccoli.

Moroccan-style Chickpea Stew

(Serves 2)

- 1 teaspoon of ground cumin
- 1 teaspoon of paprika
- 1 teaspoon of turmeric
- 1 red onion, peeled and diced
- 1 red pepper, deseeded and diced
- 2 garlic cloves, crushed
- 400ml tin chopped tomatoes
- 400ml tin (240ml drained weight) chickpeas, drained and rinsed
- 2 large handfuls of spinach

- 1 small bunch of coriander, leaves removed and roughly chopped
- Flaked almonds (lightly toasted if you prefer)
- 1 packet of wholegrain/wild pre-steamed rice
- Optional: Greek yoghurt to serve
- Olive oil

Method: heat some olive oil in a pan over a medium heat, add the spices and allow them to take colour in the oil for about one minute. Add the onion, pepper and garlic and cook until softened. Add the chopped tomatoes and chickpeas and simmer for five minutes. Heat up the pre-steamed rice according to the packet instructions. At this point I like to take the stew off the heat and lightly mash it so that some of the chickpeas burst (your choice whether you want to do this). Stir in the spinach so that it wilts without really cooking it, and add half the coriander. Season with salt and black pepper. Serve the stew alongside the rice with (the optional Greek yoghurt), flaked almonds and remaining coriander on top.

Mix-it-up Chilli

(Serves 2–4)

Classic comfort food with all the right nutrients for a mood boost. I advocate alternating between the beef and the bean version, or adding both to bulk it out and create additional servings. If you don't plan to serve this with any additional veg, then I would sneak some chopped kale in there for a nutritional boost. I like my chilli with a bit of a kick and have been known in the past to add tabasco sauce. Nowadays I have converted to chipotle paste as I love the depth of flavour this provides.

- 1 teaspoon of cumin powder
- 1 teaspoon of chilli powder

- ½ teaspoon of cinnamon powder
- 2 garlic cloves, crushed
- 1 red onion, diced
- 1 yellow or orange pepper, diced
- 300g organic minced beef *or/and*
- 400g tin (240g drained weight) mixed beans (drained)
- 400ml tin chopped tomatoes
- Optional spicy extra, e.g. 1 tablespoon of chipotle paste
- Olive oil

Method: heat a tablespoon of olive oil in a pan and add the spices. As the pan starts to warm, stir in the onion, pepper and garlic and allow them to infuse with the spices. Then add the beef, breaking it up. Once it has started to brown add the chopped tomatoes and a little additional water to cover the chilli. If using beans add them now too. If you like it spicy, add some chipotle, which gives it a nice smoky flavour and rich colour. Simmer with the lid on at a low heat for 45 minutes. If it looks too watery, take the lid off and simmer until it has thickened.

Serve with wholegrain rice/a large handful of green veg/ home-made sweet potato wedges/smashed avocado, lime and sour cream/home-made nachos (cut a large corn tortilla into triangles and bake in the oven for 8–10 minutes until crisp).

Simple Roast Chicken and Tahini Dressing

This is as simple as it sounds: it takes five minutes of minimal effort to prep the bird and then you can chill while it roasts. A roasted chicken will provide 4–6 meals and the cooked meat will keep in the fridge for 3–4 days or 2–6 months in the freezer.

- 1 organic/free-range chicken (shop local for this)
- 1 lemon
- 1 small garlic bulb
- Large handful of fresh mixed herbs

For the dressing:

- Juice of ½ lemon
- 2 tablespoons of tahini
- 1 garlic clove, crushed
- Warm water
- Olive oil

Method: preheat the oven to 200°C (180°C fan, gas mark 6). Cut the lemon in half and break up the garlic bulb. Place inside the cavity along with the mixed herbs. Season the outside of the bird thoroughly with salt and pepper and rub it in with olive oil. Cook for 20 minutes at 200°C (180°C fan, gas mark 6). Then turn the oven down to 180°C (160°C fan, gas mark 4) and roast for a further 40 minutes per kilogram. Once cooked, leave it for at least 30 minutes to rest before carving.

To make the tahini dressing, add the tahini, lemon juice and garlic to a bowl with a splash of warm water and whisk together. Add more water to loosen, until the dressing is to your desired consistency (I like it quite thick).

Note: you do not have to make a huge roast dinner with all the trimmings to go with this. When I'm short on time I will grab some cooked chicken from the fridge, along with a bag of green salad leaves. I'll heat up a packet of pre-steamed rice (takes two minutes), while I make the tahini dressing. Then mix it all in a bowl. I'll add some sliced pepper and tomatoes and done!

Thai Curry Your Way

(Serves 2)

You decide on the protein and build your meal from there. The method shown here uses prawns, but you can equally use chicken or tofu and adapt the method to suit. In terms of amount, a palm size is a typical portion of protein, so you need 2–3 portions in this recipe to make two servings.

- Tablespoon of coconut oil
- 1 heaped tablespoon of Thai curry paste (shop bought is fine, look for the ones with ingredients you recognize and without any sugar or hydrogenated fats)
- Protein (your choice: chicken breast, tiger prawns, tofu, lentils)
- 1 large handful mange tout
- 1 large handful baby sweetcorn, halved lengthways
- 400ml coconut milk
- Small bunch of coriander, chopped

Method: heat the coconut oil in a pan on a medium heat (I tend to use a wok, but it isn't necessary) and add the peeled tiger prawns. Cook until they turn pink and then set aside. Next add the Thai curry paste to the pan; once it begins to sizzle add a small amount of coconut milk and mix them together thoroughly. Then add the remaining milk. Add the vegetables to the pan and simmer for 6–8 minutes (you want the veg to be cooked but not soggy). Return the prawns to the pan to warm through and stir through half of the coriander. Serve on its own as a hearty soup or with wholegrain rice, with the remaining coriander on top.

Snacks

Snacking is not essential but healthy snacks can be useful if you know there will be a long period between meals – for example on nights when you will be home later, you're feeding the kids or you intend to exercise before dinner. If you are at Stage 3 of burnout, then I would recommend consuming food every three hours. At Stages 1–2 of burnout, or once recovered, aim to increase the space between your meals to every 4–5 hours.

These snack ideas can also be a healthy dessert if you find you need something extra after dinner. Essentially, they all contain a source of protein and / or healthy fats.

Boiled egg

Simples!

Mixed nuts

- Small handful of mixed, unsalted (raw) nuts such as Brazil nuts, walnuts, almonds, pecans or pistachios.
- Can also be consumed alongside a square of (minimum 70%) dark chocolate or a piece of low-sugar fruit such as an apple or a pear.

Nut butters (almond/cashew)

1–2 teaspoons of nut butter spread on:

- 1–2 rice cakes
- A celery stick
- Sliced apple

Hummus

Spread on/served with:

- Oatcakes
- Mixed vegetable crudités

Mackerel Pâté

Get this from your local fishmonger.

Serve as hummus, above, or spread onto a slice of sourdough, or wrapped up in lettuce leaf 'boats'.

Stewed Apple with Cinnamon

A great one if you have apple trees. Stew peeled, cored and chopped cooking or baking apples in a splash of water. Keep an eye on them to avoid burning them and stir to break them down to your desired consistency. Sprinkle in cinnamon (a natural blood sugar balancing spice) and serve with full-fat Greek or coconut yoghurt.

Tips: your spicy stewed apple can also be frozen and defrosted as needed. Stewed apple can be used as a topping on protein pancakes, chia pudding or overnight oats. Sweeten with a little maple syrup or honey if needed.

Banana 'Nice-Cream'

Dice several bananas and freeze. Take approximately half a frozen banana per person and blend with an equivalent heaped tablespoon of full-fat Greek yoghurt. Add other natural ingredients to create flavours, for example:

- Vanilla extract
- Raw cacao powder
- Strawberries

- Raspberries
- Mint leaves and cacao nibs

Smoothies

See above recipes.

Protein balls

You need a small hand blender for these.

Makes about eight balls, depending on how big you roll them!

- 60g nuts/seeds (ground or whole)
- 60g dried fruit
- 1 tablespoon of nut/seed butter
- Splash of nut/oat milk
- Optional extras: vanilla extract, unsweetened desiccated coconut, cacao powder, cinnamon powder

Method: if the nuts aren't ground, add them to the blender first and blitz to a powder consistency. Add all the remaining ingredients to the blender and pulse until combined. Next, get your hands in there and press the mixture together. Divide into eight portions and roll into balls. Repeat until complete. Chill in the fridge for 30 minutes.

Tip: this is the basic recipe. The combinations are limitless. Here are some examples:

- Raw cacao, raisins and hazelnut (ground and butter)
- Cherry and almond (ground and butter)
- Pecan, fig and tahini
- Dates and cashew (ground and butter)

Experiment until you find one you like.

RESOURCES

My website

www.re-nutrition.co.uk

On my website you will find companion resources for this book, including:

- My burnout quiz.
- All the recipes in this book in a standalone, colourful guide.
- Simple belief-change tool.
- Tried and tested brand recommendations.
- My supplement recommendations and discount codes.

Book recommendations and weblinks

Restore

Ted Talk: Sleep is your superpower – Matt Walker.

www.ted.com/talks/matt_walker_sleep_is_your_superpower?language=en

Books
Why We Sleep by Mathew Walker

A Mindfulness Guide for The Frazzled by Ruby Wax

Full Catastrophe Living by Jon Kabat-Zinn

Breath by James Nestor

Exploratory Writing by Alison Jones

Nourish

Books
The Food Mood Connection by Uma Naidoo

The Better Brain by Julia Ruckledge and Bonnie Kaplan

Eat to Beat Depression and Anxiety by Drew Ramsey

The Anxiety Food Solution by Julia Scott

Recipe Books
Eat Happy by Melissa Helmsley

Simply Good For You by Amelia Freer

The Midlife Kitchen by Mimi Spencer and Sam Rice

Engage

Ted Talk: The brain-changing benefits of exercise – Wendy Suzuki. https://ed.ted.com/best_of_web/X93aZK9s

Reframe

Books
The Chimp Paradox by Prof. Steve Peters

Awaken the Giant Within by Anthony Robins

The Big Leap by Gay Hendriks

Other book recommendations

Burnout by Emily & Amelia Nagoski

The Stress Solution by Dr Rangan Chatterjee

The Hacking of the American Mind by Robert Lustig

Fix Your Period by Nicole Jardim

It's Not You It's Your Hormones by Nicki Williams

Dirty Genes by Dr Ben Lynch

Why We Get Fat by Gary Taube

The Obesity Code by Zoe Harcombe

Staying Alive in Toxic Times by Dr Jenny Goodman

Other weblinks

Dr Louise Newson: www.balance-menopause.com – for resources on menopause and HRT.

REFERENCES

Abbasi, Behnood, Masud Kimiagar, Khosro Sadeghniiat, Minoo M. Shirazi, Mehdi Hedayati, and Bahram Rashidkhani. "The Effect of Magnesium Supplementation on Primary Insomnia in Elderly: A Double-Blind Placebo-Controlled Clinical Trial." *Journal of Research in Medical Sciences: The Official Journal of Isfahan University of Medical Sciences* 17, no. 12 (2012): 1161–69. https://pubmed.ncbi.nlm.nih.gov/23853635/.

Abraham, Guy E, and Jorge D Flechas. "Management of Fibromyalgia: Rationale for the Use of Magnesium and Malic Acid." *http://Dx.Doi.Org/10.3109/13590849208997961* 3, no. 1 (January 2009): 49–59. https://doi.org/10.3109/13590849208997961.

Addolorato, G, E Capristo, G Ghittoni, C Valeri, R Mascianà, C Ancona, and G Gasbarrini. "Anxiety but Not Depression Decreases in Coeliac Patients after One-Year Gluten-Free Diet: A Longitudinal Study." *Scandinavian Journal of Gastroenterology* 36, no. 5 (May 2001): 502–6. https://doi.org/10.1080/00365520119754.

Akbari-Fakhrabadi, Maryam, Mohammad Najafi, Soudabehsadat Mortazavian, Amir-Hossein Memari, Farzad Shidfar, Ali Shahbazi, and Javad Heshmati. "Saffron *(Crocus Sativus L.)*, Combined with Endurance Exercise, Synergistically Enhances BDNF, Serotonin, and NT-3 in Wistar Rats." *Reports of Biochemistry & Molecular Biology* 9, no. 4 (January 1, 2021): 426–34. https://doi.org/10.52547/rbmb.9.4.426.

Andel, Ross, Michael Crowe, Ingemar Kareholt, Jonas Wastesson, and Marti G. Parker. "Indicators of Job Strain at Midlife and Cognitive Functioning in Advanced Old Age." *The Journals of Gerontology. Series B, Psychological Sciences and Social Sciences* 66, no. 3 (2011): 287–91. https://doi.org/10.1093/GERONB/GBQ105.

Ansari, Walid El, Hamed Adetunji, and Reza Oskrochi. "Food and Mental Health: Relationship between Food and Perceived Stress and Depressive Symptoms among University Students in the United Kingdom." *Central European Journal of Public Health* 22, no. 2 (2014): 90–97. https://doi.org/10.21101/CEJPH.A3941.

Armon, Galit, Samuel Melamed, Arie Shirom, and Itzhak Shapira. "Elevated Burnout Predicts the Onset of Musculoskeletal Pain among Apparently Healthy Employees." *Journal of Occupational Health Psychology* 15, no. 4 (October 2010): 399–408. https://doi.org/10.1037/A0020726.

Arnsten, Amy F.T., and Tait Shanafelt. "Physician Distress and Burnout, the Neurobiological Perspective." *Mayo Clinic Proceedings* 96, no. 3 (March 1, 2021): 763-769. https://doi.org/10.1016/J.MAYOCP.2020.12.027.

Astrup, A, A Raben, and N Geiker. "The Role of Higher Protein Diets in Weight Control and Obesity-Related Comorbidities." *International Journal of Obesity (2005)* 39, no. 5 (May 2015): 721–26. https://doi.org/10.1038/ijo.2014.216.

Baguley, Brenton J., Tina L. Skinner, David G. Jenkins, and Olivia R.L. Wright. "Mediterranean-Style Dietary Pattern Improves Cancer-Related Fatigue and Quality of Life in Men with Prostate Cancer Treated with Androgen Deprivation Therapy: A Pilot Randomised Control Trial." *Clinical Nutrition (Edinburgh, Scotland)* 40, no. 1 (January 1, 2021): 245–54. https://doi.org/10.1016/J.CLNU.2020.05.016.

Bains, Gurinder Singh, Lee S. Berk, Everett Lohman, Noha Daher, Jerrold Petrofsky, Ernie Schwab, and Pooja Deshpande. "Humors Effect on Short-Term Memory in Healthy and Diabetic Older Adults." *Alternative Therapies in Health and Medicine* 21, no. 3 (May 1, 2015): 16–25. https://pubmed.ncbi.nlm.nih.gov/26026141/.

Baker, Carl, and Esme Kirk-Wade. "Mental Health Statistics: Prevalence, Services, and Funding in England." House of Commons Library, 13 March, 2023. https://researchbriefings.files.parliament.uk/documents/SN06988/SN06988.pdf.

Bear, Tracey, Julie Dalziel, Jane Coad, Nicole Roy, Christine Butts, and Pramod Gopal. "The Microbiome-Gut-Brain Axis and Resilience to Developing Anxiety or Depression under Stress." *Microorganisms* 9, no. 4 (April 1, 2021). https://doi.org/10.3390/MICROORGANISMS9040723.

Beauregard, Nancy, Alain Marchand, Jaunathan Bilodeau, Pierre Durand, Andrée Demers, and Victor Y Haines. "Gendered Pathways to Burnout: Results from the SALVEO Study." *Annals of Work Exposures and Health* 62, no. 4 (2018): 426–37. https://doi.org/10.1093/annweh/wxx114.

Bedel, Hatice Asli, Ceren Kencebay Manas, Gül Özbey, and Coşkun Usta. "The Antidepressant-like Activity of Ellagic Acid and Its Effect on Hippocampal Brain Derived Neurotrophic Factor Levels in Mouse Depression Models." *Natural Product Research* 32, no. 24 (December 2018): 2932–35. https://doi.org/10.1080/1 4786419.2017.1385021.

Bektaş, Atilla, Harun Erdal, Meltem Ulusoy, and Tayfun Uzbay. "Does Serotonin in the Intestines Make You Happy?" *The Turkish Journal of Gastroenterology* 31, no. 10 (October 1, 2020): 721-723. https://doi.org/10.5152/TJG.2020.19554.

Belujon, Pauline, and Anthony A. Grace. "Dopamine System Dysregulation in Major Depressive Disorders." *International Journal of Neuropsychopharmacology* 20, no. 12 (December 1, 2017): 1036-1046. https://doi.org/10.1093/IJNP/PYX056.

Bendall, C L, H L Mayr, R S Opie, M Bes-Rastrollo, C Itsiopoulos, and C J Thomas. "Central Obesity and the Mediterranean Diet: A Systematic Review of Intervention Trials." *Critical Reviews in Food Science and Nutrition* 58, no. 18 (December 12, 2018): 3070–84. https://doi.org/10.1080/10408398.2017.1351917.

Beydoun, May A, Monal R Shroff, Hind A Beydoun, and Alan B Zonderman. "Serum Folate, Vitamin B-12, and Homocysteine and Their Association with Depressive Symptoms among U.S. Adults." *Psychosomatic Medicine* 72, no. 9 (November 2010): 862–73. https://doi.org/10.1097/PSY.0b013e3181f61863.

Bitarafan, Sama, Aliakbar Saboor-Yaraghi, Mohammad-Ali Sahraian, Danesh Soltani, Shahriar Nafissi, Mansoureh Togha, Nahid Beladi Moghadam, Tina Roostaei, Niyaz Mohammadzadeh Honarvar, and Mohammad-Hossein Harirchian. "Effect of Vitamin A Supplementation on Fatigue and Depression in Multiple Sclerosis Patients: A Double-Blind Placebo-Controlled Clinical Trial." *Iranian Journal of Allergy, Asthma, and Immunology* 15, no. 1 (February 2016): 13–19. www.ncbi.nlm.nih.gov/pubmed/26996107.

Boucher, Jackie L. "Mediterranean Eating Pattern." *Diabetes Spectrum : A Publication of the American Diabetes Association* 30, no. 2 (March 1, 2017): 72-76. https://doi.org/10.2337/DS16-0074.

Boyle, Neil, Clare Lawton, and Louise Dye. "The Effects of Magnesium Supplementation on Subjective Anxiety and Stress—A Systematic Review." *Nutrients* 9, no. 5 (April 26, 2017): 429. https://doi.org/10.3390/nu9050429.

Brzozowski, Bartosz, Agnieszka Mazur-Bialy, Robert Pajdo, Slawomir Kwiecien, Jan Bilski, Malgorzata Zwolinska-Wcislo, Tomasz Mach, and Tomasz Brzozowski. "Mechanisms by Which Stress Affects the Experimental and Clinical Inflammatory Bowel Disease (IBD): Role of Brain-Gut Axis." *Current Neuropharmacology* 14, no. 8 (April 6, 2016): 892–900. https://doi.org/10.2174/1570159X14666160404124127.

Burnford, Joy. *Don't Fix Women: The Practical Path to Gender Equality at Work.* Practical Inspiration Publishing, 2022.

Cardinali, Daniel P, Daniel E Vigo, Natividad Olivar, María F Vidal, and Luis I Brusco. "Melatonin Therapy in Patients with Alzheimer's Disease." *Antioxidants (Basel, Switzerland)* 3, no. 2 (April 10, 2014): 245–77. https://doi.org/10.3390/antiox3020245.

Cayres, Leonardo César de Freitas, Larissa Vedovato Vilela de Salis, Guilherme Siqueira Pardo Rodrigues, André van Helvoort Lengert, Ana Paula Custódio Biondi, Larissa Donadel Barreto Sargentini, João Luiz Brisotti, Eleni Gomes, and Gislane Lelis Vilela de Oliveira. "Detection of Alterations in the Gut Microbiota and Intestinal Permeability in Patients With Hashimoto Thyroiditis." *Frontiers in Immunology* 12 (March 5, 2021). https://doi.org/10.3389/FIMMU.2021.579140.

Cervantes, Pablo, Stephen Gelber, François N.K. Ng Ying Kin, Vasavan N.P. Nair, and George Schwartz. "Circadian Secretion of Cortisol in Bipolar Disorder." *Journal of Psychiatry & Neuroscience : JPN* 26, no. 5 (2001): 411–16. https://pubmed.ncbi.nlm.nih.gov/11762208/.

Chang, Lin. "The Role of Stress on Physiologic Responses and Clinical Symptoms in Irritable Bowel Syndrome." *Gastroenterology* 140, no. 3 (2011): 761-5. https://doi.org/10.1053/J.GASTRO.2011.01.032.

Chang, Shao-Min, and Chung-Hey Chen. "Effects of an Intervention with Drinking Chamomile Tea on Sleep Quality and Depression in Sleep Disturbed Postnatal Women: A Randomized Controlled Trial." *Journal of Advanced Nursing* 72, no. 2 (February 2016): 306–15. https://doi.org/10.1111/jan.12836.

Chang, Soon-Bok, Hee-Sook Kim, Yun-Hee Ko, Choon-Hee Bae, and Sung-Eun An. "Effects of Abdominal Breathing on Anxiety, Blood Pressure, Peripheral Skin Temperature and Saturation Oxygen of Pregnant Women in Preterm Labor." *Korean Journal of Women Health Nursing* 15, no. 1 (March 31, 2009): 32–42. https://doi.org/10.4069/KJWHN.2009.15.1.32.

Chen, Wendy Y, Bernard Rosner, Susan E Hankinson, Graham A Colditz, and Walter C Willett. "Moderate Alcohol Consumption During Adult Life, Drinking Patterns, and Breast Cancer Risk." *JAMA* 306, no. 17 (November 2, 2011): 1884-1890. https://doi.org/10.1001/jama.2011.1590.

Cheng, Shu Li, Fu Chi Yang, Hsuan Te Chu, Chia Kuang Tsai, Shih Chieh Ku, Yu Ting Tseng, Ta Chuan Yeh, and Chih Sung Liang. "Incongruent Expression of Brain-Derived Neurotrophic Factor and Cortisol in Schizophrenia: Results from a Randomized Controlled Trial of Laughter Intervention." *Psychiatry Investigation* 17, no. 12 (December 1, 2020): 1191–99. https://doi.org/10.30773/PI.2020.0269.

Chiovato, Luca, Flavia Magri, and Allan Carlé. "Hypothyroidism in Context: Where We've Been and Where We're Going." *Advances in Therapy* 36, no. Suppl 2 (September 1, 2019): 47-58. https://doi.org/10.1007/S12325-019-01080-8.

Choi, Byoung O., Yeon Ji Lee, Ji Ho Choi, Se Wook Cho, Hyun Jung Im, and Jee Eun An. "The Association between Stress Level in Daily Life and Age at Natural Menopause in Korean Women: Outcomes of the Korean National Health and Nutrition Examination Survey in 2010-2012." *Korean Journal of Family Medicine* 36, no. 6 (2015): 305–9. https://doi.org/10.4082/KJFM.2015.36.6.305.

Choudhary, Arbind Kumar, and Yeong Yeh Lee. "Neurophysiological Symptoms and Aspartame: What is the Connection?" *Nutritional Neuroscience* 21, no. 5 (May 28, 2018): 306–16. https://doi.org/10.1080/1028415X.2017.1288340.

Chueh, Ke-Hsin, Christian Guilleminault, and Chia-Mo Lin. "Alcohol Consumption as a Moderator of Anxiety and Sleep Quality." *The Journal of Nursing Research : JNR* 27, no. 3 (June 2019): e23. https://doi.org/10.1097/jnr.0000000000000300.

Clark, Ian, and Hans Peter Landolt. "Coffee, Caffeine, and Sleep: A Systematic Review of Epidemiological Studies and Randomized Controlled Trials." *Sleep Medicine Reviews* 31 (February 2017): 70–78. https://doi.org/10.1016/j.smrv.2016.01.006.

Cohen, Sheldon, David A J Tyrrell, and Andrew P Smith. "Psychological Stress and Susceptibility to the Common Cold." *The New England Journal of Medicine* 325, no. 9 (January 14, 2010): 606–12. https://doi.org/10.1056/NEJM199108293250903.

Converso, Daniela, Sara Viotti, Ilaria Sottimano, Barbara Loera, Giorgia Molinengo, and Gloria Guidetti. "The Relationship between Menopausal Symptoms and Burnout. A Cross-Sectional Study among Nurses." *BMC Women's Health* 19, no. 1 (November 27, 2019). https://doi.org/10.1186/S12905-019-0847-6.

Convit, Antonio, Oliver T Wolf, Chaim Tarshish, and Mony J De Leon. "Reduced Glucose Tolerance is Associated with Poor Memory Performance and Hippocampal Atrophy among Normal Elderly." *Proceedings of the National Academy of Sciences of the United States of America* 100, no. 4 (February 2, 2003): 2019-2022. https://doi.org/10.1073/PNAS.0336073100.

Dashorst, Patricia, Trudy M Mooren, Rolf J Kleber, Peter J de Jong, and Rafaele J C Huntjens. "Intergenerational Consequences of the Holocaust on Offspring Mental Health: A Systematic Review of Associated Factors and Mechanisms." *European Journal of Psychotraumatology* 10, no. 1 (2019): 1654065. https://doi.org/10.1080/20008198.2019.1654065.

Deloitte. "Poor Mental Health Costs UK Employers up to £56 Billion a Year | Deloitte UK," 2022. www2.deloitte.com/uk/en/pages/press-releases/articles/poor-mental-health-costs-uk-employers-up-to-pound-56-billion-a-year.html.

Dietz, Christina, Matthijs Dekker, and Betina Piqueras-Fiszman. "An Intervention Study on the Effect of Matcha Tea, in Drink and Snack Bar Formats, on Mood and Cognitive Performance." *Food Research International (Ottawa, Ont.)* 99, no. Pt 1 (September 1, 2017): 72–83. https://doi.org/10.1016/J.FOODRES.2017.05.002.

Drake, Amanda J, Justin I Tang, and Moffat J Nyirenda. "Mechanisms Underlying the Role of Glucocorticoids in the Early Life Programming of Adult Disease."

Clinical Science (London, England : 1979) 113, no. 5 (September 2007): 219–32. https://doi.org/10.1042/CS20070107.

Emmons, Robert A, and Michael E McCullough. "Counting Blessings versus Burdens: An Experimental Investigation of Gratitude and Subjective Well-Being in Daily Life." *Journal of Personality and Social Psychology* 84, no. 2 (2003): 377–89. https://doi.org/10.1037//0022-3514.84.2.377.

Erickson, Kirk I, Destiny L Miller, and Kathryn A Roecklein. "The Aging Hippocampus." *The Neuroscientist* 18, no. 1 (February 29, 2012): 82–97. https://doi.org/10.1177/1073858410397054.

Fancourt, Daisy, Aaron Williamon, Livia A Carvalho, Andrew Steptoe, Rosie Dow, and Ian Lewis. "Singing Modulates Mood, Stress, Cortisol, Cytokine and Neuropeptide Activity in Cancer Patients and Carers." *Ecancermedicalscience* 10 (April 5, 2016): 631. https://doi.org/10.3332/ECANCER.2016.631.

Fasano, Alessio. "All Disease Begins in the (Leaky) Gut: Role of Zonulin-Mediated Gut Permeability in the Pathogenesis of Some Chronic Inflammatory Diseases." *F1000Research* 9 (2020): 69. https://doi.org/10.12688/F1000RESEARCH.20510.1/DOI.

Fasano, Alessio. "Zonulin, Regulation of Tight Junctions, and Autoimmune Diseases." *Annals of the New York Academy of Sciences* 1258, no. 1 (July 2012): 25–33. https://doi.org/10.1111/j.1749-6632.2012.06538.x.

Foster, Jane A, Linda Rinaman, and John F Cryan. "Stress & the Gut–Brain Axis: Regulation by the Microbiome." *Neurobiology of Stress* 7 (December 1, 2017): 124–36. https://doi.org/10.1016/J.YNSTR.2017.03.001.

Fresán, Ujué, Maira Bes-Rastrollo, Gina Segovia-Siapco, Almudena Sanchez-Villegas, Francisca Lahortiga, Pedro-Antonio de la Rosa, and Miguel-Angel Martínez-Gonzalez. "Does the MIND Diet Decrease Depression Risk? A Comparison with Mediterranean Diet in the SUN Cohort." *European Journal of Nutrition* 58, no. 3 (April 2019): 1271–82. https://doi.org/10.1007/s00394-018-1653-x.

Freudenberger, Herbert J. "Staff Burn-Out." *Journal of Social Issues* 30, no. 1 (1974): 159–65. https://doi.org/10.1111/J.1540-4560.1974.TB00706.X.

Furman, David, Judith Campisi, Eric Verdin, Pedro Carrera-Bastos, Sasha Targ, Claudio Franceschi, Luigi Ferrucci, et al. "Chronic Inflammation in the Etiology of Disease across the Life Span." *Nature Medicine* 25, no. 12 (December 1, 2019): 1822-1832. https://doi.org/10.1038/S41591-019-0675-0.

Gangwisch, James E, Lauren Hale, Lorena Garcia, Dolores Malaspina, Mark G Opler, Martha E Payne, Rebecca C Rossom, and Dorothy Lane. "High Glycemic Index Diet as a Risk Factor for Depression: Analyses from the Women's Health Initiative." *The American Journal of Clinical Nutrition* 102, no. 2 (August 2015): 454–63. https://doi.org/10.3945/ajcn.114.103846.

Gascon, Mireia, Wilma Zijlema, Cristina Vert, Mathew P White, and Mark J Nieuwenhuijsen. "Outdoor Blue Spaces, Human Health and Well-Being: A Systematic Review of Quantitative Studies." *International Journal of Hygiene and Environmental Health* 220, no. 8 (November 1, 2017): 1207–21. https://doi.org/10.1016/J.IJHEH.2017.08.004.

Gaynes, Bradley N, A John Rush, Madhukar H Trivedi, Stephen R Wisniewski, Donald Spencer, and Maurizio Fava. "The STAR*D Study: Treating Depression in the Real World." *Cleveland Clinic Journal of Medicine* 75, no. 1 (2008): 57–66. https://doi.org/10.3949/CCJM.75.1.57.

Ghisari, Mandana, Hans Eiberg, Manhai Long, and Eva C Bonefeld-Jørgensen. "Polymorphisms in Phase I and Phase II Genes and Breast Cancer Risk and Relations to Persistent Organic Pollutant Exposure: A Case-Control Study in Inuit Women." *Environmental Health: A Global Access Science Source* 13, no. 1 (March 16, 2014): 19. https://doi.org/10.1186/1476-069X-13-19.

Ginde, Adit A, Jonathan M Mansbach, and Carlos A Camargo. "Association Between Serum 25-Hydroxyvitamin D Level and Upper Respiratory Tract Infection in the Third National Health and Nutrition Examination Survey." *Archives of Internal Medicine* 169, no. 4 (February 23, 2009): 384–90. https://doi.org/10.1001/ARCHINTERNMED.2008.560.

Glaser, Ronald, and Janice K Kiecolt-Glaser. "Stress-Induced Immune Dysfunction: Implications for Health." *Nature Reviews. Immunology* 5, no. 3 (March 2005): 243–51. https://doi.org/10.1038/NRI1571.

Gordon, Brett R, Cillian P McDowell, Mats Hallgren, Jacob D Meyer, Mark Lyons, and Matthew P Herring. "Association of Efficacy of Resistance Exercise Training With Depressive Symptoms: Meta-Analysis and Meta-Regression Analysis of Randomized Clinical Trials." *JAMA Psychiatry* 75, no. 6 (2018): 566–76. https://doi.org/10.1001/jamapsychiatry.2018.0572.

Guszkowska, Monika. "Effects of Exercise on Anxiety, Depression and Mood." *Psychiatria Polska* 38, no. 4 (2004): 611–20. https://pubmed.ncbi.nlm.nih.gov/15518309/.

Hackett, Ruth A, Mika Kivimäki, Meena Kumari, and Andrew Steptoe. "Diurnal Cortisol Patterns, Future Diabetes, and Impaired Glucose Metabolism in the Whitehall II Cohort Study." *The Journal of Clinical Endocrinology and Metabolism* 101, no. 2 (February 1, 2016): 619–25. https://doi.org/10.1210/JC.2015-2853.

Häuser, Winfried, Karl-Heinz Janke, Bodo Klump, Michael Gregor, and Andreas Hinz. "Anxiety and Depression in Adult Patients with Celiac Disease on a Gluten-Free Diet." *World Journal of Gastroenterology* 16, no. 22 (June 14, 2010): 2780–87. https://doi.org/10.3748/wjg.v16.i22.2780.

He, Jing wen, Zhi hao Tu, Lei Xiao, Tong Su, and Yun xiang Tang. "Effect of Restricting Bedtime Mobile Phone Use on Sleep, Arousal, Mood, and Working Memory: A Randomized Pilot Trial." *PLoS ONE* 15, no. 2 (February 1, 2020): e0228756. https://doi.org/10.1371/JOURNAL.PONE.0228756.

Hendricks, Gay. *The Big Leap: Conquer Your Hidden Fear and Take Life to the Next Level*. HarperOne, 2010.

Hermes, Gretchen L, Bertha Delgado, Maria Tretiakova, Sonia A Cavigelli, Thomas Krausz, Suzanne D Conzen, and Martha K McClintock. "Social Isolation Dysregulates Endocrine and Behavioral Stress While Increasing Malignant Burden of Spontaneous Mammary Tumors." *Proceedings of the National Academy of Sciences of the United States of America* 106, no. 52 (December 12, 2009): 22393-22398. https://doi.org/10.1073/PNAS.0910753106.

Hidese, Shinsuke, Shintaro Ogawa, Miho Ota, Ikki Ishida, Zenta Yasukawa, Makoto Ozeki, and Hiroshi Kunugi. "Effects of L-Theanine Administration on Stress-Related Symptoms and Cognitive Functions in Healthy Adults: A Randomized Controlled Trial." *Nutrients* 11, no. 10 (October 1, 2019): 2362. https://doi.org/10.3390/NU11102362.

Hölzel, Britta K, James Carmody, Mark Vangel, Christina Congleton, Sita M Yerramsetti, Tim Gard, and Sara W Lazar. "Mindfulness Practice Leads to Increases in Regional Brain Gray Matter Density." *Psychiatry Research* 191, no. 1 (January 1, 2011): 36-43. https://doi.org/10.1016/J.PSCYCHRESNS.2010.08.006.

Hu, Danqing, Lixiao Cheng, and Wenjie Jiang. "Sugar-Sweetened Beverages Consumption and the Risk of Depression: A Meta-Analysis of Observational Studies." *Journal of Affective Disorders* 245 (2019): 348-55. https://doi.org/10.1016/j.jad.2018.11.015.

Huang, Qingyi, Huan Liu, Katsuhiko Suzuki, Sihui Ma, and Chunhong Liu. "Linking What We Eat to Our Mood: A Review of Diet, Dietary Antioxidants, and Depression." *Antioxidants (Basel, Switzerland)* 8, no. 9 (September 5, 2019): 376. https://doi.org/10.3390/antiox8090376.

Huo, Meng, Lisa M Soederberg Miller, Kyungmin Kim, and Siwei Liu. "Volunteering, Self-Perceptions of Aging, and Mental Health in Later Life." *The Gerontologist* 61, no. 7 (October 1, 2021): 1131-40. https://doi.org/10.1093/GERONT/GNAA164.

IFM. "Good Sleep Hygiene May Help Protect Against Infectious Diseases | The Institute for Functional Medicine," 2023. www.ifm.org/news-insights/good-sleep-hygiene-may-help-protect-infectious-diseases/.

Ilchmann-Diounou, Hanna, and Sandrine Menard. "Psychological Stress, Intestinal Barrier Dysfunctions, and Autoimmune Disorders: An Overview." *Frontiers in Immunology* 11 (August 25, 2020): 1823. https://doi.org/10.3389/FIMMU.2020.01823.

Jacka, Felice N, Nicolas Cherbuin, Kaarin J Anstey, Perminder Sachdev, and Peter Butterworth. "Western Diet is Associated with a Smaller Hippocampus: A Longitudinal Investigation." *BMC Medicine* 13, no. 1 (September 8, 2015): 215. https://doi.org/10.1186/S12916-015-0461-X.

Jacka, Felice N, Adrienne O'Neil, Rachelle Opie, Catherine Itsiopoulos, Sue Cotton, Mohammedreza Mohebbi, David Castle, et al. "A Randomised Controlled Trial of Dietary Improvement for Adults with Major Depression (the 'SMILES' Trial)." *BMC Medicine* 15, no. 1 (January 30, 2017): 23. https://doi.org/10.1186/s12916-017-0791-y.

Janssen, Math, Yvonne Heerkens, Wietske Kuijer, Beatrice Van Der Heijden, and Josephine Engels. "Effects of Mindfulness-Based Stress Reduction on Employees' Mental Health: A Systematic Review." *PLoS ONE* 13, no. 1 (January 1, 2018): e0191332. https://doi.org/10.1371/JOURNAL.PONE.0191332.

Jones, Alison. *Exploratory Writing: Everyday Magic for Life and Work.* Practical Inspirations Publishing, 2022.

Jones, Sara K, Deirdre M McCarthy, Cynthia Vied, Gregg D Stanwood, Chris Schatschneider, and Pradeep G. Bhide. "Transgenerational Transmission of Aspartame-Induced Anxiety and Changes in Glutamate-GABA Signaling and

Gene Expression in the Amygdala." *Proceedings of the National Academy of Sciences of the United States of America* 119, no. 49 (December 6, 2022): e2213120119. https://doi.org/10.1073/PNAS.2213120119.

Kabat-Zinn, Jon. *Full Catastrophe Living, Revised Edition: How to Cope with Stress, Pain and Illness Using Mindfulness Meditation.* Revised. Piatkus, 2013.

Kasckow, J W, Baker, and T D Geracioti. "Corticotropin-Releasing Hormone in Depression and Post-Traumatic Stress Disorder." *Peptides* 22, no. 5 (2001): 845–51. https://doi.org/10.1016/S0196-9781(01)00399-0.

Kasper, Siegfried, and Angelika Dienel. "Multicenter, Open-Label, Exploratory Clinical Trial with Rhodiola Rosea Extract in Patients Suffering from Burnout Symptoms." *Neuropsychiatric Disease and Treatment* 13 (March 22, 2017): 889–98. https://doi.org/10.2147/NDT.S120113.

Kaufman, Harvey W, Justin K Niles, Martin H Kroll, Caixia Bi, and Michael F Holick. "SARS-CoV-2 Positivity Rates Associated with Circulating 25-Hydroxyvitamin D Levels." *PloS One* 15, no. 9 (2020): e0239252. https://doi.org/10.1371/journal.pone.0239252.

Kelly, John R, Paul J Kennedy, John F Cryan, Timothy G Dinan, Gerard Clarke, and Niall P Hyland. "Breaking down the Barriers: The Gut Microbiome, Intestinal Permeability and Stress-Related Psychiatric Disorders." *Frontiers in Cellular Neuroscience* 9 (2015): 392. https://doi.org/10.3389/fncel.2015.00392.

Keys, A, and F Grande. "Role of Dietary Fat in Human Nutrition. III. Diet and the Epidemiology of Coronary Heart Disease." *American Journal of Public Health and the Nation's Health* 47, no. 12 (December 1957): 1520–30. https://doi.org/10.2105/ajph.47.12.1520.

Kumari, Meena, Tarani Chandola, Eric Brunner, and Mika Kivimaki. "A Nonlinear Relationship of Generalized and Central Obesity with Diurnal Cortisol Secretion in the Whitehall II Study." *The Journal of Clinical Endocrinology and Metabolism* 95, no. 9 (2010): 4415–23. https://doi.org/10.1210/JC.2009-2105.

Lambertini, Luca, Jia Chen, and Yoko Nomura. "Mitochondrial Gene Expression Profiles Are Associated with Maternal Psychosocial Stress in Pregnancy and Infant Temperament." *PLoS ONE* 10, no. 9 (September 29, 2015): e0138929. https://doi.org/10.1371/JOURNAL.PONE.0138929.

Lamers, F, N Vogelzangs, K R Merikangas, P De Jonge, A T F Beekman, and B W J H Penninx. "Evidence for a Differential Role of HPA-Axis Function, Inflammation and Metabolic Syndrome in Melancholic versus Atypical Depression." *Molecular Psychiatry* 18, no. 6 (June 2013): 692–99. https://doi.org/10.1038/MP.2012.144.

Langkamp-Henken, Bobbi, Cassie C Rowe, Amanda L Ford, Mary C Christman, Carmelo Nieves, Lauren Khouri, Gretchen J Specht, Stephanie Anne Girard, Samuel J Spaiser, and Wendy J Dahl. "Bifidobacterium Bifidum R0071 Results in a Greater Proportion of Healthy Days and a Lower Percentage of Academically Stressed Students Reporting a Day of Cold/Flu: A Randomised, Double-Blind, Placebo-Controlled Study." *The British Journal of Nutrition* 113, no. 3 (February 14, 2015): 426–34. https://doi.org/10.1017/S0007114514003997.

Larrieu, Thomas, and Sophie Layé. "Food for Mood: Relevance of Nutritional Omega-3 Fatty Acids for Depression and Anxiety." *Frontiers in Physiology* 9, no. AUG (August 6, 2018): 1047. https://doi.org/10.3389/FPHYS.2018.01047.

Leal, G, C R Bramham, and C B Duarte. "BDNF and Hippocampal Synaptic Plasticity." *Vitamins and Hormones* 104 (January 1, 2017): 153–95. https://doi.org/10.1016/BS.VH.2016.10.004.

Lee, Ji Soo, and Soo Kyoung Lee. "The Effects of Laughter Therapy for the Relief of Employment-Stress in Korean Student Nurses by Assessing Psychological Stress Salivary Cortisol and Subjective Happiness." *Osong Public Health and Research Perspectives* 11, no. 1 (2020): 44–52. https://doi.org/10.24171/J.PHRP.2020.11.1.07.

Lieber, Charles S. "The Influence of Alcohol on Nutritional Status." *Nutrition Reviews* 46, no. 7 (1988): 241–54. https://doi.org/10.1111/J.1753-4887.1988. TB05443.X.

Losso, Jack N, John W Finley, Namrata Karki, Ann G Liu, Alfredo Prudente, Russell Tipton, Ying Yu, and Frank L Greenway. "Pilot Study of Tart Cherry Juice for the Treatment of Insomnia and Investigation of Mechanisms." *American Journal of Therapeutics* 25, no. 2 (March 1, 2018): e194. https://doi.org/10.1097/MJT. 0000000000000584.

Louca, Panayiotis, Benjamin Murray, Kerstin Klaser, Mark S Graham, Mohsen Mazidi, Emily R Leeming, Ellen Thompson, et al. "Modest Effects of Dietary Supplements during the COVID-19 Pandemic: Insights from 445 850 Users of the COVID-19 Symptom Study App." *BMJ Nutrition, Prevention & Health*, 4, no. 1 (April 19, 2021): 149-157. https://doi.org/10.1136/bmjnph-2021-000250.

Loughrey, David G, Sara Lavecchia, Sabina Brennan, Brian A Lawlor, and Michelle E Kelly. "The Impact of the Mediterranean Diet on the Cognitive Functioning of Healthy Older Adults: A Systematic Review and Meta-Analysis." *Advances in Nutrition (Bethesda, Md.)* 8, no. 4 (July 2017): 571–86. https://doi.org/10.3945/an.117.015495.

Love, Tiffany M. "The Impact of Oxytocin on Stress: The Role of Sex." *Current Opinion in Behavioral Sciences* 23 (October 2018): 136-142. https://doi.org/10.1016/J. COBEHA.2018.06.018.

Luo, Jingyi, Xiaoxia Wang, Li Yuan, and Lixin Guo. "Iron Deficiency, a Risk Factor of Thyroid Disorders in Reproductive-Age and Pregnant Women: A Systematic Review and Meta-Analysis." *Frontiers in Endocrinology* 12 (February 25, 2021): 629831. https://doi.org/10.3389/FENDO.2021.629831.

Lynch, Ben. *Dirty Genes: A Breakthrough Program to Treat the Root Cause of Illness and Optimize Your Health*. 1st. HarperOne, 2018.

Ma, Gou Ping, Qun Zheng, Meng Bei Xu, Xiao Li Zhou, Lin Lu, Zuo Xiao Li, and Guo Qing Zheng. "Rhodiola Rosea L. Improves Learning and Memory Function: Preclinical Evidence and Possible Mechanisms." *Frontiers in Pharmacology* 9 (December 4, 2018): 1415. https://doi.org/10.3389/FPHAR.2018.01415.

Ma, Xiao, Zi Qi Yue, Zhu Qing Gong, Hong Zhang, Nai Yue Duan, Yu Tong Shi, Gao Xia Wei, and You Fa Li. "The Effect of Diaphragmatic Breathing on Attention, Negative Affect and Stress in Healthy Adults." *Frontiers in Psychology* 8, no. JUN (June 6, 2017): 874. https://doi.org/10.3389/FPSYG.2017.00874.

Maghbooli, Zhila, Mohammad Ali Sahraian, Mehdi Ebrahimi, Marzieh Pazoki, Samira Kafan, Hedieh Moradi Tabriz, Azar Hadadi, et al. "Vitamin D Sufficiency, a Serum 25-Hydroxyvitamin D at Least 30 Ng/ML Reduced Risk for Adverse Clinical Outcomes in Patients with COVID-19 Infection." *PloS One* 15, no. 9 (2020): e0239799. https://doi.org/10.1371/journal.pone.0239799.

Maguire, Eleanor A, David G Gadian, Ingrid S Johnsrude, Catriona D Good, John Ashburner, Richard S J Frackowiak, and Christopher D Frith. "Navigation-Related Structural Change in the Hippocampi of Taxi Drivers." *Proceedings of the National Academy of Sciences of the United States of America* 97, no. 8 (April 4, 2000): 4398-4403. https://doi.org/10.1073/PNAS.070039597.

Manning, Lydia, Morgan Ferris, Carla Narvaez Rosario, Molly Prues, and Lauren Bouchard. "Spiritual Resilience: Understanding the Protection and Promotion of Well-Being in the Later Life." *Journal of Religion, Spirituality & Aging* 31, no. 2 (April 3, 2019): 168-186. https://doi.org/10.1080/15528030.2018.1532859.

Mantella, Rose C, Meryl A Butters, Janet A Amico, Sati Mazumdar, Bruce L Rollman, Amy E Begley, Charles F Reynolds, and Eric J Lenze. "Salivary Cortisol is Associated with Diagnosis and Severity of Late-Life Generalized Anxiety Disorder." *Psychoneuroendocrinology* 33, no. 6 (July 2008): 773–81. https://doi.org/10.1016/J.PSYNEUEN.2008.03.002.

Mao, Jun J, Sharon X Xie, Jarcy Zee, Irene Soeller, Qing S Li, Kenneth Rockwell, and Jay D Amsterdam. "Rhodiola Rosea versus Sertraline for Major Depressive Disorder: A Randomized Placebo-Controlled Trial." *Phytomedicine : International Journal of Phytotherapy and Phytopharmacology* 22, no. 3 (March 15, 2015): 394–99. https://doi.org/10.1016/J.PHYMED.2015.01.010.

Marsland, Anna L, Peter J Gianaros, Sarah M Abramowitch, Stephen B Manuck, and Ahmad R Hariri. "Interleukin-6 Covaries Inversely with Hippocampal Grey Matter Volume in Middle-Aged Adults." *Biological Psychiatry* 64, no. 6 (September 9, 2008): 484-490. https://doi.org/10.1016/J.BIOPSYCH.2008.04.016.

Marsland, Anna L, Karen L Petersen, Rama Sathanoori, Matthew F Muldoon, Serina A Neumann, Christopher Ryan, Janine D Flory, and Stephen B Manuck. "Interleukin-6 Covaries Inversely with Cognitive Performance among Middle-Aged Community Volunteers." *Psychosomatic Medicine* 68, no. 6 (November 2006): 895–903. https://doi.org/10.1097/01.PSY.0000238451.22174.92.

Maslach, C, W B Schaufeli, and M P Leiter. "Job Burnout." *Annual Review of Psychology* 52 (2001): 397–422. https://doi.org/10.1146/annurev.psych.52.1.397.

McEwen, Bruce S. "Structural Plasticity of the Adult Brain: How Animal Models Help Us Understand Brain Changes in Depression and Systemic Disorders Related to Depression." *Dialogues in Clinical Neuroscience* 6, no. 2 (2004): 119-133. https://doi.org/10.31887/DCNS.2004.6.2/BMCEWEN.

McLean, Carmen P, Anu Asnaani, Brett T Litz, and Stefan G Hofmann. "Gender Differences in Anxiety Disorders: Prevalence, Course of Illness, Comorbidity and Burden of Illness." *Journal of Psychiatric Research* 45, no. 8 (August 2011): 1027–35. https://doi.org/10.1016/J.JPSYCHIRES.2011.03.006.

Mechan, Annis O, Ann Fowler, Nicole Seifert, Henry Rieger, Tina Wöhrle, Stéphane Etheve, Adrian Wyss, et al. "Monoamine Reuptake Inhibition and Mood-

Enhancing Potential of a Specified Oregano Extract." *The British Journal of Nutrition* 105, no. 8 (April 2011): 1150–63. https://doi.org/10.1017/S0007114510004940.

Messaoudi, Michaël, Nicolas Violle, Jean François Bisson, Didier Desor, Hervé Javelot, and Catherine Rougeot. "Beneficial Psychological Effects of a Probiotic Formulation (Lactobacillus Helveticus R0052 and Bifidobacterium Longum R0175) in Healthy Human Volunteers." *Gut Microbes* 2, no. 4 (2011): 256-261. https://doi.org/10.4161/GMIC.2.4.16108.

Miller, Andrew H, and Charles L Raison. "The Role of Inflammation in Depression: From Evolutionary Imperative to Modern Treatment Target." *Nature Reviews. Immunology* 16, no. 1 (January 1, 2016): 22 34. https://doi.org/10.1038/NRI.2015.5.

Mizokami, Tetsuya, Audrey Wu Li, Samer El-Kaissi, and Jack R Wall. "Stress and Thyroid Autoimmunity." *Thyroid: Official Journal of the American Thyroid Association* 14, no. 12 (December 2004): 1047–55. https://doi.org/10.1089/THY.2004.14.1047.

Moncrieff, Joanna, Ruth E Cooper, Tom Stockmann, Simone Amendola, Michael P Hengartner, and Mark A Horowitz. "The Serotonin Theory of Depression: A Systematic Umbrella Review of the Evidence." *Molecular Psychiatry*, (2022). https://doi.org/10.1038/S41380-022-01661-0.

Mund, Marcus, and Kristin Mitte. "The Costs of Repression: A Meta-Analysis on the Relation between Repressive Coping and Somatic Diseases." *Health Psychology: Official Journal of the Division of Health Psychology, American Psychological Association* 31, no. 5 (September 2012): 640–49. https://doi.org/10.1037/A0026257.

Nepomnaschy, Pablo A, Kathleen B Welch, Daniel S McConnell, Bobbi S Low, Beverly I Strassmann, and Barry G England. "Cortisol Levels and Very Early Pregnancy Loss in Humans." *Proceedings of the National Academy of Sciences of the United States of America* 103, no. 10 (March 3, 2006): 3938-3942. https://doi.org/10.1073/PNAS.0511183103.

Ng, Qin Xiang, Shawn Shao Hong Koh, Hwei Wuen Chan, and Collin Yih Xian Ho. "Clinical Use of Curcumin in Depression: A Meta-Analysis." *Journal of the American Medical Directors Association* 18, no. 6 (June 1, 2017): 503–8. https://doi.org/10.1016/j.jamda.2016.12.071.

Nikolova, Viktoriya L, Megan R B Hall, Lindsay J Hall, Anthony J Cleare, James M Stone, and Allan H Young. "Perturbations in Gut Microbiota Composition in Psychiatric Disorders: A Review and Meta-Analysis." *JAMA Psychiatry* 78, no. 12 (December 1, 2021): 1-12. https://doi.org/10.1001/JAMAPSYCHIATRY.2021.2573.

Nourse, R, P Adamshick, and J Stoltzfus. "College Binge Drinking and Its Association with Depression and Anxiety: A Prospective Observational Study." *East Asian Archives of Psychiatry: Official Journal of the Hong Kong College of Psychiatrists = Dong Ya Jing Shen Ke Xue Zhi: Xianggang Jing Shen Ke Yi Xue Yuan Qi Kan* 27, no. 1 (March 2017): 18–25. www.ncbi.nlm.nih.gov/pubmed/28387209.

Novotny, Janet A, Sarah K Gebauer, and David J Baer. "Discrepancy between the Atwater Factor Predicted and Empirically Measured Energy Values of Almonds in Human Diets." *The American Journal of Clinical Nutrition* 96, no. 2 (August 1, 2012): 296–301. https://doi.org/10.3945/AJCN.112.035782.

Office for National Statistics. "Healthcare Expenditure, UK Health Accounts: 2020," 2022. www.ons.gov.uk/peoplepopulationandcommunity/healthandsoci alcare/healthcaresystem/bulletins/ukhealthaccounts/2020.

Olsson, Erik M, Bo von Schéele, and Alexander G Panossian. "A Randomised, Double-Blind, Placebo-Controlled, Parallel-Group Study of the Standardised Extract Shr-5 of the Roots of Rhodiola Rosea in the Treatment of Subjects with Stress-Related Fatigue." *Planta Medica* 75, no. 2 (February 2009): 105–12. https://doi.org/10.1055/s-0028-1088346.

Parletta, Natalie, Catherine M Milte, and Barbara J Meyer. "Nutritional Modulation of Cognitive Function and Mental Health." *The Journal of Nutritional Biochemistry* 24, no. 5 (May 1, 2013): 725–43. https://doi.org/10.1016/J.JNUTBIO.2013.01.002.

Pascoe, Michaela C, David R Thompson, and Chantal F Ski. "Yoga, Mindful-ness-Based Stress Reduction and Stress-Related Physiological Measures: A Me-ta-Analysis." *Psychoneuroendocrinology* 86 (December 2017): 152–68. https://doi.org/10.1016/j.psyneuen.2017.08.008.

Patriota, Erika S O, Isis C C Lima, Eduardo A F Nilson, Sylvia C C Franceschini, Vivian S S Gonçalves, and Nathalia Pizato. "Prevalence of Insufficient Iodine Intake in Pregnancy Worldwide: A Systematic Review and Meta-Analysis." *European Journal of Clinical Nutrition 2021 76:5* 76, no. 5 (September 20, 2021): 703–15. https://doi.org/10.1038/s41430-021-01006-0.

Pepino, M Yanina, Courtney D Tiemann, Bruce W Patterson, Burton M Wice, and Samuel Klein. "Sucralose Affects Glycemic and Hormonal Responses to an Oral Glucose Load." *Diabetes Care* 36, no. 9 (September 2013): 2530–35. https://doi.org/10.2337/DC12-2221.

Peters, Steve. *The Chimp Paradox: The Mind Management Programme to Help You Achieve Success, Confidence and Happiness.* 1st ed. Vermilion, 2012.

Picard, Martin, and Bruce S McEwen. "Psychological Stress and Mitochondria: A Systematic Review." *Psychosomatic Medicine* 80, no. 2 (February 1, 2018): 141-153. https://doi.org/10.1097/PSY.0000000000000545.

Pierce, Matthias, Holly Hope, Tamsin Ford, Stephani Hatch, Matthew Hotopf, Ann John, Evangelos Kontopantelis, et al. "Mental Health before and during the COVID-19 Pandemic: A Longitudinal Probability Sample Survey of the UK Population." *The Lancet. Psychiatry* 7, no. 10 (July 21, 2020): 883-892. https://doi.org/10.1016/S2215-0366(20)30308-4.

Pratte, Morgan A, Kaushal B Nanavati, Virginia Young, and Christopher P Morley. "An Alternative Treatment for Anxiety: A Systematic Review of Human Trial Results Reported for the Ayurvedic Herb Ashwagandha *(Withania Somnifera)*." *Journal of Alternative and Complementary Medicine* 20, no. 12 (December 12, 2014): 901-908. https://doi.org/10.1089/ACM.2014.0177.

Pullar, Juliet M, Anitra C Carr, Stephanie M Bozonet, and Margreet C M Vissers. "High Vitamin C Status Is Associated with Elevated Mood in Male Tertiary Students." *Antioxidants (Basel, Switzerland)* 7, no. 7 (July 16, 2018): 91. https://doi.org/10.3390/antiox7070091.

Rajan, Kumar B, Robert S Wilson, Jennifer Weuve, Lisa L Barnes, and Denis A Evans. "Cognitive Impairment 18 Years before Clinical Diagnosis of Alzheimer

Disease Dementia." *Neurology* 85, no. 10 (September 9, 2015): 898-904. https://doi.org/10.1212/WNL.0000000000001774.

Samel Alexander, Vejvoda Martin, and Maass Hartmut. "Sleep Deficit and Stress Hormones in Helicopter Pilots on 7-Day Duty for Emergency Medical Services - PubMed." Accessed November 28, 2022. https://pubmed.ncbi.nlm.nih.gov/15558991/.

Sánchez-Villegas, A Cabrera-Suárez, P Molero, A González-Pinto, C Chiclana-Actis, C Cabrera, F Lahortiga-Ramos, et al. "Preventing the Recurrence of Depression with a Mediterranean Diet Supplemented with Extra-Virgin Olive Oil. The PREDI-DEP Trial: Study Protocol." *BMC Psychiatry* 19, no. 1 (February 11, 2019): 347. https://doi.org/10.1186/S12888-019-2036-4.

Sandman, Curt A, Pathik Wadhwa, Laura Glynn, Aleksandra Chicz-Demet, Manuel Porto, and Thomas J Garite. "Corticotrophin-Releasing Hormone and Fetal Responses in Human Pregnancy." *Annals of the New York Academy of Sciences* 897, no. 1 (1999): 66–75. https://doi.org/10.1111/j.1749-6632.1999.tb07879.x.

Sategna-Guidetti, Carla, Mauro Bruno, Enrico Mazza, Alessandra Carlino, Stefania Predebon, Milena Tagliabue, and Claudio Brossa. "Autoimmune Thyroid Diseases and Coeliac Disease." *European Journal of Gastroenterology & Hepatology* 10, no. 11 (1998): 927–31. https://doi.org/10.1097/00042737-199811000-00005.

Savic, I, A Perski, and W Osika. "MRI Shows That Exhaustion Syndrome Due to Chronic Occupational Stress Is Associated with Partially Reversible Cerebral Changes." *Cerebral Cortex (New York, N.Y.: 1991)* 28, no. 3 (March 1, 2018): 894–906. https://doi.org/10.1093/CERCOR/BHW413.

Seeman, Teresa E, Burton H Singer, Carol D Ryff, Gayle Dienberg Love, and Lené Levy-Storms. "Social Relationships, Gender, and Allostatic Load across Two Age Cohorts." *Psychosomatic Medicine* 64, no. 3 (2002): 395–406. https://doi.org/10.1097/00006842-200205000-00004.

Sephton, Sandra E, Robert M Sapolsky, Helena C Kraemer, and David Spiegel. "Diurnal Cortisol Rhythm as a Predictor of Breast Cancer Survival," n.d. https://academic.oup.com/jnci/article/92/12/994/2905796.

Sharma, Ashish, Vishal Madaan, and Frederick D Petty. "Exercise for Mental Health." *Primary Care Companion to the Journal of Clinical Psychiatry* 8, no. 2 (2006): 106-107. https://doi.org/10.4088/pcc.v08n0208a.

Sharman, Leah S, Genevieve A Dingle, Ad M J J Vingerhoets, and Eric J Vanman. "Using Crying to Cope: Physiological Responses to Stress Following Tears of Sadness." *Emotion (Washington, D.C.)* 20, no. 7 (October 1, 2020): 1279–91. https://doi.org/10.1037/EMO0000633.

Shoba, G, D Joy, T Joseph, M Majeed, R Rajendran, and P S Srinivas. "Influence of Piperine on the Pharmacokinetics of Curcumin in Animals and Human Volunteers." *Planta Medica* 64, no. 4 (May 1998): 353–56. https://doi.org/10.1055/s-2006-957450.

Sorriento, Daniela, Eugenio Di Vaia, and Guido Iaccarino. "Physical Exercise: A Novel Tool to Protect Mitochondrial Health." *Frontiers in Physiology* 12 (April 27, 2021): 660068. https://doi.org/10.3389/FPHYS.2021.660068.

Spring, B. "Recent Research on the Behavioral Effects of Tryptophan and Carbohydrate." *Nutrition and Health* 3, no. 1–2 (1984): 55–67. https://doi.org/10.1177/026010608400300204.

Sterling, P, and J Eyer. "Allostasis: A New Paradigm to Explain Arousal Pathology." In *Handbook of Life Stress, Cognition and Health*, edited by S Fisher and J Reason, 629–49. John Wiley & Sons, 1988.

Streeter, Chris C, H Whitfield Theodore, Liz Owen, Tasha Rein, Surya K Karri, Aleksandra Yakhkind, Ruth Perlmutter, et al. "Effects of Yoga versus Walking on Mood, Anxiety, and Brain GABA Levels: A Randomized Controlled MRS Study." *Journal of Alternative and Complementary Medicine (New York, N.Y.)* 16, no. 11 (November 1, 2010): 1145–52. https://doi.org/10.1089/ACM.2010.0007.

Strickland, Justin C, and Mark A Smith. "The Anxiolytic Effects of Resistance Exercise." *Frontiers in Psychology* 5 (2014): 753. https://doi.org/10.3389/fpsyg.2014.00753.

Sudo, Nobuyuki, Yoichi Chida, Yuji Aiba, Junko Sonoda, Naomi Oyama, Xiao-Nian Yu, Chiharu Kubo, and Yasuhiro Koga. "Postnatal Microbial Colonization Programs the Hypothalamic-Pituitary-Adrenal System for Stress Response in Mice." *The Journal of Physiology* 558, no. Pt 1 (July 1, 2004): 263–75. https://doi.org/10.1113/jphysiol.2004.063388.

Świątkowska-Stodulska, Renata, Agata Berlińska, Katarzyna Stefańska, Maciej Zieliński, Sebastian Kwiatkowski, Joanna Połom, Elżbieta Andrysiak-Mamos, Piotr Wydra, and Krzysztof Sworczak. "Endocrine Autoimmunity in Pregnancy." *Frontiers in Immunology* 13 (June 29, 2022): 907561. https://doi.org/10.3389/FIMMU.2022.907561.

Tarleton, Emily K, and Benjamin Littenberg. "Magnesium Intake and Depression in Adults." *Journal of the American Board of Family Medicine: JABFM* 28, no. 2 (2015): 249–56. https://doi.org/10.3122/jabfm.2015.02.140176.

Tawakol, Ahmed, Amorina Ishai, Richard A P Takx, Amparo L Figueroa, Abdelrahman Ali, Yannick Kaiser, Quynh A Truong, et al. "Relation between Resting Amygdalar Activity and Cardiovascular Events: A Longitudinal and Cohort Study." *The Lancet* 389, no. 10071 (February 25, 2017): 834–45. https://doi.org/10.1016/S0140-6736(16)31714-7.

Taylor, Andrew M, and Hannah D Holscher. "A Review of Dietary and Microbial Connections to Depression, Anxiety, and Stress." *Nutritional Neuroscience* 23, no. 3 (March 2020): 237–50. https://doi.org/10.1080/1028415X.2018.1493808.

Taylor, Shelley E, Laura Cousino Klein, Brian P Lewis, Tara L Gruenewald, Regan A R Gurung, John A Updegraff, Brian P Lewis, Tara L Gruenewald, et al. "Biobehavioral Responses to Stress in Females: Tend-and-Befriend, Not Fight-or-Flight." *Psychological Review* 107, no. 3 (2000): 411–29. https://doi.org/10.1037/0033-295X.107.3.411.

Taylor, Terry, Robert G Dluhy, and Gordon H Williams. "Beta-Endorphin Suppresses Adrenocorticotropin and Cortisol Levels in Normal Human Subjects." *The Journal of Clinical Endocrinology and Metabolism* 57, no. 3 (1983): 592–96. https://doi.org/10.1210/JCEM-57-3-592.

Tolahunase, Madhuri, Rajesh Sagar, and Rima Dada. "Impact of Yoga and Meditation on Cellular Aging in Apparently Healthy Individuals: A Prospective, Open-Label Single-Arm Exploratory Study." *Oxidative Medicine and Cellular Longevity* 2017 (January 16, 2017): 1–9. https://doi.org/10.1155/2017/7928981.

Tóth, Barbara, Péter Hegyi, Tamás Lantos, Zsolt Szakács, Beáta Kerémi, Gábor Varga, Judit Tenk, et al. "The Efficacy of Saffron in the Treatment of Mild to Moderate Depression: A Meta-Analysis." *Planta Medica* 85, no. 1 (2019): 24–31. https://doi.org/10.1055/A-0660-9565.

Unno, Keiko, Ayane Hara, Aimi Nakagawa, Kazuaki Iguchi, Megumi Ohshio, Akio Morita, and Yoriyuki Nakamura. "Anti-Stress Effects of Drinking Green Tea with Lowered Caffeine and Enriched Theanine, Epigallocatechin and Arginine on Psychosocial Stress Induced Adrenal Hypertrophy in Mice." *Phytomedicine* 23, no. 12 (November 15, 2016): 1365–74. https://doi.org/10.1016/j.phymed.2016.07.006.

Varatharaj, Aravinthan, and Ian Galea. "The Blood-Brain Barrier in Systemic Inflammation." *Brain, Behavior, and Immunity* 60 (February 1, 2017): 1–12. https://doi.org/10.1016/J.BBI.2016.03.010.

Vieira, Renata Teles, Leonardo Caixeta, Sergio Machado, Adriana Cardoso Silva, Antonio Egidio Nardi, Oscar Arias-Carrión, and Mauro Giovanni Carta. "Epidemiology of Early-Onset Dementia: A Review of the Literature." *Clinical Practice and Epidemiology in Mental Health: CP & EMH* 9, no. 1 (July 19, 2013): 88-95. https://doi.org/10.2174/1745017901309010088.

Wahbeh, Helané, and Barry S Oken. "Salivary Cortisol Lower in Posttraumatic Stress Disorder." *Journal of Traumatic Stress* 26, no. 2 (April 2013): 241–48. https://doi.org/10.1002/JTS.21798.

Wainstock, Tamar, Liat Lerner-Geva, Saralee Glasser, Ilana Shoham-Vardi, and Eyal Y Anteby. "Prenatal Stress and Risk of Spontaneous Abortion." *Psychosomatic Medicine* 75, no. 3 (2013): 228–35. https://doi.org/10.1097/PSY.0B013E318280F5F3.

Wang, Sheng-Min, Changsu Han, Won-Myoung Bahk, Soo-Jung Lee, Ashwin A Patkar, Prakash S Masand, and Chi-Un Pae. "Addressing the Side Effects of Contemporary Antidepressant Drugs: A Comprehensive Review." *Chonnam Medical Journal* 54, no. 2 (2018): 101-112. https://doi.org/10.4068/CMJ.2018.54.2.101.

Wang, Siwen, Luwei Quan, Jorge E Chavarro, Natalie Slopen, Laura D Kubzansky, Karestan C Koenen, Jae Hee Kang, Marc G Weisskopf, Westyn Branch-Elliman, and Andrea L Roberts. "Associations of Depression, Anxiety, Worry, Perceived Stress, and Loneliness Prior to Infection With Risk of Post–COVID-19 Conditions." *JAMA Psychiatry* 79, no. 11 (2022): 1081-1091. https://doi.org/10.1001/JAMAPSYCHIATRY.2022.2640.

Westover, Arthur N, and Lauren B Marangell. "A Cross-National Relationship between Sugar Consumption and Major Depression?" *Depression and Anxiety* 16, no. 3 (2002): 118–20. https://doi.org/10.1002/da.10054.

Whitehead, William E, Olafur Palsson, and Kenneth R Jones. "Systematic Review of the Comorbidity of Irritable Bowel Syndrome with Other Disorders: What Are the Causes and Implications?" *Gastroenterology* 122, no. 4 (2002): 1140–56. https://doi.org/10.1053/GAST.2002.32392.

Wilckens, Kristine A, Chelsea M Stillman, Aashna M Waiwood, Chaeryon Kang, Regina L Leckie, Jamie C Peven, Jill E Foust, Scott H Fraundorf, and Kirk I Erickson. "Exercise Interventions Preserve Hippocampal Volume: A Meta-Analysis." *Hippocampus* 31, no. 3 (March 1, 2021): 335–47. https://doi.org/10.1002/HIPO.23292.

Wood, Gwendolyn E, and Tracey J Shors. "Stress Facilitates Classical Conditioning in Males, but Impairs Classical Conditioning in Females through Activational Effects of Ovarian Hormones." *Proceedings of the National Academy of Sciences of the United States of America* 95, no. 7 (March 3, 1998): 4066-4071. https://doi.org/10.1073/PNAS.95.7.4066.

World Health Organization. "ICD-11 for Mortality and Morbidity Statistics," 2023. https://icd.who.int/browse11/l-m/en#/http://id.who.int/icd/entity/129180281.

Wu, Yao, Kristina M Espinosa, Scott D Barnett, Anushree Kapse, Jessica Lynn Quistorff, Catherine Lopez, Nickie Andescavage, et al. "Association of Elevated Maternal Psychological Distress, Altered Fetal Brain, and Offspring Cognitive and Social-Emotional Outcomes at 18 Months." *JAMA Network Open* 5, no. 4 (April 29, 2022): E229244. https://doi.org/10.1001/JAMANETWORKOPEN.2022.9244.

Yehuda, Rachel, Nikolaos P Daskalakis, Linda M Bierer, Heather N Bader, Torsten Klengel, Florian Holsboer, and Elisabeth B Binder. "Holocaust Exposure Induced Intergenerational Effects on FKBP5 Methylation." *Biological Psychiatry* 80, no. 5 (September 1, 2016): 372–80. https://doi.org/10.1016/J.BIOPSYCH.2015.08.005.

Zarrindast, Mohammad Reza, and Fatemeh Khakpai. "The Modulatory Role of Dopamine in Anxiety-like Behavior." *Archives of Iranian Medicine* 18, no. 9 (September 1, 2015): 591–603. https://doi.org/0151809/AIM.009.

Zhang, Ji-Chun, Wei Yao, and Kenji Hashimoto. "Brain-Derived Neurotrophic Factor (BDNF)-TrkB Signaling in Inflammation-Related Depression and Potential Therapeutic Targets." *Current Neuropharmacology* 14, no. 7 (2016): 721–31. www.ncbi.nlm.nih.gov/pubmed/26786147.

Zou, Shenglong, and Ujendra Kumar. "Cannabinoid Receptors and the Endocannabinoid System: Signaling and Function in the Central Nervous System." *International Journal of Molecular Sciences* 19, no. 3 (March 13, 2018): 833. https://doi.org/10.3390/IJMS19030833.

GLOSSARY OF TERMS

Acetylcholine	Our cognition neurotransmitter
Adaption	A natural biological process: making internal biochemical adjustments to enable survival in response to stressors
Adrenaline	Our fight or flight neurotransmitter that raises the threat level to high when under stress
Adrenals	Small, fluffy glands that produce our stress hormones, located at the top of the kidneys
Allostasis	The ability to adapt through change
Amygdala	The fear centre of your brain, highly active under conditions of chronic stress
Antioxidants	Neutralize reactive oxygen species
Autonomic nervous system	The part of the nervous system that sends signals without you having to think about it. Divides into the sympathetic and parasympathetic nervous systems
BDNF	Brain-derived neurotrophic factor, a signalling protein that supports brain plasticity: the formation of new neurons, cell growth, cell survival and synapse formation.
Burnout	The end point following a long period of stress; characterized by emotional exhaustion, occupational cynicism and reduced personal achievement
Central nervous system	The brain and the spinal cord
Circadian rhythm	Our innate sleep–wake cycle
Cortisol	Our stress hormone that initiates adaption in other biological systems
Dopamine	Our pleasure, motivation and reward neurotransmitter

Endocannabinoids	Signalling chemicals thought to play a role in regulating stress, mood, cognitive function and sleep
Endocrine glands	Where hormones are produced and secreted
Endorphins	'Feel-good' hormones that are released in your brain in response to pain or stress
Epigenetics	The science of environmental modification to gene expression
Gamma-aminobutryic acid (GABA)	Our calming neurotransmitter
Glutamate	Our excitatory neurotransmitter
Glutathione	The master antioxidant
Gut–brain axis	The bidirectional communication between the gut and the brain
Hippocampus	The learning and memory part of our brain, susceptible to damage under conditions of chronic stress
Hormones	Communication chemicals that, unlike neurotransmitters, travel outside of the nervous system
HPA-axis	The hypothalamic–pituitary–adrenal axis, part of our neuroendocrine system that controls our response to stress. Can become dysregulated under conditions of chronic stress and burnout
Hypothalamus	The part of the brain that controls homeostasis and connects the nervous system to the endocrine system
Inflammation	A natural part of our immune system that helps us to fight off invading microbes and repair damaged tissue
Insulin	Our blood sugar regulating hormone, produced in the pancreas
Kefir	Soured yoghurt containing live bacteria
Kimchi	Korean pickle containing live bacteria

Kombucha	A fermented tea drink containing live bacteria
Leaky gut	Colloquial term for impaired gut barrier function
Melatonin	Our sleep neurotransmitter that also acts as a hormone and antioxidant
Methylation	A ubiquitous biochemical process that supports many biological functions including neurotransmitter synthesis and metabolism, hormone metabolism, detoxification, energy production, immune function, DNA synthesis and repair and gene expression
Microbiome	A vast microbial ecosystem that lives alongside us supporting stress resilience and many other biological functions. Composition can become imbalanced when under stress
Mitochondrion	The energy engine room of every cell in the human body (plural: mitochondria)
Neurons	Cells found in the nervous system
Neurotransmitters	Signalling molecules that relay messages from one neuron to the next in the nervous system. Some neurotransmitters act as mood-regulating chemicals
Noradrenaline	The precursor neurotransmitter to adrenaline
Nutrigenomics	A scientific field examining the effect of food and nutrition on gene expression
Oxytocin	Our social-bonding and connection hormone, aka the 'cuddle hormone'
Parasympathetic nervous system	Part of the autonomic nervous system, active when we are at rest and feeling calm
Peripheral nervous system	Everything outside of your central nervous system
Pituitary gland	The master endocrine gland
Plasticity	The brain's ability to rewire itself, or change as a result of experience

Prebiotics	Indigestible fibre that our microbiome feeds on
Probiotics	Live bacteria
Prefrontal cortex	The part of your brain that controls the highest levels of cognitive function
Reactive oxygen species (ROS)	Harmful chemicals present in environmental toxins, also produced as a by-product of energy production in the body
Resilience	Your body's ability to adapt and cope with stressors
Serotonin	Our 'happy' neurotransmitter; also acts as a hormone
SIBO	Small intestinal bacterial overgrowth; whereby microbes have migrated from the large intestine to the small intestine
SNPs	Single nucleotide polymorphisms: variations on the genetic code that may offer a protective effect or increase susceptibility to disease
Somatic nervous system	Controlling voluntary movement
Stress	A physiological state occurring in response to an internal or external challenge or threat
Stressed-out	The feelings associated with an overload of stressors
Stressor	An external or internal challenge or threat
Sympathetic nervous system	Part of the autonomic nervous system, active when we are in a state of alert or responding to a stressor
Thyroid	An endocrine gland that regulates metabolism
Vagus nerve	Part of the parasympathetic nervous system, connecting the brain to the gut

ACKNOWLEDGEMENTS

There are so many people to thank, I could really get carried away. I am also writing this on manuscript submission day, so I think my elation at having completed the book may have made this into more of an Oscars speech than I originally intended! It's an emotional process writing a book, and I am so grateful to so many. It is important to me that I acknowledge them.

First and foremost, thank you to my publisher, Alison, and all the team at PIP. You helped me to take the seed of an idea and nourish it into the book you see today. Thanks also to my fabulous editors Sophie and Erin for all of their efforts in bringing my manuscript to life.

Next, I would like to thank my beta-readers: Lauren, Katie, Leanne and Angela. They selflessly gave up their time to wade through an early version of this book and their feedback was invaluable. Thank you, ladies.

Thanks also to Tracey, Sam, Nicki, Clare, Carolyn, Emily, Sam and Satu for taking the time to read the book and write such kind endorsements.

To my growing clinic team: you basically protected me from burning out while I did this. Thank you. And to all of our wonderful clients, thank you for putting your trust in me and my team.

Becky! You absolute nutter! You keep me sane and make me do lunge jumps. I literally couldn't have done this (or them) without you.

To my mentor, Nicki. You inspire so many of us to follow where you lead.

To my business coach, Una, and the rest of the Unleashed crew: thank you for keeping me accountable and for opening my eyes to Focus Mate. What a game changer that was!

To the super-talented Kayleigh from Wild Kind Photography, who captured the front cover image of me, and Louise from Louise

Mora Creative, who helped create the additional resources for the book – thank you both.

To all my friends and family who have cheered me on during my book-writing journey, thank you. Special mentions go to Mum and Dad, just for being you; and to Saul and Hayley who encouraged me to share my story and put up with me writing the beta-draft while we were on holiday. Thanks guys.

To all the little ones in my life, this is for you. I hope you never have to experience burnout. RaRa is always here for you with food and a hug.

Finally, the biggest thank you of all must go to my husband, Paul, who has tirelessly supported me through it all. You're the Sonny to my Cher; I love you, babe.

INDEX

9 781788 603768